The Open University

Book 4

Contexts

Edited by Donna Loftus and Paul-François Tremlett

This publication forms part of the Open University module A105 *Voices, texts and material culture*. Details of this and other Open University modules can be obtained from the Student Registration and Enquiry Service, The Open University, PO Box 197, Milton Keynes MK7 6BJ, United Kingdom (tel. +44 (0)300 303 53 03; email general-enquiries@open.ac.uk).

Alternatively, you may visit the Open University website at www.open.ac.uk where you can learn more about the wide range of modules and packs offered at all levels by The Open University.

To purchase a selection of Open University materials visit www.ouw.co.uk, or contact Open University Worldwide, Walton Hall, Milton Keynes MK7 6AA, United Kingdom for a catalogue (tel. +44 (0)1908 274066; fax +44 (0)1908 858787; email ouw-customer-services@open.ac.uk).

The Open University, Walton Hall, Milton Keynes MK7 6AA

First published 2015

Edited and designed by The Open University.

Typeset by The Open University.

Printed and bound in the United Kingdom by Bell and Bain Ltd, Glasgow.

ISBN 978 1 7800 7823 6

1.1

Contents

Introduction

This book is divided into two parts, each of which takes a different approach to the study of context. The first part is centred on industrialisation in mid-nineteenth-century Lancashire. It brings History and Literature together to show how context emerges when we rebuild a conversation between voices, texts and disciplines in a specific time and place. The second part takes a broader geographical and subject focus in considering how meanings and context change when people, things and interpretation are disrupted. Instead of seeing context as the fixed background in which texts, voices and objects are interpreted, this book looks in greater depth at how context itself is shaped. Your study of this book as a whole explores how meanings may be produced, changed and challenged when a broader range of voices, texts and objects are brought into a debate.

As you begin Book 4, you may be wondering why the study of mid-nineteenth-century Lancashire is important. From the eighteenth century onwards, industrialisation and urbanisation were transforming many parts of Britain, but nowhere more so than Lancashire, the centre of the cotton industry. By the 1830s and 1840s visitors were flocking to Manchester to witness a wholly new kind of city. What they saw both fascinated and appalled them. The nature and speed of change, and uncertainties about the future, caused an enormous outpouring of comment, as people confronted and responded to the social and economic problems thrown up by these changes. These debates became known as the 'condition of England' question, and in exploring them you will be able to see how texts of various kinds interact with each other. Commentators responded not only to what they observed, but also to what they heard and read. Responses came in the form of official inquiries, speeches, political pamphlets, newspaper articles, even novels and ballads. In the words of historian Simon Gunn, the effort to encapsulate the significance of industrial cities such as Manchester 'strained the language of contemporaries to its limits' (2000, p. 36). The chronological and geographical focus of the first part of Book 4 should enable you to develop a detailed understanding of the issues under debate. Texts produced in, or relating to, a society in turmoil are often characterised by a kind of urgency as they reach out for new language and forms through which to articulate disturbing new realities and describe new kinds of social relationships.

In the first part of the book you will find two chapters written by historians and one by a literature specialist. In Chapter 1 there are also two short sections on Philosophy, while there is some discussion of Music in Chapter 3. Together these four weeks of study make up a case study on nineteenth-century industrial Lancashire. The first week has been set aside for you to read Charles Dickens's *Hard Times*, a fictional work that arguably continues to influence our assumptions about life in nineteenth-century factory towns. Chapter 1 explores responses to the rapid changes in industrial Lancashire by looking at texts from the 1830s and 1840s. Chapter 2 focuses on *Hard Times*. Chapter 3 looks at how some of the problems about relations between classes were resolved in the 1850s and 1860s, in what has been described as 'the age of equipoise', a mid Victorian oasis between the conflicts of the 1840s and the growing tensions of the end of the century. (There is a timeline that you can use to help you locate some of the voices and texts you will study in these three chapters. You can access this from the Study Planner on the A105 website.) There is thus a chronological progression through the first three chapters of the book, but the switch from History to Literature and then back again, together with the inserts from Philosophy, should enable us to see more easily how connections can emerge across texts and between the disciplines. So although much of your time in Book 4 will be spent practising the analytical skills specific to History and Literature, you will also be building your understanding of how interdisciplinary study works, by bringing to bear knowledge and methodologies from different subjects on a single topic.

The following three chapters (Chapters 4–6) take a different approach to context. Written by specialists in Religious Studies, Art History and Philosophy, respectively, these chapters address difficult questions of ownership, identity and memorialisation that have emerged as a consequence of war, colonialism, consumerism and tourism. They develop your understanding of context by showing how the movement, dislocation and disruption of people, settings and things can change the meaning and significance of objects. In particular, they show how different contexts can coexist, sometimes peacefully and sometimes in conflict, as different interests, beliefs and experiences are brought together in spaces such as tourist sites and museums.

Chapter 4 focuses on religious objects that are visited by pilgrims and tourists. Two case studies, one on the icon of St Sara and annual assemblages of pilgrims and tourists in the small village of Les-Saintes-Maries-de-la-Mer in southern France, the other on the standing stones in Catholic villages on the island of Flores in Indonesia, ask you to consider the different meanings religious objects have for tourists and villagers. In both case studies, the focus is on the effects of the 'tourist gaze': that is, the way tourists view, categorise and define religious objects, conferring on them new layers of meaning and significance. A key issue is whether this tourist gaze threatens the authenticity of religious objects and transforms them into commodities or, alternatively, whether tourism provides opportunities for the revitalisation of minority religious practices. As you will see, the meaning of religious objects depends on the shifting contexts in which they are perceived.

The next two chapters return to the subject of objects and museums. They offer alternative perspectives from ones you have encountered so far in the module by looking at the impact of dislocation and disruption caused by war, persecution and imperialism on museums, memorials and material culture. Chapter 5 considers the ways in which museum curators, architects and artists have memorialised the attempted extermination of Europe's Jewish populations by the Nazis during the 1930s and the 1940s. Chapter 6 examines the museum as a site of ethical concern and asks who has the right to hold and display material culture removed from countries in the age of colonialism and empire.

These last two chapters take different approaches to difficult and contentious issues. They bring your study of A105 to a close through a detailed examination of two highly contested debates about context, objects and display. Chapter 5 shows how context is actively shaped in museums and memorials to help express core ideas. In this case, you will see how the appalling violence of the Nazis is communicated through museums, monuments and counter-monuments, and how spaces are organised with the purpose of generating particular reactions and affects. For example, your study of the Jewish Museum in Berlin will show how brutal architecture is used to unsettle the visitor and so-called counter-monuments are designed for visceral discomfort rather than any conventional educational or museographic purpose. Chapter 6 follows with a discussion of Kwame Anthony Appiah's argument about cosmopolitanism and cultural patrimony. It asks you to consider whether objects and material culture removed from localities in the context of empire and colonialism belong to specific peoples or to the whole of humanity, and whether these kinds of argument have a greater emotional impact when the material culture on display is a human body or human body parts. In particular, it explores what happens when precise arguments about places and objects are re-contextualised as part of a broader discussion about culture and humanity.

Book 4 deals with the large and difficult topics resulting from industrialisation and globalisation. Some of the issues are emotive: they involve questions about power and authority and ask who has the right to represent the past, whose meaning should be given precedence and who can claim ownership of objects. Through careful analysis of voices, texts, objects and context you will scrutinise the arguments of others and uncover their claims and assumptions. As Chapter 4 makes clear, you are part of the world that these chapters address. You need to think about your own assumptions and think critically about your own position. Why do you hold the views you do? What evidence do you have to support your claims?

Through the examination of context, this book shows you how debate in the Arts and Humanities develops. Different voices and new questions can challenge existing interpretations of voices, texts and objects. This final book of A105 also shows that there are few simple answers to these questions. However, through the development of your analytical skills and through the careful examination of arguments and assumptions, including your own, it is possible to clarify reasoning and participate in complex and difficult debates.

Reference

Gunn, S. (2000) *The Public Culture of the Victorian Middle Class*, Manchester, Manchester University Press.

Chapter 1
Manchester: 'shock city'

Robin Mackie with Cristina Chimisso

Contents

Aims

This chapter will:

- explore how contemporaries discussed Manchester in the 1830s and 1840s and, in particular, why many saw the city as representing a society in crisis
- enhance your skills in reading texts as historical sources
- help you develop the ability to explore the relationship between texts – specifically, you will explore how texts are written in response to other texts and how our understanding of the past is enhanced by this skein of different voices.

Materials you will need

In this chapter, you will need to watch the following films, which can be found on the module website:

- Interview with Tristram Hunt.

- Manchester and the factory: Quarry Bank Mill and Ancoats.

You will also be directed to the module website for an online activity.

Introduction

This chapter is the first of three to focus on texts about Lancashire in the mid nineteenth century. In this first chapter, you will explore why contemporaries were so interested in Manchester and the surrounding area in the 1830s and 1840s. In the opening section, we shall look at a very famous text about Manchester, *The Condition of the Working-Class in England*, written by Friedrich Engels (1820–1895), and explore how historians approach a **source**. The second section will broaden the discussion, by comparing this text with others, and discuss why Manchester in the 1840s attracted such attention. The third section will consider why contemporaries were so keen to investigate **working-class** poverty in the city, and the nature of the evidence this has left us. In the fourth and final section, we shall explore how texts about Manchester fitted into a wider debate about the 'condition of England', and the boundaries of this debate. As one of the two chapters in the first half of Book 4 to concentrate on the academic discipline of History, this chapter also aims to help you develop your skills in analysing texts as historical sources.

1.1 *The Condition of the Working-Class in England*

I'd like you to start your exploration of texts about Lancashire by focusing on Engels's book, *The Condition of the Working-Class in England*.

Activity

You should allow about 30 minutes for this activity.

Look at Reading 1.1, which consists of extracts from Engels's book. We shall be studying the document in greater depth later on; at this stage, I'd like you simply to read the text and think about the following:

1   Some questions to place the document in its historical context:

Who wrote it?

When was it written?

What type of document is it (for instance, an official document; a public or private document)?

Who was it written for?

2   How useful is Engels's text as a source for understanding Manchester in the 1840s?

Discussion

1   If you have studied AA100, you may recall such questions as ones a historian might use when first working with a historical source. They help us to understand the source by placing it in its historical context: they enable us to start rebuilding the set of circumstances in which the source was produced.
A good starting point when answering questions like these is always the source itself and any linked information (for example, details provided in the source reference). In this case, the information I have provided about Engels, such as his date of birth, given in the Introduction above, and the source reference at the beginning of Reading 1.1, will have told you that the reading consists of extracts taken from a book by a young German man (Engels was just 24 when he wrote it). The dedication was completed in March 1845 and the book was first published in the same year. As a published source, it was clearly a public one and, indeed, the dedication makes clear who the intended audience is. Although the book is dedicated to 'Working Men' in general, and the first paragraph reveals that the author means the working men of England in particular, the target readership is identified as Engels's 'German Countrymen'. As you may have noted from

looking at the source reference, the book was first published in German and only translated into English much later.

2   I imagine you may have found this question rather more difficult to answer. On the one hand, you may well have been impressed (and appalled!) by Engels's description. If you have read *Hard Times*, it may also have reminded you of the way in which Charles Dickens describes Coketown (for instance, the opening section of Chapter 5 of the novel). On the other hand, you may have wondered how accurate Engels's description is. Coketown is fictional; how factual is this? In this respect, you may have noted how anxious Engels is to emphasise that his account is based on first-hand knowledge. This is evident from his book's subtitle (*From Personal Observation and Authentic Sources*) and from its dedication, in which the author explains he wanted to create 'a faithful picture' based on more than 'abstract knowledge'. Furthermore, Engels concentrates on Manchester partly 'because I know it as intimately as my own native town'. He repeatedly draws on – and reminds us of – this detailed knowledge; for instance, in the passage about the slums above DucieBridge.

This first-hand knowledge may well have inclined you to conclude that the sections drawing directly on personal experience are likely to be accurate. However, you might equally have decided to be more cautious. Engels might have misunderstood what he observed, or exaggerated it in some way. Indeed, since the violent revolution that Engels predicts at the end of his book did not happen, you may have been inclined to suspect that he got other things wrong too.

Much of what we know about the past is based on texts written at the time. *The Condition of the Working-Class* has been described by a recent biographer of Engels as 'one of the greatest works on the British industrial experience', responsible for 'much of what we think we know of Victorian Manchester' (Hunt, 2009, pp. 80–1). Yet in using such texts we have a problem: most were created for contemporaries; they were not written to tell later readers how things were. Hence the importance of placing texts in context by asking questions about why they were written and who they were written for. Internal evidence can often help us get started. In this case, the question in the activity about what type of document this is (or, to use a word used elsewhere in A105 but more rarely used by historians, its 'genre') may be particularly helpful. I imagine you may have found *The Condition of the Working-Class* quite hard to classify. It is not simply a description, but is also an analysis –

perhaps the most useful way to describe it would be as a political pamphlet or treatise: so, a text that uses evidence to support an argument and persuade. Indeed, this may explain why Engels is so keen to stress that his account is based on first-hand knowledge. By doing so, he may wish to convince us not only of the evidence but also of the argument.

Yet we shall only get so far by looking at the text on its own. One obvious approach to Engels's description of Manchester would be to compare it with others. We are more likely to be convinced by details if they are confirmed elsewhere. As we shall see, drawing on many texts allows us to build up a more detailed and complex picture. But there is another reason why it is useful to compare texts. Texts are written in a context that includes other texts. Writers read what others have written, pick up ideas, cite their peers in order to provide evidence, disagree with others, sometimes even copy from them. In turn, their writings influence others. As a result, texts do not exist in isolation but form part of a developing conversation, which, like most conversations, does not always develop as a logical progression but has many twists and turns and not a few dead ends.

In considering *The Condition of the Working-Class*, therefore, we might want to look at other texts written at the time, not only to find out if Engels was right in what he wrote about Manchester but also to understand why he wrote it. What was Engels doing in Manchester? What led him to write such an impassioned denunciation? And what was its impact? More broadly, how does his text fit into this ongoing conversation, this network of ideas?

An interesting place to start is with Engels's audience. As we have noted, *The Condition of the Working-Class* was first published in Germany; it was not translated into English until the 1880s. We have no evidence of it being widely known in Britain in the mid nineteenth century (Hunt, 2004, p. 44), but this does not mean it had no impact. Engels (shown in Figure 1.1) was the son of a Rhineland textile manufacturer. He had been sent to Manchester in 1842 to gain business experience in a firm in which his father was a partner, but he had previously been active in radical political circles in Germany, and among such circles his book was an immediate success (Hunt, 2009, p. 116). In particular, it made a great impression on Karl Marx (1818–1883), who was to become Engels's close friend and intellectual collaborator. Out of their partnership was to develop a set of ideas now usually described as **Marxism**, which has had a major impact in the twentieth century.

Figure 1.1 Friedrich Engels, *c*.1860. Photo: Mary Evans Picture Library/Imagno

Marx and Marxism: history and philosophy

Cristina Chimisso and Donna Loftus

Karl Marx was born in Trier, Prussia (now part of Germany), in 1818, and died in London in 1883. His writings can be understood as a contemporary response to the problems of his own day and as the foundation of Marxism, an intellectual tradition that has had a major influence on the study of History and Philosophy.

Marx did not produce a general theory of history. Nevertheless, a key component of his writing, known as 'historical materialism', has been used by twentieth-century scholars as a method for analysing society past, present and future. In very simple terms, historical materialism explains the world through economic systems. It argues that the way things are manufactured or grown, distributed and consumed, explains existing social relations and political structures. Tensions and contradictions between economic systems and social relations are, in turn, the fundamental driver of historical change. You saw this in Reading 1.1 when Engels argues that increasing inequality in industrial Manchester would unite the mass of workers against the bourgeoisie and lead to revolution and change.

In its consideration of history and change, Marxism offers a way for all scholars to think about the relationship between economic and social structures and human agency. Are we products of our material environment, or do we have control over our own actions? Philosophers have drawn this into a broader question about human nature. Some philosophers (and scientists) think that ultimately the way we are (for example selfish or altruistic, driven by desire or by rationality) is given once and for all and that our human nature is immutable. Marx and Engels did not share this view. For them, material and social circumstances are crucial in the shaping of human beings. Indeed, they thought that there is no 'human nature' that is given once and for all. In fact, they criticised philosophers and economists of their time, including John Stuart Mill (who you will come across later), because he based his ethical and economic views on an abstract conception of the individual, separated from the society in which she lives.

In the twentieth century many political parties were founded in Marx's name, and regimes were created, notably in the USSR and

China, that despite their differences claimed to be Marxist. Philosophers, historians, sociologists, economists and scientists all over the world have called themselves Marxist. Marxism has also been combined with other doctrines, including Catholicism, Islam and nationalism. The variety of positions and policies that have been labelled Marxist can be bewildering. This multifarious legacy often makes people forget that Marx lived in the nineteenth century. Crucially, what he knew and commented on was the social, economic and political reality of his time, but some of the questions raised about the relationship between economic, social and political life are still relevant today, and can be used to understand society and inform political solutions to poverty and inequality.

Engels used his time in Manchester to explore the city and make contacts with radical political groups, such as the **Chartists**. He drew on this experience in writing *The Condition of the Working-Class*, in which he identified a growing polarisation between a small number of **capitalists** and the increasingly exploited working classes. This analysis formed the basis of the Marxist idea of class conflict as the dynamic driving history forward towards a final revolution in which the **proletariat** would overthrow the **bourgeoisie**. Engels later moderated his views. It is generally agreed, however, that *The Condition of the Working-Class in England* was Engels's greatest intellectual contribution to Marxism. For now, the main point to note is how long Engels's book, barely noted in Britain at the time, has continued to resonate. If texts form part of a conversation, it is one which may last over centuries.

Activity

Find the audio recording 'Interview with Tristram Hunt' on the module website. Hunt is a historian and politician who has studied the writings of Engels and Marx. In this interview, Hunt discusses Engels's time in Manchester, his relationship with Marx and the legacy of Marxism. This interview will help you to understand Engels's contribution to the history of Manchester and the relationship between Marxism and history. Listen to the audio now.

You should allow about 30 minutes for this activity.

But what about the texts that Engels drew on? In the next sections we shall look at some other texts written about Manchester in this period and learn that, although Engels's analysis and conclusions were strikingly different, he was far from alone in his fascination with the city. *The Condition of the Working-Class* can be seen as part of a body of writing about a city in turmoil.

1.2 Visitors to Manchester

Engels was by no means the only foreigner to visit Manchester in the first half of the nineteenth century. From the turn of the century onwards, the city attracted a stream of visitors who have left accounts of it. Their descriptions are dramatic. The German novelist Johanna Schopenhauer (1766–1838) described Manchester as 'this famous, great factory town. Dark and smoky from the coal vapours, it resembles a huge forge or workshop. ... The clatter of the cotton mills and the looms can be heard everywhere' (quoted in Bradshaw, 1987, p. 28). Another traveller, William Cooke Taylor (1800–1849), wrote of 'the forest of chimneys pouring forth volumes of steam and smoke, forming an inky canopy which seemed to embrace and involve the whole place' (quoted in Bradshaw, 1987, p. 36). In the words of the historian Asa Briggs, Manchester was the 'shock city of the 1840s' (1968 [1963], p. 56).

As these quotations show, it was Manchester's industry that first struck visitors. Factories and chimneys figure prominently in descriptions, and also in contemporary pictures of the city, such as Figures 1.2 and 1.3. Engels came to Manchester to work in a cotton business, and cotton was central to the city's rapid industrial development. British cotton production was already concentrated in the counties of Lancashire and Cheshire in the eighteenth century, but became more so as new inventions made possible first the mechanisation of spinning and later that of weaving. It is difficult to get figures that accurately reflect this growth, but British net imports of raw cotton increased one-hundredfold from an annual average of 5.1 million pounds in weight in the 1770s to an annual average of 555.7 million pounds in the 1840s (Timmins, 1998, pp. 159, 179). Most of this cotton was spun and woven in Manchester and the surrounding industrial districts.

Activity

Watch the film 'Manchester and the factory: Quarry Bank Mill and Ancoats', which you can find on the module website. This explores the impact of changes in the production of cotton in terms of two spinning mills: Quarry Bank Mill near Wilmslow in Cheshire, and Murray's Mill in Ancoats, Manchester.

At the end of the film, it is suggested that, over time, the advantage lay with urban mills such as Murray's Mill, rather than rural ones. Why was this?

You should allow about 15 minutes for this activity.

Figure 1.2 William Wyld, *Manchester from Kersal Moor*, 1852, watercolour, 32cm x 49cm. The Royal Collection © 2010, Her Majesty Queen Elizabeth II

Discussion

There were essentially two reasons: one negative, one positive. At first, mills such as Quarry Bank were sited beside fast-flowing rivers, since water power was needed to drive the machinery. With the advent of steam engines in the 1780s and 1790s, this advantage was lost. At this point, the positive advantages of urban locations came into play. Urban mills such as Murray's had better transport links, such as canals, and were closer to markets. Above all, they had a better supply of labour. Finding workers was always a problem at Quarry Bank Mill, and the film explains how Samuel Greg and his descendants brought in **pauper** apprentices to work in their mill. Later, they turned to adult workers but needed to provide housing for them. All this meant that the labour supply was less flexible than in Manchester, which was a disadvantage in the fluctuating economic conditions of the first half of the nineteenth century.

COTTON FACTORIES, UNION STREET, MANCHESTER.

Figure 1.3 'Cotton Factories, Union Street, Manchester', from E. Baines (1835) *History of the Cotton Manufacture in Great Britain: with a Notice of its Early History in the East, and In All the Quarters of the Globe*, London, Fisher, Fisher and Jackson. Photo: © Science Museum Library/Science and Society Picture Library

If the Ancoats spinning firms were among the largest in the industry, Manchester was always more than just a centre for the production of cotton. The real mill towns were those around the city. Manchester itself also developed ancillary engineering and chemical industries and became the hub of the region's transport network (first canals; later railways). Above all, it became the commercial centre of the cotton industry. The warehouses of the merchants who bought and sold raw cotton, yarn and finished cotton goods were as large and imposing as the factories. It was the Royal Exchange, where cotton goods were traded – 'the parliament house of the lords of cotton' – that was 'the real heart of the city' (quoted in Farnie, 1979, p. 64).

The attention that Manchester attracted was therefore not simply because of its industrial development. This was indeed without precedent, and the rapid population growth that accompanied

it – the population of the city more than tripled between
1801 and 1841, from 76,788 to 242,983 (Kidd, 2006 [1993], p. 14) –
also had few contemporary parallels. Figure 1.4 shows how new
industrial and residential suburbs pushed out in all directions from the
city's medieval core. But the city, with its factories, chimneys and slums,
was also seen as representing something new and alarming: a city
dedicated to the creation of wealth, regardless of the costs.

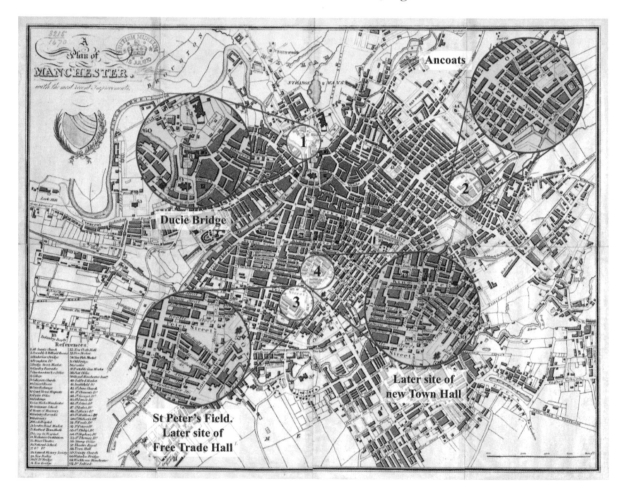

Figure 1.4 Map of Manchester in 1840, showing some of the locations discussed in this chapter and in
Chapter 3. British Library map collection, maps 3215 (8). Photo: © British Library Board

I'd like now to turn to another text that explores these connections. The
French economist Léon Faucher (1803–1854) wrote a number of
articles for a leading French liberal journal, the *Revue des Deux Mondes*,
after visiting Manchester. A shortened version of the articles was
translated into English and published in 1844. Unlike Engels's work,

therefore, Faucher's writings were immediately available in Britain. Engels, who read Faucher in French, thought he gave 'a better account than any hitherto given either by an English or a German author' (quoted in Marcus, 1974, p. 57).

Activity

Reading 1.2 consists of extracts from Faucher's pamphlet, *Manchester in 1844: Its Present Condition and Future Prospects*. Read this now and compare it with Engels's account of Manchester in Reading 1.1. You should consider the following questions:

You should allow about 30 minutes for this activity.

1   How do Faucher and Engels describe the economic role of the city?

2   What are the main problems in Manchester, as discussed by the two writers? Do they identify the same ones?

3   Is there any difference in the ways the two authors present their case?

Discussion

1   Both writers identify Manchester closely with cotton. Engels writes that the cotton industry is in advance of all others, so that 'The modern art of manufacture has reached its perfection in Manchester'. Faucher describes the city as a 'diligent spider' sending out orders to the surrounding Lancashire towns and controlling the trade. Both are clearly awestruck by the enormous vitality of the city's industrial development. Both also stress the economic ups and downs resulting from fluctuating demand for cotton goods.

2   In the extracts selected, Engels writes of the slums and the associated squalor, of depressed and uncertain wages, of poor health. Faucher, too, makes reference to poor housing and insanitary conditions, although he presents this almost as an unfortunate side-effect of efficient production (consider the paragraph starting 'From this apparently indifferent combination ...'). He goes on to describe unhealthy workers; uncontrolled sexual behaviour; outspoken factory girls; alcohol abuse; overwork; and mothers who have no time to care for their children.

3   Although it would be easy to exaggerate the contrast, there is a difference in the ways the two authors present their case. Engels's style is polemic: everything he writes about fits into an argument; when he describes, he is marshalling evidence. Faucher is more discursive: he touches on one point and moves on to another, sometimes even within one paragraph. Although he, too, is concerned about the consequences of industrialisation, he presents the city in terms of a dense web of interlocking problems.

Part of the contrast between the two texts is due to my editing. The two books are both long: 285 and 152 pages, respectively, in the editions I am using. Inevitably it was necessary to select which passages to quote. Engels is also concerned by alcohol abuse, while Faucher describes insanitary living conditions. Both also address the employment of women and children in factories, which was one of the many features that alarmed observers. As you will have noted, Faucher is concerned about the effect of factory work on young women – their lack of 'modesty' – and the way that working mothers neglected young children. This was part of a broader fear that employment of women outside the home would undermine the family and the authority of husbands and fathers. In other sections of *The Condition of the Working-Class*, Engels expresses similar concerns. He deplores the 'moral consequences' of employing women in factories, and the way it turned the whole family 'upside down', with men 'condemned to domestic occupations'. Yet in the same section he argues that 'if the reign of wife over the husband, as inevitably brought about by the factory system, is inhuman, the pristine rule of the husband over the wife must have been inhuman too' (Engels, 1975 [1845], pp. 441, 438, 439).

This surprising twist points to a difference in the problems the two authors identify, or perhaps rather in the way they identify them. Although they are describing the same city, and despite the fact that Engels has clearly drawn on Faucher's writings, their analyses are very different. For Engels, the problems are consequences, while Faucher places much more emphasis on the role of the workers in their own misery. This is not to say that Engels denies that the way people behave may make their lives worse. But he goes on immediately to ask: 'When a class can purchase few and only the most sensual pleasures by its wearying toil, must it not give itself over blindly and madly to those pleasures?' (Engels, 1975 [1845], p. 424). If both authors use the term 'degradation' to describe what is happening to the working classes in the new city, Engels adds a second one, 'demoralisation', to mean specifically how many of the poor respond to their situation: 'they are tossed about by fate, lose their moral hold upon themselves as they have already lost their economic hold, live along from day to day, drink and fall into licentiousness' (pp. 414–15). He even considers the effect of monotonous factory work on their mental state: 'nothing is more terrible than being constrained to do some one thing every day from morning until night against one's will' (p. 415). As a result of this distinction, whereas Faucher discusses crime and public disorder in terms of the consequences of industrialisation, Engels suggests they might also be a response, a form of resistance. Crime itself might be 'the earliest, crudest, and least fruitful form of rebellion' (p. 502), but it soon led on to other more effective types of resistance, such as opposition to new machines, strikes for higher wages and better working conditions, and political protests (Marcus, 1974, pp. 220–6).

Manchester was indeed a centre of popular protest in the early nineteenth century. In 1819 a massive political meeting at St Peter's Field in Manchester calling for **electoral reform** was violently broken up by soldiers, resulting in at least 11 deaths. Only four years after Waterloo, the event was immediately dubbed 'Peterloo' and became a great symbol of the repression of working-class political aspirations. The first decades of the nineteenth century also saw conflicts about work and wages, culminating in many strikes and lockouts. By the 1830s, many of these forms of protest were coalescing into the greatest working-class political movement of the nineteenth century: Chartism.

In 1832 the Great Reform Act widened the franchise so as to give most middle-class and some working-class men the vote. But (as at Peterloo) there had always been agitation for much broader electoral reform, and working-class leaders pushed for a further widening of the franchise, against what they saw as middle-class betrayal by settling for the Reform Act. The six-point Charter, drawn up in 1838, included demands for universal adult male suffrage, secret ballots and annual elections – the widespread assumption in Victorian Britain was that this would yield a permanent working-class majority in Parliament. Although the Charter was first launched in London, Manchester soon became a centre of protest. The Manchester Political Union and later the National Charter Association coordinated huge protests and petitions in 1838–42. Events came to a head in 1842, when a slump led to strikes against wage reductions, which spontaneously developed into huge protests in Manchester and elsewhere. These were usually known as the Plug Strikes, since the strikers attempted to bring factories to a standstill by removing the plugs from engine boilers. For several days in August, marches and protests dominated the city. Although these protests were not organised by the Chartists, it was inevitable that members of this group should emerge as spokesmen, since they were the best-known working-class leaders. But fears of revolution led the government to move large numbers of troops to Manchester (Kidd, 2006 [1993], pp. 93–7; Mather, 1974). Even though the protests soon subsided, Manchester remained tense. Such was the immediate background to Engels's and Faucher's texts.

Class

The early nineteenth century was when the term 'class' first came to be widely used to distinguish different groups in a hierarchically organised society. You may have noted that in Reading 1.1 Engels uses the term 'working class', while in Reading 1.2 Faucher prefers the term 'operatives'. Other words used to describe workers include 'labourers', or, as in *Hard Times*, 'hands'. These terms all emphasise what was seen as central to the concept of a working class – that they worked. The contrast was with an upper class of gentlemen and women, who, conspicuously, did not work – and indeed looked down on 'trade'.

In the twentieth century, historians influenced by Marx tried to identify the emergence of class **identity** and politics. Perhaps the most influential book written in this tradition (indeed one of the most influential works on British history published in the last half century or so) is E.P. Thompson's *The Making of the English Working Class*, first published in 1963. In it, Thompson explores the emergence in England, in the years between 1780 and 1832, of a working class with a clear sense of identity. Class, he argues, is 'a relationship'. It 'happens when some men [*sic*], as a result of common experiences (inherited or shared), feel and articulate the identity of their interests as between themselves, and as against other men whose interests are different from (and usually opposed to) theirs' (Thompson, 1980 [1963], pp. 8–9). In this, Thompson's debt to Engels, and to his description of an increasingly polarised society, is clear.

What of the middle class? Contemporaries were clear that there were many groups between the aristocracy and the workers, although whether these formed one middle class or many was open to debate. In the early nineteenth century manufacturers, merchants and professional men in cities such as Manchester came to see themselves as different from those above and beneath them. For a start, they worked, if not manually, and were proud of their productivity in comparison with the 'idle rich'. The middle class, too, had its political movements, such as the movement for electoral reform before 1832 and the **Anti-Corn Law League** in the 1840s.

1.3 Investigating Manchester

The first major report on Manchester was written by James Phillip Kay (1804–1877), a young medical graduate who was appointed physician at the Ardwick and Ancoats Dispensary in the heart of Manchester in 1828. Almost immediately, he was involved in combating a major epidemic of cholera, which had reached Britain in November 1831 and Manchester in May 1832. The disease caused real panic, not least because it was feared it would spread from working-class areas to more affluent districts. Without any cure, or indeed a real understanding of cholera's causes and spread, the authorities relied solely on public health measures to stop it spreading.

Activity

Kay's report, *The Moral and Physical Condition of the Working Classes Employed in the Cotton Manufacture in Manchester,* was his attempt to understand the spread of the disease and find ways of combating it. Sections of the report are printed as Reading 1.3. Read the opening two paragraphs now.

Who does Kay blame for the disease's spread?

You should allow about 10 minutes for this activity.

Discussion

The first paragraph makes a crucial connection between disease and poverty. Cholera develops in the 'most loathsome haunts'; it is a disease of the poor – even if, as we have seen, the disease caused such alarm because it threatened to spread to the wealthy too. Yet, despite the way that Kay links poverty and 'vice', he rejects the suggestion that the poor can be blamed. Even when their habits encourage the spread of disease, this is due to ignorance, the want of good examples and the 'desperate straits of a perverted spirit battling with hunger and toil'.

The link made between disease and poverty is central to Kay's pamphlet; indeed the title is quite precise: it is a text about the 'moral and physical condition' of the working classes, not about cholera itself. Yet Kay uses his medical background to add authority to what he has to say. He adopts a scientific tone; he seeks to provide evidence to back his claims; he is not seeking to blame, but to demonstrate what is happening and what should be done about it. The historian Christopher Hamlin argues that 'it reflects a medical view of society' in which

'Manchester workers are victims of a social, moral, and physical disease which they no more choose than we choose the flu' (1998, pp. 76–7). Kay may write about living conditions rather than cholera itself, but the way he discusses them is very much in terms of contagion.

Activity

You should allow about 10 minutes for this activity.

Now read the remaining sections of Reading 1.3 and answer the following:

1   What is Kay trying to show?
2   How well does his evidence support his claims?

Discussion

1   In these paragraphs, Kay discusses the streets and houses where the working classes live. He starts by stating that an 'intimate connexion' exists between cleanliness and bad habits. The two tables provided show the number of streets and houses in poor condition. We may find some of the measures rather vague, but this was the product of a real attempt to measure poverty.

2   Kay himself admits that 'even these numerical results fail to exhibit a perfect picture of the ills which are suffered by the poor'. They are inadequate indicators: the figures for houses requiring whitewashing, for instance, give only a very partial idea of how dirty they really were. To give a fuller impression, Kay resorts to description.

The historian Mary Poovey points out that virtually all of Kay's tables are accompanied by a similar apology (1995, p. 83). Kay sometimes seems to suggest that more detailed investigation would provide better figures, but, as in Reading 1.3, he also hints at a frustration that society is in fact quite difficult to measure. His descriptions are also quite normative. Terms such as 'ill-ventilated' and 'uncleanliness' suggest a comparison with a normal – presumably middle-class – standard of hygiene (Poovey, 1995, p. 83).

Ten years after Kay's pioneering report, another survey of Manchester was printed. This was based on investigations carried out over the previous two years during a slump in trade, and was linked to the distribution of a charitable fund. The report on this survey was written by Joseph Adshead and was entitled *Distress in Manchester: Evidence (Tabular and Otherwise) of the State of the Labouring Classes in 1840–42*. As the title suggests, it contained considerable statistical material, some of which was compared with Kay's findings. But it also contained a chapter entitled 'Narratives of Suffering', extracts from which are presented here as Reading 1.4.

Activity

Read Reading 1.4 now. (References in the reading to the 'Overseer' and the 'Night Asylum' are to the agents and institutions of the **Poor Law**, which provided relief for the destitute.)

How does this compare with Kay's report in Reading 1.3?

You should allow about 10 minutes for this activity.

Discussion

The most obvious difference is that the survey in Reading 1.4 names working-class people. The effect is quite striking, because none of the reports we have looked at so far do this: the working classes have remained anonymous. Providing names and describing circumstances makes the hardship faced by the families listed suddenly more real.

This was no doubt deliberate: Adshead surely had donations to the relief fund in mind. The fact that the examples are provided by a 'military gentleman', and so presumably a writer unlikely to be swayed by emotion, is probably also significant. You may have noticed, too, how Adshead stresses that the families are respectable, or are in need because of circumstances beyond their control. One might think of the distinction between the 'able-bodied' and those unable to work that was central to the Poor Law.

Is there a contrast here with Kay's report? Whereas Kay uses scientific language, Adshead is appealing for an emotional response. The difference is certainly there. Yet you might also have felt that the difference is more apparent than real. Both writers make moral judgements.

Adshead's report may seem to us a curious mixture of hard facts (such as the figures for wages) and individual stories. Contemporaries in the 1830s and 1840s were concerned that personal contacts between people of different classes, which they believed existed in the past and still existed in rural areas, were no longer possible in the anonymous cities. The social reporting of the 1830s and 1840s represented a new way of knowing about other classes, a form of writing which was apparently more detached and objective, and in which individual names and circumstances were no longer appropriate. Adshead's report combines this new type of knowledge with older ways of writing about the poor. The new investigations did create a great deal of information about working-class living conditions in Manchester, information which is still widely used by historians today. Clearly, this evidence was created for a purpose, and the purpose shapes its form. But this is true of most of the evidence we have about the past. Historians are accustomed to using texts in ways that were not the intention of the writer and talk of reading sources 'against the grain'. Furthermore, understanding these intentions and how they shaped texts gives us an insight into how their writers saw their world.

Official inquiries were another means by which concerns about social conditions in the mid nineteenth century led to the collection of evidence. Parliament set up a number of Royal Commissions and other public inquiries as a first step towards possible legislation. The data they collected, including the evidence of witnesses, was printed and was used by Engels and others. (You will find a reference to the 'Blue Books', in which the data was published, in your copy of *Hard Times*. See p. 59 and the footnote on p. 310.)

As you know from watching the film 'Manchester and the factory: Quarry Bank Mill and Ancoats', many children were employed in early factories. By the 1830s and 1840s the use of child labour was becoming increasingly controversial, and inquiries were set up to look into this issue.

Activity

You should allow about 40 minutes for this activity.

You should now complete the online activity 'Official inquiries into the employment of children in factories', which you can find on the Study Planner of the module website. In this activity, you will hear statements about the employment of children in factories, taken from two separate inquiries.

1.4 Manchester and the 'condition of England'

So far, we have focused on the problems identified by the different texts we have looked at, but have said little about the solutions they proposed. This is as it should be: all the writers we have considered had much less to say about what should be done.

One reason for this is that all the writers saw Manchester's social problems as indissolubly tied to the economic vitality which so impressed them. In the words of a French commentator, Alexis de Tocqueville (1805–1859), quoted by Professor Gunn in the film 'Manchester and the factory: Quarry Bank Mill and Ancoats': 'From this foul drain the greatest stream of human industry flows out to fertilise the whole world. From this filthy sewer pure gold flows' (De Tocqueville, 1977 [1835], p. 119).

This was compounded by a set of ideas about society and economics usually termed **political economy**. Building on the ideas of Adam Smith (1723–1790) about the operation of the market, and Robert Malthus (1766–1834) about the relationship between economic development and population growth, many early nineteenth-century political economists were highly critical of all attempts to control the market. They were suspicious of government activity because they thought it could be partisan, biased or corrupt. For these political economists, freedom from restrictions on commercial activity was not an end in itself but a way of achieving greater freedom in all aspects of life. Jeremy Bentham (see box) drew these ideas into a broader philosophy called utilitarianism. Utilitarians were optimistic about the fate of unrestrained human activity and believed a natural equilibrium, or balance, would be found through commercial exchange. Malthus's conclusions were grimmer. Arguing that the growth in population would always outstrip that in the food supply, he feared that the increased opportunity for work that came with the growth of commercial society and any rise in wages would encourage the poor to have more children than they could support. Combined, these arguments led to a belief that attempts to regulate market forces or intervene to mitigate some of its more damaging effects could have dire long-term consequences.

The debates about political economy and moral philosophy were complex; however, aspects of them were taken up by factory employers and used to describe their role and defend their interests. Their influence is well brought out in the following extract from the writings of William Rathbone Greg (1809–1881), a son of Samuel Greg, the founder of Quarry Bank Mill and himself a noted writer on political issues (see Rose, 1986, pp. 126–8):

> The first duty which the great employer of labour owes to those who work for him is to make his business succeed. […]
>
> In the second place, this obligation of success imposes upon the employer the duty of not allowing any benevolent plans or sentiments of lax kindness to interfere with the main purpose in view. […] He must not scruple to reduce wages where the well-being of the undertaking renders this change indispensible; nor must he gratify himself with the luxury of paying higher wages than his neighbours, either out of vanity or from benevolence. […]
>
> The plain truth is, that neither the most boundless benevolence, nor the most consummate ability, can fight against the clear moral and material laws of the universe. If the field of employment is too limited for the numbers who crowd into it, no power and no goodness can prevent wages from falling; and all schemes, whether old or new, *for enabling labourers to be redundant, and yet to evade the consequences of their redundancy*, must come to nought.
>
> (Greg, 1853, pp. 282, 284, 290; original emphasis)

In this passage, Greg likens the operation of the market to the laws of the universe. Thus, resistance to the natural order of the market is pointless. The good employer has more than a right – he has a duty – to reduce wages or lay off workers if his business requires it. This faith in the market came to be particularly associated with Manchester and was termed 'Manchester school' economic liberalism. In the name of political economy, **Factory Acts** (legislation to limit hours of work or improve working conditions), restrictions on trade and attempts by workers to combine in trade unions were all attacked as unwarranted limitations on the freedom of employers to act in the best interests of their firms, and ultimately of society.

Utilitarianism: a moral philosophy

Cristina Chimisso

Versions of utilitarianism can be found throughout the history of philosophy. However, the classic formulations of this philosophy are credited to Jeremy Bentham (1748–1832) and John Stuart Mill (1806–1873). Bentham's *Introduction to the Principles of Morals and Legislation* (1798) is often regarded as the work that laid the foundations of utilitarianism. Bentham was a close friend of Mill's father, the Scottish philosopher and historian James Mill (1773–1836), who raised his son according to utilitarian principles. John Stuart Mill's main works are *Utilitarianism* (1863), *On Liberty* (1859) and *The Subjection of Women* (1861). Bentham, Mill and the members of nineteenth-century utilitarian circles were concerned not only with philosophical speculation but also with current affairs, and campaigned for legal, social and political reform. Politically, their theories are part of the tradition of liberalism, because of the fundamental importance that individual liberty occupies in them.

Utilitarianism is a moral theory. Moral theories provide us with principles that are intended to tell us *how* we ought to behave and also *why* we ought to behave in a certain manner. For instance, we may want to decide whether lying is wrong. A moral theory should tell us not only whether lying is right or wrong (or perhaps right in some cases and wrong in others), but also why it is right or wrong. Let us assume that I think that lying is wrong. Which principles could I invoke to support my view? I could say that it is my moral principle never to lie, because I regard telling the truth as an inescapable moral duty (I may need to justify this further, but we shall stop here). Or I could say that I intend to be a virtuous person, and I have observed that virtuous people do not lie. I could also say that lying is wrong because if people normally lie, mutual trust would collapse and with it the very fabric of our society. Note that the last answer focuses on the consequences of lying. In this case, lying is not considered intrinsically wrong; in theory, if it were good for society, it could be considered good. Philosophies that judge acts or moral rules according to their consequences are unsurprisingly called 'consequentialist'. Utilitarianism is one such philosophy.

In order to judge actions by their consequences, it is necessary to establish which consequences are desirable and which are not. For utilitarians, happiness is the most desirable consequence. But be careful: for utilitarians, our actions are right when they promote not just my or your happiness, but rather when they promote the greatest amount of happiness for the greatest number of people. An expert conman may derive great happiness from swindling millions out of many unsuspecting victims, but he will thereby maximise only his own happiness – or possibly also that of his associates. At the same time, he will cause a great amount of unhappiness to a considerable number of people. For this reason, utilitarians would consider his actions wrong, as they will bring about more unhappiness than happiness.

This simple principle of maximisation of happiness, if applied in a strict manner, may lead to highly controversial judgements. Let us consider, for instance, a scenario like that in Kazuo Ishiguro's *Never Let Me Go* (2005). In this novel a number of young people (who are clones) are raised in order to provide organs for people who may need them. Each young person will save many individuals, although this will lead to her or his own premature death. If we are concerned only with maximisation of happiness, this system appears to be acceptable, as it saves the lives of a great number of people while sacrificing a small minority. However, I am sure I am not alone in finding it repugnant.

There is further difficulty with utilitarian theories, namely the definition of their central concept: happiness. Happiness sounds like a desirable aim, but it is also rather vague, as people have very different conceptions of it. Utilitarians hold that their theory should guide public policy. But how would politicians determine what counts as happiness for the general population? The utilitarians' answer appears straightforward: happiness is pleasure and the absence of pain. But how do you assess the pleasure that an action is likely to bring about? Bentham thought he had an answer, and indeed developed a 'hedonic calculus', that is to say a method to calculate pleasure (*hedone* means 'pleasure' in Greek). Bentham considered all types of pleasure as qualitatively the same: there is no difference between the pleasure derived from eating a delicious dish, listening to good music, gambling, drinking, or studying an OU module. In fact, studying an OU module may not be very pleasurable. Should we then be trying to maximise our pleasure by eating and drinking as much as we can, rather than studying? Similar objections, and indeed eyebrows, were raised in Bentham's time. Indeed, John Stuart Mill, without mentioning Bentham directly, judged the latter's quantitative approach fit for swine, rather than human beings. He accepted that happiness should be equated with pleasure and the absence of pain, but also believed that not all pleasures are the same. His own approach was qualitative rather than quantitative, as he distinguished what may be termed 'higher pleasures' from so-called 'lower pleasures'. For him, physical pleasures, such as eating, which in fact swine can enjoy, belong to the latter category. By contrast, the pleasures of the intellect and the imagination are more properly human and, as such, 'higher'. In his view, reading a good book affords a higher pleasure than eating cake. Mill's revision of Bentham's approach solves important problems, but arguably introduces other difficulties. In particular, the assessment of what counts as higher or lower pleasure can be rather difficult and indeed controversial.

One major demand of the Manchester school was for free trade, and especially repeal of the **Corn Laws**, legislation that limited imports of grain to Britain. To the supporters of political economy this was the height of iniquity – class-based legislation that restricted trade and kept the price of grain high in the interests of the landed aristocracy. During the 1830s and 1840s Manchester was at the heart of the Anti-Corn Law League, one of the most effective campaigning groups in British history (Howe, 1984, pp. 209–15). Removing restrictions on trade, it was believed, would stimulate the economy and thereby raise employment and wages. Both Kay and Adshead argued that ending the Corn Laws was part of the solution to urban poverty. Beyond this, political economy offered little comfort. One common theme was the need for better education, not least in the principles of political economy, so that the working classes would better understand and learn to cope with their situation.

All the voices we have so far heard came from within the tradition of political economy. All belonged to urban, middle-class writers who accepted the primacy of economic 'laws'. For all their disagreements, there were boundaries to the debate.

In the final pages of this chapter I should like to turn briefly to two voices outside this consensus. The first is that of Thomas Carlyle

Figure 1.5 Thomas Carlyle, photographed by Robert S. Tait, salt print, 1851. National Portrait Gallery, London, NPG P171(7). Photo: © National Portrait Gallery, London

(1795–1881), a highly influential writer and critic, admired by both Engels and Dickens. It was Carlyle (1965 [1843], p. 1) who coined the phrase 'condition of England' that was used to define a debate about what was happening to Britain in this period.

Carlyle (shown in Figure 1.5) was the son of a labourer from Dumfriesshire. When he set off (on foot) at the age of 14 to study in Edinburgh, he left not only his home but the whole rural world of his parents. When he established himself in literary London in the 1830s, therefore, his background meant that he was an outsider, and he was always happy to cultivate this pose. Much of his writing takes the form of a denunciation from the margins of society.

In the following passage, Carlyle addresses the argument that British manufacturers constantly needed to reduce wages and prices to remain competitive:

Cotton-cloth is already two-pence a yard or lower; and yet bare backs were never more numerous among us. [...] Let inventive men consider, Whether the Secret of this Universe, and of Man's Life there, does, after all, as we rashly fancy it, consist in making money? There is One God, just, supreme, almighty: but is Mammon the name of him? [...]

All this dire misery, [...] – may we not regard it as a voice from the dumb bosom of Nature, saying to us: 'Behold! Supply-and-demand is not the one Law of Nature; Cash-payment is not the sole nexus of man with man, – how far from it!'

(1965 [1843], pp. 189, 192)

(Note that 'Mammon' is an old name for a false god, used to personify the desire for earthly wealth.) In questioning the importance of acting competitively, Carlyle was challenging one of the fundamental principles of political economy from a moral perspective. He was very concerned by the influence of political economy on contemporary thought. He saw the political economists as trying to impose unbending laws that were far too narrow to encompass the breadth of human aspirations (Morrow, 2006, pp. 85–6). What was required was moral leadership that would show Britain the way out of its current impasse. Unlike many contemporary commentators, Carlyle did not condemn Chartism or other working-class movements; however, this did not mean he was sympathetic to their goals. Chartism, he argued, was simply a cry of distress from men who required leadership. His writings were not addressed to the working classes but to those he thought should provide this leadership: the upper and middle classes (Morrow, 2006, p. 81).

A second voice outside the consensus of political economy theory is that of David Ross, a Chartist lecturer in Manchester. The text I should like you to focus on in the next activity is from a speech made by Ross in Manchester in April 1842, just months before the Plug Strikes. We have no dates for Ross, but we do know he was from Ireland and a Catholic. He first came to prominence as a speaker against the Corn Laws, but from 1841 onwards he was making his reputation as a powerful speaker for the Chartists. He was arrested after the Plug Strikes, but was acquitted when no evidence was brought against him (Pickering, 1995, p. 204).

You should allow about
10 minutes for this
activity.

Activity

You will find Ross's speech, 'The State of the Country, as the Effect of
Class Legislation; and the Charter as a Remedy', reproduced as Reading
1.5. Read this now, and then answer the following question:

Why, according to Ross, is the Charter so essential?

Discussion

The importance of the Charter is explained in this speech in economic
terms. The working classes are the producers of all wealth, and are
deprived of it by bad laws. Implementing the Charter would mean
Parliament making laws of benefit to all – the implication is that this
would include laws to limit exploitation in factories.

If Carlyle's writings can be seen as an attack on the dominance of
political economy from a moral perspective, Chartism can be seen as an
argument from a political one. The historian Robert Gray talks of an
'alternative political economy' in which legislation would be used to
protect workers from the worst excesses of the market (1996, p. 28).
Just as middle-class reformers railed against the Corn Laws as class
legislation to protect the upper class, speakers such as Ross argued that
laws passed by a Parliament that excluded working-class representatives
favoured manufacturers and merchants. Only the Charter, and its
promise of universal male suffrage, would ensure that the balance
between masters and men was restored. In his speech, Ross sets up a
contrast between the handloom weavers, who controlled their own
labour, and the factories, source of 'poverty, wretchedness, and
discontent'.

Both Carlyle and Ross challenged political economy. Furthermore, both
came from humble origins in the smaller nations of the United
Kingdom. But there the similarities end. Carlyle's voice was heard in the
'condition of England' debate, and that of Ross was not. This was
partly because of what they said. Carlyle's writings spoke to many
audiences – his denunciations of Mammonism appealed to working-
class radicals, and his glorification of work to factory-owners – while his
calls for a newly morally inspired leadership also appealed to
conservative reformers within Britain's elite. But Carlyle was also heard
because of who he was. By the late 1830s he was established in London
and part of the literary world. Ross, on the other hand, was a Chartist

lecturer speaking to working-class audiences in a divided city. The Chartists were the subject of the debate about the condition of England, but not participants within it. Nor were working-class voices the only ones excluded. As I am sure you will have noted, all the texts selected here are by male writers.

Conclusion

Ross's desire to return to an age without factories may seem as strange to us as Carlyle's suggestion that manufacturers should cease to compete. This is perhaps partly because we still live in the shadow of these times: the boundaries then established between economics and politics are ones we have inherited and, perhaps, no longer question. As you saw at the beginning of this chapter, historians try to understand the past in its own terms by putting sources in their historical context. Rebuilding the conversations and circumstances of which voices and texts were a part helps us to understand how contemporaries made sense of their times. In Manchester in the 1830s and 1840s, commentators confronted a new industrial and urban world. The texts we have studied reveal them trying to understand this new world, sometimes using new philosophies and ways of writing, such as utilitarianism and statistics, sometimes drawing on old ideas and motifs, and often borrowing from each other. In the next two chapters we shall explore how Britain came to terms with this new world.

References

Adshead, J. (1972 [1842]) *Distress in Manchester: Evidence (Tabular and Otherwise) of the State of the Labouring Classes in 1840–42*, in Carpenter, K. E. (ed.) *Conditions of Working and Living: The Reawakening of the English Conscience. Five Pamphlets: 1838–1844*, New York, Arno Press.

Bradshaw, L.D. (1987) *Visitors to Manchester*, Manchester, self-published.

Briggs, A. (1968 [1963]) *Victorian Cities*, Harmondsworth, Penguin.

Carlyle, T. (1965 [1843]) *Past and Present*, London, Oxford University Press.

De Tocqueville, A. (1977 [1835]) 'Journeys to England and Ireland', in Clayre, A. (ed.) *Nature and Industrialization*, Oxford, Oxford University Press in association with Open University Press.

Engels, F. (1975 [1845]) *The Condition of the Working-Class in England: From Personal Observation and Authentic Sources*, in Marx, K. and Engels, F. *Collected Works*, vol. 4, London, Lawrence & Wishart.

Farnie, D.A. (1979) *The English Cotton Industry and the World Market, 1815–1896*, Oxford, Clarendon.

Faucher, L. (1969 [1844]) *Manchester in 1844: Its Present Condition and Future Prospects. Translated from the French with Copious Notes Appended by a Member of the Manchester Athenaeum*, London, Frank Cass.

Gray, R. (1996) *The Factory Question and Industrial England, 1830–1860*, Cambridge, Cambridge University Press.

Greg, W.R. (1853) *Essays on Political and Social Science*, London, Longman, Brown & Green.

Hamlin, C. (1998) *Public Health and Social Justice in the Age of Chadwick*, Cambridge, Cambridge University Press.

Howe, A. (1984) *The Cotton Masters 1830–1860*, Oxford, Clarendon.

Hunt, T. (2004) *Building Jerusalem: The Rise and Fall of the Victorian City*, London, Weidenfeld & Nicolson.

Hunt, T. (2009) *The Frock-Coated Communist: The Revolutionary Life of Friedrich Engels*, London, Allen Lane.

Ishiguro, K. (2005) *Never Let Me Go*, London, Faber and Faber.

Kay, J.P. (1969 [1832]) *The Moral and Physical Condition of the Working Classes Employed in the Cotton Manufacture in Manchester*, Manchester, E.J. Morten.

Kidd, A. (2006 [1993]) *Manchester: A History*, Lancaster, Carnegie Publishing.

Marcus, S. (1974) *Engels, Manchester and the Working Class*, London, Weidenfeld & Nicolson.

Mather, F.C. (1974) 'The General Strike of 1842: a study in leadership, organisation and the threat of revolution during the Plug Plot disturbances', in Quinault, R. and Stevenson, J. (eds) *Popular Protest and Public Order: Six Studies in British History, 1790–1920*, London, George Allen and Unwin.

Morrow, J. (2006) *Thomas Carlyle*, London, Hambledon Continuum.

Pickering, P.A. (1995) *Chartism and the Chartists in Manchester and Salford*, Basingstoke, Macmillan.

Poovey, M. (1995) *Making a Social Body: British Cultural Formation, 1830– 1864*, Chicago and London, University of Chicago Press.

Rose, M.B. (1986) *The Gregs of Quarry Bank Mill: The Rise and Decline of a Family Firm, 1750–1914*, Cambridge, CambridgeUniversity Press.

Ross, D. (2001 [1842]) 'The State of the Country, as the Effect of Class Legislation; and the Charter as a Remedy: a Lecture, delivered in the Chartist Room, Manchester, April 10th, 1842' in Claeys, G. (ed.) *The Chartist Movement in Britain, 1838–1850*, London, Pickering & Chatto, vol. 3.

Thompson, E.P. (1980 [1963]) *The Making of the English Working Class*, Harmondsworth, Penguin.

Timmins, G. (1998) *Made in Lancashire: A History of Regional Industrialisation*, Manchester, Manchester University Press.

Further reading

The most useful histories of the industrial city of Manchester combine economic, social, political and cultural history and consider the working and middle classes; for example Alan Kidd (2006) and Martin Hewitt (1996). Tristram Hunt's *Building Jerusalem* gives a good overview of the great Victorian industrial cities covering Sheffield, Birmingham and Leeds as well as Manchester. Emma Griffin (2010) offers a good introduction to the history of industrialisation and a good overview of the existing scholarship. For further details on the condition of England debate, see Levin (1998).

Griffin, E. (2010) *A Short History of the British Industrial Revolution*, Basingstoke, Palgrave Macmillan.

Hewitt, M. (1996) *The Emergence of Stability in the Industrial City: Manchester, 1832–67*, Aldershot, Scolar Press.

Hunt, T. (2004) *Building Jerusalem: The Rise and Fall of the Victorian City*, London, Weidenfeld & Nicolson (paperback edn 2005, London, Phoenix).

Kidd, A. (2006 [1993]) *Manchester: A History*, Lancaster, Carnegie Publishing.

Levin, M. (1998) *The Condition of England Question: Carlyle, Mill, Engels*, Basingstoke, Macmillan.

Reading 1.1 *The Condition of the Working-Class in England: From Personal Observation and Authentic Sources*

Source: Engels, F. (1975 [1845]) *The Condition of the Working-Class in England: From Personal Observation and Authentic Sources,* **in Marx, K. and Engels, F.,** *Collected Works,* **vol. 4, London, Lawrence & Wishart, pp. 300–1, 320, 344–5, 352–3, 381–2, 403, 562–3, 580, 583. (First published in German; first English publications in the USA in 1887 and in the UK in 1892)**

[Dedication]

Working Men!

To you I dedicate a work, in which I have tried to lay before my German Countrymen a faithful picture of your condition, of your sufferings and struggles, of your hopes and prospects. I have lived long enough amidst you to know something about your circumstances; I have devoted to their knowledge my most serious attention, I have studied the various official and non-official documents as far as I was able to get hold of them – I have not been satisfied with this. I wanted more than a mere *abstract* knowledge of my subject, I wanted to see you in your own homes, […] to witness your struggles against the social and political power of your oppressors. I have done so: I forsook the company and the dinner-parties, the port-wine and the champagne of the middle-classes, and devoted my leisure-hours almost exclusively to the intercourse with plain Working Men; I am both glad and proud of having done so. […]

Barmen, March 15th, 1845

The great towns

[…] The modern art of manufacture has reached its perfection in Manchester. In the cotton industry of South Lancashire, the application of the forces of Nature, the superseding of hand-labour by machinery (especially by the power-loom and the self-acting mule), and the division of labour, are seen at their highest point [...] The effects of modern manufacture upon the working-class must necessarily develop here most freely and perfectly, and the manufacturing proletariat present itself in its fullest classic perfection. [...] Because Manchester is the classic type of a modern manufacturing town, and because I know it as intimately as my own native town, more intimately than most of its residents know it, we shall make a longer stay here.

[...]

Above Ducie Bridge [...] the condition of the dwellings on both banks grows worse rather than better. [...] Everywhere heaps of debris, refuse, and offal; standing pools for gutters, and a stench which alone would make it impossible for a human being in any degree civilised to live in such a district. The newly built extension of the Leeds railway, which crosses the Irk here, has swept away some of these courts and lanes, laying others completely open to view. Immediately under the railway bridge there stands a court, the filth and horrors of which surpass all the others by far, just because it was hitherto so shut off [...] This whole collection of cattle-sheds for human beings was surrounded on two sides by houses and factory, and on the third by the river, and besides the narrow stair up the bank, a narrow doorway led out into another almost equally ill-built, ill-kept labyrinth of dwellings.

Enough! The whole side of the Irk is built in this way, a planless, knotted chaos of houses, more or less on the verge of uninhabitableness, whose unclean interiors fully correspond with their filthy external surroundings. [...]

Competition

[...] In spite of the extension of industry, in spite of the demand for working-men which, in general, has increased, there is, according to the confession of all the official political parties (Tory, Whig, and Radical), permanent surplus, superfluous population; the competition among the workers is constantly greater than the competition to secure workers.

Whence comes this incongruity? It lies in the nature of industrial competition and the commercial crises which arise from it. In the present unregulated production and distribution of the means of subsistence, which is carried on not directly for the sake of supplying needs, but for profit, in the system in which everyone works for himself to enrich himself, disturbances inevitably arise at every moment. [...]

Everything is done blindly, as guess-work, more or less at the mercy of accident. Upon the slightest favourable report, each one exports what he can, and before long, such markets are glutted, sales stop, capital remains inactive, prices fall, and English manufacture has no further employment for its hands. […] The small manufacturers and merchants who cannot survive a prolonged [period of] inactivity of their invested capital fail, the larger ones suspend business during the worst season, close the mills or work short time, perhaps half the day; wages fall […]; want becomes universal among the workers […], the number of the starving increases, and the whole multitude of [the] 'surplus' population presses in terrific numbers into the foreground. […]

Results

The result of all these influences is a general enfeeblement of the frame in the working-class. There are few vigorous, well-built, healthy persons among the workers […] Nearly all suffer from indigestion, and consequently from a more or less hypochondriac, melancholy, irritable, nervous condition. Their enfeebled constitutions are unable to resist disease, and are therefore seized by it on every occasion. Hence they age prematurely and die early. On this point the mortality statistics supply unquestionable testimony. […]

The attitude of the bourgeoisie towards the proletariat

[…] I have never seen a class […] so incurably debased by selfishness, so corroded within, so incapable of progress, as the English bourgeoisie […] For it nothing exists in this world, except for the sake of money […] It knows no bliss save that of rapid gain, no pain save that of losing gold. […] I once went into Manchester with such a bourgeois, and spoke to him of the bad, unwholesome method of building, the frightful condition of the working-people's quarters, and asserted that I had never seen so ill-built a city. The man listened quietly to the end, and said at the corner where we parted: 'And yet there is a great deal of money made here; good morning, sir'. […]

But assuming that England retained the monopoly of manufactures, that its factories perpetually multiply, what must be the result? The commercial crises would continue, and grow more violent, more terrible, with the extension of industry and the multiplication of the proletariat. The proletariat would increase in geometrical proportion, in consequence of the progressive ruin of the lower middle-class and the giant strides with which capital is concentrating itself in the hands of the few; and the proletariat would soon embrace the whole nation, with the exception of a few millionaires. But in this development there comes a stage at which the proletariat perceives how easily the existing power may be overthrown, and then follows a revolution. [...]

[...]

The classes are divided more and more sharply, the spirit of resistance penetrates the workers, the bitterness intensifies, the guerrilla skirmishes become concentrated in more important battles, and soon a slight impulse will suffice to set the avalanche in motion. Then, indeed, will the war-cry resound through the land: 'War to the mansion, peace to the cottage!' – but then it will be too late for the rich to beware.

Reading 1.2 *Manchester in 1844: Its Present Condition and Future Prospects*

Source: Faucher, L. (1969 [1844]) *Manchester in 1844: Its Present Condition and Future Prospects. Translated from the French with Copious Notes Appended by a Member of the Manchester Athenaeum,* **London, Frank Cass, pp. 15–18, 45–6, 57, 72–9, 90–3**

Nothing is more curious than the industrial topography of Lancashire. Manchester, like a diligent spider, is placed in the centre of the web, and sends forth roads and railways towards its auxiliaries, formerly villages, but now towns, which serve as outposts to the grand centre of industry. [...]

An order sent from Liverpool in the morning, is discussed by the merchants in the Manchester Exchange at noon, and in the evening is distributed amongst the manufacturers in the environs. In less than eight days, the cotton spun at Manchester, Oldham, or Ashton, is woven in the sheds of Bolton, Stalybridge, or Stockport; dyed and printed at Blackburn, Chorley, or Preston, and finished, measured, and packed at Manchester. By this division of labour amongst the towns, and amongst the manufacturers in the towns, and amongst the operatives in the manufactories; the water, coal, and machinery work incessantly. Execution is almost as quick as thought. [...]

Manchester, which holds under its sway these industrial agglomerations, is itself an agglomeration the most extraordinary, the most interesting, and in some respects, the most monstrous, which the progress of society has presented. The first impression is far from favourable. Its position is devoid of picturesque relief, and the horizon of clearness.

Amid the fogs which exhale from this marshy district, and the clouds of smoke vomited forth from the numberless chimneys, Labour presents a mysterious activity, somewhat akin to the subterraneous action of a volcano. [...] All the houses, all the streets, resemble each other; and yet this uniformity is in the midst of confusion. [...] The manufactories and machine shops form as it were, a girdle around the town, and follow the courses of the streams. Factories, seven stories in height, rear their lofty fronts along the banks of the Irwell, and along the borders of the canals [...] The waters of the Irk, black and fetid as they are, supply numerous tanneries and dye-works [...]

From this apparently indifferent combination, there results a great economy both of time and wealth in production. There is perhaps good reason for complaint that too little attention has been paid to the health and convenience of the inhabitants; of the want of public squares, fountains, trees, promenades, and well-ventilated buildings; but it is certain that it would be a difficult task to devise a plan by which the various products of Industry could be more concentrated, or by which the manufactories should be brought nearer to the fuel which feeds them, or more accessible to facilities for disposing of the goods when manufactured. [...]

The manufacturing system, as conducted at the present day, is far from encouraging regularity of conduct. In congregating so many men, women, and children, together without any other object than Labour, there is full scope for the birth and growth of passions which eventually refuse to submit to constraint, and which end in unbridled license. The union of the sexes, and the high temperature of the manufactories, act upon the organisation like the tropical sun; and puberty is developed before age and education have matured the moral sentiments. The factory girls are strangers to modesty. Their language is gross, and often obscene, and when they do not marry early, they form illicit connexions, which degrade them still more than premature marriage. It is a common occurrence to meet in the intervals of labour, in the back streets, couples of males and females, which the caprice of the moment has brought together. Sometimes they accompany each other to the beer shop, and thus accustom themselves to a double debauch. All the public inquiries on this subject since 1832, bear witness to this corruption of manners. [...]

In the manufacturing districts the operatives are exposed to periodical crises, which put a stop to labour, throw whole families out of employment, and produce the same effect that a bad harvest does in the rural districts. Excluding the accidental cause of distress, there yet remains in all the great manufacturing towns a mass of misery which increases from year to year. [...]

The operatives are pale and meagre in their appearance, and their physiognomy has not that animation which indicates health and vigour. Female beauty is not to be found amongst them, and the declining vigour of the men is replaced by febrile energy. The officers of the regiments, raised in Lancashire, affirm that the men cannot bear much fatigue. It is evident that the race is degenerating.

The women, working under the same circumstances as the men, are subject to similar influences. There are factories in Manchester which are open seventeen hours daily, of which fifteen and a half hours are occupied with effective labour. As to the children in the manufacturing districts […], they recruit the exhaustion of the week's toil, by lying in bed the whole of Sunday. There is no order in the family, and education is a thing unthought of. The mothers, who are working at the mule jenny all the day, administer to their infants a preparation of opium, to keep them quiet, or leave them under the care of younger children; and thus is explained the fact that out of 407 violent deaths, 110 were of children who were burnt or scalded to death. Those who escape these accidental deaths receive no instruction or culture […]

The manufacturing system in England and elsewhere is in this period of trial. […] Industry is evidently in a state of anarchy; but it will, sooner or later, make a better use of its liberty.

Amongst the causes which prolong this temporary malady, none act more strongly than the agglomeration of manufactories and operatives in the towns. The centres of industry are seats of corruption […]

Reading 1.3 *The Moral and Physical Condition of the Working Classes Employed in the Cotton Manufacture in Manchester*

Source: Kay, J.P. (1969 [1832]) *The Moral and Physical Condition of the Working Classes Employed in the Cotton Manufacture in Manchester,* **Manchester, E.J. Morten, pp. 4–6, 29–32**

Thus occupied in tracing the means by which the contagious principle of cholera is disseminated, I have felt surprise at the singular frequency with which I have been led to the most loathsome haunts of poverty and vice. [...]

It is melancholy to perceive how many of the evils suffered by the poor flow from their own ignorance or errors. [...] Ignorance, dissolute habits, imprudence and idle extravagance prevail. Some prejudiced men, accustomed to examine only one side of the shield, are hence eager to attribute all the evils suffered by the poor, solely to their ignorance or moral deviations. On the contrary, not only do they suffer under the pressure of extraneous grievances, but even those which immediately flow from their own habits, may often be traced to the primary influence of the imperfect institutions of society on their character – to the combined effects of an untutored ignorance – bad example, uncounteracted by a system of moral instruction – and the desperate straits of a perverted spirit battling with hunger and toil. Their errors are not more their fault than their misfortune [...]

An intimate connexion subsists, among the poor, between the cleanliness of the street and that of the house and person. Uneconomical habits, and dissipation are almost inseparably allied; and they are so frequently connected with uncleanliness, that we cannot regard their concomitance as altogether accidental. The first step to recklessness may often be traced in a neglect of that self-respect, and of the love of domestic enjoyments, which are indicated by personal slovenliness, and discomfort of the habitation. [...]

The following table, arranged by the Committee of Classification appointed by the Special Board of Health, from the reports of Inspectors of the various District Boards of Manchester, shows the extent to which the imperfect state of the streets of Manchester may tend to promote demoralization and disease among the poor.

[No. of] District	No. of streets inspected	No. of streets unpaved	No. of streets partially paved	No. of streets ill ventilated	No. of streets containing heaps of refuse, stagnant pools, ordure, &c
1	114	63	13	7	64
2	180	93	7	23	92
3	49	2	2	12	28
4	66	37	10	12	52
5	30	2	5	5	12
6	2	1	0	1	2
7	53	13	5	12	17
8	16	2	1	2	7
9	48	0	0	9	20
10	29	19	0	10	23
11	0	0	0	0	0
12	12	0	1	1	4
13	55	3	9	10	23
14	33	13	0	8	8
Total	687	248	53	112	352

[…] We discover in those districts which contain a large proportion of the poor, namely, in Nos. 1, 2, 3, 4, 7, 10, 13, and 14, that among 579 streets inspected, 243 were altogether unpaved – 46 partially paved – 93 ill-ventilated – and 307 containing heaps of refuse, deep ruts, stagnant pools, ordure, &c. […]

The replies to the questions proposed in the second table relating to houses, contain equally remarkable results, which have been carefully arranged by the Classification Committee of the Special Board of Health as follows.

[No. of] District	No. of houses inspected	No. of houses reported as requiring whitewashing	No. of houses reported as requiring repair	No. of houses in which the soughs wanted repair	No. of houses damp	No. of houses reported as ill ventilated	No. of houses wanting privies
1	850	399	128	112	177	70	326
2	2489	898	282	145	497	109	755
3	213	145	104	41	61	52	96
4	650	279	106	105	134	69	250
5	413	176	82	70	101	11	66
6	12	3	5	5			5
7	343	76	59	57	86	21	79
8	132	35	30	39	48	22	20
9	128	34	32	24	39	19	25
10	370	195	53	123	54	2	232
11							
12	113	33	23	27	24	16	52
13	757	218	44	108	146	54	177
14	481	74	13	83	68	7	138
Total	6951	2565	961	939	1435	452	2221

It is however to be lamented, that even these numerical results fail to exhibit a perfect picture of the ills which are suffered by the poor [...] Some idea of the want of cleanliness prevalent in their habitations may be obtained from the report of the number of houses requiring whitewashing; but this column fails to indicate their gross neglect of order, and absolute filth. Much less can we obtain satisfactory statistical results concerning the want of furniture, especially of bedding, and of food, clothing, and fuel. In these respects the habitations of the Irish are most destitute. [...] Frequently, the inspectors found two or more families crowded into one small house, containing only two apartments, one in which they slept, and another in which they eat; and often more than one family lived in a damp cellar, containing only one room, in whose pestilential atmosphere from twelve to sixteen person were crowded. To these fertile sources of disease were sometimes added the keeping of pigs and other animals in the house, with other nuisances of the most revolting character.

Reading 1.4 *Distress in Manchester: Evidence (Tabular and Otherwise) of the State of the Labouring Classes in 1840–42*

Source: Adshead, J. (1972 [1842]) *Distress in Manchester: Evidence (Tabular and Otherwise) of the State of the Labouring Classes in 1840–42*, **in Carpenter, K.E. (ed.)** *Conditions of Working and Living: The Reawakening of the English Conscience. Five Pamphlets: 1838–1844*, **Arno Press, New York, pp. 30–1**

The following cases are the result of a personal examination by a benevolent military gentleman of rank and experience, who took a deep interest in the state of the poor at that period: […]

Elizabeth Curry, Thackery's-buildings, Oldham-road. They are five in [a] family, only one able to work, who earns 1s. 6d. per week. She has been twenty years in Manchester, and is now unable to work from sickness. She receives 3s. from the Overseer, and pays in rent 2s.

Sarah Cunningham, Pot-street, Ancoats. An Irish family, nine in number; one of the children earns 4s. 6d. They pay in rent 1s. 6d. The husband cannot obtain work; and is disqualified to receive relief, having only resided four years in Manchester. […]

John Maycock, 15 years of age, piecer by trade, laying at the Night Asylum. He is an orphan without home or work. He was received a few days since at the Night Asylum, and will die if sent from it. He is in an utter state of destitution, and no prospect of obtaining work. His master brought him to the Night Asylum, having no work for him.

Reading 1.5 'The State of the Country, as the Effect of Class Legislation; and the Charter as a Remedy'

Source: Ross, D. (2001 [1842]) 'The State of the Country, as the Effect of Class Legislation; and the Charter as a Remedy: a Lecture, delivered in the Chartist Room, Manchester, April 10th, 1842', in Claeys, G. (ed.) *The Chartist Movement in Britain, 1838–1850*, London, Pickering & Chatto, vol. 3, pp. 104–13

Respected Sir, And Fellow Labourers in the Cause of Truth, Justice and Freedom.

On a former occasion I declared, as my firm conviction, that the 'People's Charter' was the remedy for the manifold existing evils and abuses which distract, unsettle, and threaten with inevitable ruin, this unhappy country […]

Labour being the source from which all wealth is derived, permit me to ask, what would be the condition of the manufacturers if deprived of our assistance? How could they employ, to advantage, the capital which they so highly value, and about which they are so solicitous? […] Even the most exquisite and skilfully arranged, and ingeniously executed machinery is powerless, without being aided by the wisdom and labour of man […]

But suppose the 'Charter' obtained; labour would then be governed by firm and immutable laws; the poor man would not then be compelled to carry his child to the factory, with scarce a rag to cover its shivering limbs on a winter's morning. The poor child would not have, from morning to night, to keep pace with never-tiring machinery, as at the present day. Mothers would not have to weep over the mangled remains of their murdered children, who sink into premature graves through the severity of their labour. The factory system is, moreover, the prolific parent of vice and immorality […]

I never behold a poor factory child, but I instinctively picture to myself the misery which the cursed system entails upon the human family. I was once in the habit of visiting the hand-loom weavers, about ten or twelve years ago, and I invariably found them a happy and contented people; their cottages were comfortable homes; they had hours of relaxation, and gardens for profit and amusement; but now the factories are at work in those districts in which they resided, and poverty, wretchedness, and discontent are the inmates of every dwelling.

Many impute to bad trade, the cause of our unexampled distress; such, my friends, is a palpable delusion. Bad laws have effected this. If want of trade had brought this present ruin upon our country, from whom have the manufacturers obtained the means to build their large warehouses, and their splendid houses? How have they been able to raise great factories, and fill them with expensive machinery? The answer is plain; from the labours of the spinner, the weaver, the dresser &c, &c, [...]

The attainment of the 'Charter' will restore things to their proper level, and pristine appearance. Labour will have its protection, equal with its child, capital, which will remove hunger and fear of it; and in its stead, bring plenty and contentment.

Chapter 2
Dickens's *Hard Times*

Lynda Prescott

Contents

Aims

This chapter will:

- explore how contemporary readers might have approached the novel *Hard Times*, by establishing its original publication context

- introduce you to some major features of nineteenth-century novels through examination of characterisation, plot, structure, setting and, most importantly, narrative voice

- help you to develop your analytical skills in the close reading of both fictional and non-fictional prose.

Materials you will need

In this chapter, you will need to listen to the following audio recording, which can be found on the module website:

- *Hard Times*, *Household Words* and Dickens's reputation.

You will need to watch the following film, which can be found on the module website:

- The Preston Lockout.

You will also be referred to the set book: Charles Dickens, *Hard Times*, edited with an introduction and notes by Kate Flint and published by Penguin Classics.

Introduction

We turn now from historical texts about Manchester in the 1830s and 1840s, some well known, some less so, to a very well-known fictional text written in the 1850s, *Hard Times* by Charles Dickens (1812–1870). There are several obvious reasons for discussing *Hard Times* in the context of a study of mid-nineteenth-century Britain. Not only was the novel written and published during the historical period we are interested in, but it is also a text that focuses very deliberately on aspects of its contemporary world – the subtitle Dickens chose for the novel is *For These Times*. But novels, however topical, do not merely offer a fictional reflection of the society in which they appear. The fabric of any novel, from the texture of its language and its internal structure to its physical form, is shaped, at least in part, by the circumstances and conventions of the world in which it is produced. At the same time, novels, like any works of art, can influence that world, leading the people who live in it to think a little differently about themselves. So we could say that meaning flows to and fro between the literary text and its contemporary context.

Another reason for choosing *Hard Times* is that it is a major novel by one of the best-known and most influential writers of the day; by focusing on it here we touch again on the theme of authority that you considered extensively in Book 2 of the module. And because Dickens is still a significant literary figure today, we can explore some of the ways in which the academic discipline of Literature provides further contextual layers for studying a text from the past.

One fairly standard way of approaching a long literary text for study purposes is to begin with analysis of the text and then add various relevant contexts to the mix. In this chapter we shall work in the opposite direction, starting from contemporary contexts and then focusing increasingly on analysis of the novel itself. However, you do need to be reasonably familiar with the novel from the outset, so if you were not able to complete your initial reading of *Hard Times* during the allocated Reading Week before starting on Book 4 it would be best to finish it now, before continuing with this chapter.

2.1 Not 'classic' but 'contemporary'

It is hard for any reader to approach a novel by Dickens without having the term 'classic' in mind, especially when the edition we have chosen comes under the banner of 'Penguin Classics'. Dickens (shown in Figure 2.1) is one of the best known of English writers, and even people who might not have read any of his novels are probably familiar with his reputation. Some of his fictional characters, too, are famous outside the books in which they first appeared (think of Ebenezer Scrooge in *A Christmas Carol*, or the young orphan hero Oliver Twist, who outraged the workhouse authorities by asking for a second helping of gruel). So when we read *Hard Times* we are likely to bring to our reading certain assumptions and expectations about both the writer and the kind of work we are encountering.

For the moment, though, I want you to try to look at Dickens's novel not through the lens of our twenty-first-century judgements, but through the eyes of his contemporary readers encountering *Hard Times* for the first time in 1854.

Activity

Study Figure 2.2, which shows the first page of *Household Words*, no. 210: the version in which Dickens's original readers would have read the opening of the novel. What are the main differences you notice between this mid-Victorian version and the edition of *Hard Times* you have been using?

Spend just a few minutes jotting down some of these differences.

Discussion

You may have thought that the *Household Words* version, with its double-columned format and inclusion of a date, looks more like the front page of a newspaper than the start of a book. This is not far from the truth, since we see from the subtitle that *Household Words*, if not exactly a newspaper, was 'a weekly journal', or magazine. So the original readers of *Hard Times* would have followed the novel in 20 weekly instalments rather than reading at their chosen pace through a single volume. There were usually 24 pages in each issue of *Household Words*, covering a range of different topics, with the most important item on the front page. Thus in the *Household Words* version the opening of Dickens's novel looks something like an opinion-forming leading article in a newspaper. You may also have noticed that there is no subtitle

Figure 2.1 Charles Dickens in 1861. Photographed by John Watkins. Photo: © The Charles Dickens Museum

('For These Times') under the heading 'Hard Times', and no book or chapter titles – Dickens added these later. Overall, the *Household Words* version is plain and compressed, and it looks physically very different from the edition of *Hard Times* we're using, with its 300 or more pages.

Perhaps the next question is: do these differences actually matter? Having explored the physical nature of the printed book in Book 1, Chapter 4 of this module, you will be aware that format is important, but you may still be thinking that what really matters in a novel is the

Figure 2.2   The first serialised page of *Hard Times* in *Household Words*

words, or 'the text'. We shall certainly be looking in detail at the text of *Hard Times*, but viewing the novel from 'outside', so to speak, can enhance our study of the text in a number of ways.

Comparing the original *Household Words* format with our modern paperback edition helps us to recognise some of our contemporary assumptions about novels and novel-reading, assumptions that are triggered even before we open the pages of the 200mm x 130mm x 20mm object that fits so easily into the hands of a reader, or perhaps download an electronic version onto a mobile device. As well as recognising our possible preconceptions about Dickens and his reputation, we should also remember that some of our expectations about the novel as a genre are different from those Dickens's original readers would have had. By the mid-nineteenth century the novel was no longer the new form of literature that its name suggests, but it was still new enough to be slightly controversial. In some quarters novel-reading was even considered to be a rather hazardous leisure activity, especially for impressionable young, and female, readers, who might be exposed to unsuitable ideas. Although this view was fading out by the middle of the century, the reading of novels was often seen as a branch of idleness. Dickens plays on this idea when he states in Chapter 8 of *Hard Times* that Mr Gradgrind 'greatly tormented his mind about what the people read' in Coketown's library (2003 [1854], p. 53). Gradgrind cannot understand why, after a long day's work, men and women should want to read 'mere fables' rather than use their time to acquire useful knowledge, such as mathematics. In the mid-nineteenth century novels were not likely to feature in the educational syllabus, either at schools like Gradgrind's, or indeed at universities, where the study of Literature still meant mostly Latin and Greek literature.

But novel-reading in the mid-nineteenth century was also enormously popular. Britain's 'reading public' was growing ever larger, thanks to improving literacy rates as well as general population increase, and demand for fiction meant that the writing, publishing and selling of novels was becoming a big, profitable business. During the first half of the nineteenth century the kinds of technological advances, underpinned by capitalist enterprise, that had earlier transformed the cotton industry in Lancashire now propelled printing and book production into a phase of rapid expansion. Steam power was applied first to paper making, leading to a dramatic increase in production, and then to printing. Although the new steam-driven printing machines were used initially for newspapers, by the 1830s books were being produced this way too. When we approach mid-nineteenth-century novels from this perspective, we are engaging in 'Book History' (a comparatively new area in the study of Literature). Book History involves paying particularly close attention to the economic, social and cultural contexts of book production, and as we do so we naturally tap into the concerns of other kinds of historians too.

Approaching our set novel 'from the outside' like this may help us to see its creator, Charles Dickens, not as the 'classic' author whose lengthy novels fill so many shelves of our bookshops and libraries, but as a dominant figure in the expanding business of mid-nineteenth-century publishing. To his contemporaries, Dickens was not simply a novelist, but a writer of short fiction and non-fiction, as well as a journalist. There were several other strands in Dickens's career, including public speaking, acting and (in a combination of these two) phenomenally successful public readings from his own works. However, the aspect of his public persona we shall explore next, because it has a direct bearing on our study of *Hard Times*, is as the 'conductor' of the weekly journal *Household Words*.

2.2 Dickens's journalism

I have already referred to the early nineteenth-century revolution in print production that led to such tremendous expansion in the newspaper industry. In 1780 there were just 76 newspapers and periodicals in England and Wales but as costs, especially taxes, gradually came down, newspapers became more numerous. Long-established titles like *The Times* (founded in 1785) were joined by new daily, weekly and monthly papers and magazines, and the reading of newspapers and periodicals became an increasingly important feature of national life.

Dickens had been involved in this explosion of journalism right from the start of his career. Based in London, he worked from 1834 to 1836 as a freelance parliamentary reporter for the *Morning Chronicle* newspaper. After that, he spent three years editing a new monthly literary magazine, *Bentley's Miscellany*, named after the owner, the publisher Richard Bentley (1794–1871). Dickens's first novel, *Pickwick Papers*, had already appeared in monthly parts (1836–37), and he serialised his second novel, *Oliver Twist*, in *Bentley's Miscellany* (1837–39).

But the pull of political journalism, rather than serial fiction-writing, was still strong, and for a brief period in 1846 Dickens acted as editor of a new liberal national newspaper. The day to day demands of this job were scarcely compatible with the other demands of his writing life, but Dickens's short-lived involvement with the *Daily News* was characteristically energetic. A more feasible opportunity to exercise his editorial skills arose in 1850 when his publishers, Bradbury and Evans, provided backing for a new venture that would make considerable profits for Dickens and his partners. This was the launch of a new weekly magazine, introduced in an advertising handbill as '*Household Words*: a miscellany of general literature' (Lohrli, 1973, p. 3), but clearly designed to be as much a platform for discussion of social questions of the day as for entertainment. The journal was to be 'conducted' by Dickens, an unusual expression in such a context, but it conveys quite effectively the way that Dickens mustered and led an ensemble of contributors that included some of the best writers of the day.

Dickens always paid a great deal of attention to the titles of his literary works, and the new journal was no exception. *Household Words*, as you may be able to make out from looking at the top of the page illustrated in Figure 2.2, is actually a Shakespearean phrase, and the full quotation, from Henry V's speech before Agincourt, appeared at the head of every edition of the journal: 'Familiar in their Mouths as *Household Words*', along with Shakespeare's name. Dickens might be seen here as drawing on Shakespeare's literary authority and, in doing so, appealing to the reasonably well-educated readers he was seeking to attract. The market for weekly magazines, at this period, mainly consisted of working-class or lower-middle-class readers, but *Household Words*, priced at 2d. (old pence) a week, was more expensive than its main rivals. It also made more ambitious claims in terms of literary quality. So Dickens and his partners seem to have been aiming to attract both middle-class and working-class readers.

Activity

You should allow about 10 minutes for this activity.

Read the short extract below from the 'Preliminary Word' in the first issue of *Household Words*. Jot down a few words or phrases from the extract that might help you to answer the following questions:

1   What kind of relationship with its readers does the new journal seek to establish?

2   Is the view of contemporary society offered in this passage positive or negative?

> We aspire to live in the Household affections, and to be numbered among the Household thoughts, of our readers. We hope to be the comrade and friend of many thousands of people, of both sexes, and of all ages and conditions, on whose faces we may never look. We seek to bring to innumerable homes, from the stirring world around us, the knowledge of many social wonders, good and evil, that are not calculated to render any of us less ardently persevering in ourselves, less faithful in the progress of mankind, less thankful for the privilege of living in this summer-dawn of time.

(Quoted in Slater, 1996, p. 177)

Discussion

1   In answer to this question you perhaps noted repetitions of the inclusive 'we', along with phrases such as 'Household affections' and 'comrade and friend' that seem to suggest a personal, even intimate, relationship in a domestic setting. To a twenty-first-century reader this may sound contrived and sentimental, but in terms of nineteenth-century **rhetoric** it is not an unfamiliar tone. In general, the

'Preliminary Word' seems to envisage an inclusive readership –
people 'of all ages and conditions'.

2   When assessing the view of contemporary society in the extract, you
    may have noted that phrases such as 'stirring world', 'progress of
    mankind', 'summer-dawn of time' have a distinctly positive ring about
    them. I wondered, though, whether the concentration of negative
    words crammed into the final sentence, where a 'not' and three
    'less'es make the syntax very complex, casts a shadow over the rosy
    picture.

Your approach to the questions in the last activity may have differed
from mine, but I have deliberately emphasised close attention to
language to demonstrate the way that this can help us to identify the
tone of a piece of writing. 'Tone' is a rather vague but still useful critical
term, often used to describe effects in a piece of writing that are more
localised than those covered under the more general heading of 'style'.
People sometimes – mistakenly – refer to style as though it is
something added to writing, like a layer of icing on a cake. However,
literary analysis shows that style and tone are integral parts of the
meaning and effects of any piece of writing.

Close reading of the kind we have just practised is particularly valuable
in teasing out tensions and ambiguities in written texts. I've implied in
my comments on the 'Preliminary Word' above that Dickens offers a
mixed picture of the state of mid-nineteenth-century society: this would
not be surprising, because although *Household Words* was advertised as
providing 'Instruction and Entertainment' (Lohrli, 1973, p. 4), it was
also a crusading magazine. Alongside often light-hearted informational
items, the journal drew attention to social ills of various kinds, both in
its general articles and in some of the fictional works it carried. In his
letters to potential contributors Dickens made this motive clear. For
example, in January 1850 he wrote to fellow-novelist Elizabeth Gaskell
(1810–1865) that 'the general mind and purpose' of *Household Words* was
'the raising up of those that are down, and the general improvement of
our social condition' (quoted in Lohrli, 1973, p. 4). The outcome of this
particular correspondence was a four-chapter story by Gaskell, to which
Dickens gave pride of place in the opening instalments of the journal.
'Lizzie Leigh' (later published in book format as *Lizzie Leigh and Other
Tales* in 1855) is the story of a country girl who goes into domestic
service in Manchester, then becomes pregnant, loses her job in
consequence, and turns to prostitution. So the first readers of *Household*

Words were immediately stirred by a moving portrayal of the plight of the 'fallen woman', a major social issue of the day.

Hard Times provides another prime example of *Household Words'* social mission. Dickens planned and wrote the novel at short notice to boost the sales of the journal, which had fallen off during 1853. Some of his ideas for *Hard Times* were clearly prompted by the long industrial dispute that had kept the cotton mills of Preston closed for many months, attracting national and even international attention. As we shall see in the next section of this chapter, the Preston Lockout represented a crisis of industrial relations, which seemed to be just the visible tip of a dangerous iceberg. The human cost of rapid industrialisation was all too apparent to Dickens and his contemporaries, in the dismal lives that industrial workers led.

As a London-based journalist and fiction-writer, Dickens had less direct experience of living conditions in the industrialised north than, for example, Gaskell, who lived and worked in Manchester. But he did travel frequently, both at home and abroad, and while he was planning and starting to write *Hard Times* he took two journeys northwards, to the Midlands and to the northwest of England. Both of these journeys would generate important new articles for *Household Words*, as well as feeding into his plans for *Hard Times*.

The first of these journeys, in December 1853, was to Birmingham. Dickens had first visited the town (it acquired city status only much later) in 1838, and was astonished at its gloomy landscape of furnaces and steam engines. He returned several times over the next 15 years, and in 1853 was invited by the Committee of the Birmingham and Midlands Institute (BMI), one of the **mechanics' institutes** springing up across Britain, to give three 'Christmas Readings' (notably from *A Christmas Carol*) at Birmingham Town Hall to raise money for the new educational institution. This was the start of Dickens's enormously popular public readings from his own works. He asked the BMI Committee to arrange for one of the evening readings to be given to a working-class audience, and made an introductory speech on this occasion calling for greater understanding between employees and employers:

> If there ever was a time when any one class could of itself do much for its own good, and for the welfare of society – which I greatly doubt – that time is unquestionably past. It is in the fusion

of different classes, without confusion; in the bringing together of employers and employed; in the creating of a better common understanding among those whose interests are identical, who depend upon each other, who are vitally essential to each other, and who can never be in unnatural antagonism without deplorable results, that one of the chief principles of a mechanics' institution should consist. In this world a great deal of the bitterness among us arises from an imperfect understanding of one another.

(Quoted in Fielding, 1960, p. 167)

The rapturous applause that greeted this speech would have helped to persuade Dickens that his call for cooperation and understanding across class boundaries, during the brief gestation period for *Hard Times*, had struck a popular note. But the most immediate literary product of his West Midlands excursion was an article called 'Fire and Snow', which appeared in the 200th edition of *Household Words* on 21 January 1854.

On the free day between his town hall readings, 28 December 1853, Dickens took the train to Wolverhampton. There had been heavy snowfall the day before, and the amazement that Dickens had felt when first seeing this blackened industrial landscape 15 years earlier was given a fresh turn by the snow-transformation. His *Household Words* article was really a travel piece, but the extracts below suggest the impact of this landscape on his imagination:

Can this be the region of cinders and coal-dust, which we have traversed before now, divers times, both by night and by day, when the dirty wind rattled as it came against us charged with fine particles of coal, and the natural colour of the earth and all its vegetation might have been black, for anything our eyes could see to the contrary in a waste of many miles? Indeed it is the same country, though so altered that on this present day when the old year is near its last, the North East wind blows white, and all the ground is white – pure white – insomuch that if our lives depended on our identifying a mound of ashes as we jar along this Birmingham and Wolverhampton Railway, we could not find a handful [...]

So, away again over the moor, where the clanking serpents usually writhing above coal-pits, are dormant and whitened over – this being holiday time – but where those grave monsters, the blast-furnaces, which cannot stoop to recreation, are awake and roaring. Now, a smoky village; now, a chimney; now, a dormant serpent who seems to have been benumbed in the act of working his way for shelter into the lonely little engine-house by the pit's mouth [...] Not altogether agreeable to think of crossing such space without a guide, and being swallowed by a long-abandoned, long-forgotten shaft.

(Slater, 1998, pp. 191–2)

In *Hard Times*, Stephen Blackpool does, of course, cross this kind of undermined country without a guide, and we can see fictional plot possibilities at work in Dickens's piece of non-fictional travel writing. You might also have noticed the 'clanking serpents' at the pit-heads, and thought of Coketown's 'serpents of smoke'. Clearly Dickens worked on this image, as he transferred the 'serpent' idea from the looming, angular outlines of winding-gear described here to the more sinuous shapes of smoke-trails over Coketown.

A month after his highly successful public readings in Birmingham, Dickens went further north, to Preston, to see for himself the effects of the long-running industrial dispute that had paralysed most of Preston's mills since the summer of 1853. Besides providing him with background material for *Hard Times*, this journey also generated, as you will read in the next section, another major article for *Household Words*.

2.3 The Preston Lockout

By the winter of 1853–54 the long-running conflict between employers and workers in Preston was bitter and deeply entrenched. Some of the historical evidence relating to this important episode in Lancashire's industrial past exists in visual and aural form, so we have compiled a short film to introduce the topic, foregrounding voices as well as texts.

Activity

Watch the film 'The Preston Lockout', which you can find on the module website. The film should help you to understand why the lockout happened, and what its impact was.

You should allow about 20 minutes for this activity.

Dickens was clearly interested in the subject of industrial relations, and in 1851 he had published an article in *Household Words* on 'Railway Strikes'. There he argued that the working men of England, specifically railwaymen in this case, were in danger of being misled by outside agitators. We can see this idea continued later through the character of Slackbridge, the trade union official, in *Hard Times*. But although the fictional workers in Coketown do not actually go on strike, Dickens did write directly about the Preston Lockout in a long article for *Household Words* which appeared in February 1854.

Activity

Read the extract from 'On Strike' that appears as Reading 2.1 at the end of this chapter. The extract focuses on Dickens's arrival in Preston, where he sees many placards and notices posted on street corners. There are lengthy quotations within Dickens's article, some of which are included in the reading. As you read, pay close attention to the language of these texts-within-a-text, from the long address undersigned by the strike committee to the short pieces accompanying subscriptions to the strike fund. Try to get a sense of what the language of the quoted texts reveals: do any particular words and phrases evoke other (non-industrial) frames of reference?

You should allow about 30 minutes for this activity.

Discussion

The power of print at this period certainly seems evident from the sheer quantity, and length, of street notices that Dickens is able to quote. We can imagine the 'groups of working people attentively reading' the address to 'Friends and Fellow Operatives' being stuck at their particular street corner for quite a long time! Dickens intersperses quotations from the ephemeral literature of the lockout with comments and judgements of his own, but in his choice of placards to report he seems concerned to play down any fears of *Household Words*' readers about the threat to public and economic order that the lockout represented. He chooses the address to the 'Friends and Fellow Operatives' as the 'worst' example of its sort, implying at the same time that its tone is not especially passionate. Certainly, the locked-out workers of Preston are 'outraged and insulted', 'down trodden' and victims of 'oppression', but by and large the language is fairly measured. One term that did stand out for me, however, was 'serfs'. Serfdom is often defined as a form of **slavery**, since under the medieval feudal system serfs were agricultural labourers bound to work their masters' lands. In Britain the feudal system had broken up centuries earlier, but in 1854 slavery had only recently been abolished in the British empire and still existed in the southern states of the USA, the main source of Lancashire's cotton. So we might expect nineteenth-century activists searching for a metaphor to express the condition of exploited factory workers to talk about slavery rather than serfdom (which persisted only in Russia and distant parts of eastern Europe), and indeed some of them did. The reference to 'serfs', however, side-steps the matter of race, a prominent issue in abolitionist debates, and in some senses is less emotive. It suggests a reversion to an older social system in which the labourers, instead of being at the mercy of all-powerful masters who owned the land, were now at the mercy of capitalists who owned the factories – and, ironically, agricultural labour, if not serfdom, was only a generation or two distant from many factory labourers. I don't want to build too much on the use of a single word here, but it does seem that the authors of this document, struggling to convey the 'unfree' condition of factory workers, have reached for a term that will evoke an entire social system.

A more general point you may have noted about the rhetoric of the strike committee's address, especially in the second half, is its use of religious terminology. 'God' and 'his blessings' make a direct appearance in the fifth paragraph, but before that we have a reference to the 'great architect', who designed the world as 'the dwelling place and the abode of peace, plenty, happiness and love'. Further on, the political message that everyone should take their share in the world's work is given the status of a 'divine precept': 'Those who will not work, shall not eat'. But the committee's address is not the only document quoted in Dickens's article to use religious references. The contributors to the strike fund whose sign-offs are given towards the end of the reading include two who draw on the words of the Christian gospels to reinforce the sentiments behind their donations: 'Bear ye one another's burthens' and

'We'll stand to our text, see that ye love one another'. These expressions of morality based on the teachings of Christ seem to be in tune with the dying words of Stephen Blackpool as he is carried, at night, from the disused pit-shaft in *Hard Times*, Book 3, Chapter 6. The image of a guiding star, which figures so prominently in the story of Christ's nativity, is echoed in the chapter's title, 'The Starlight', and in Stephen's words as he gazes 'reverently' at the star that has been visible above him during his ordeal: 'in our judgements, like as in our doins, we mun bear and forbear. [...] I ha' made it my dyin' prayer that aw th' world may o'ny coom toogether more' (p. 264). You might have been reminded of Stephen's final speech as you read this section of 'On Strike'.

You may have noted other points about the language of the texts-within-texts, but the influence of Christianity is worth pausing over. The Religious Census of 1851 showed that only about half the population of England and Wales over the age of 10 attended any kind of church on 30 March that year (many contemporaries found this a shocking statistic), and church attendance was undoubtedly lowest in the working-class areas of London and the northern industrial towns. Even so, Dickens's article implies, the language and many key values of Christianity were still very familiar, to working-class as well as middle-class Victorians.

The 'New Song of the Preston Strike' taps into a different set of traditions. We saw and heard in 'The Preston Lockout' film that ballads played an important part in working-class **culture**, helping to spread news, sometimes of a political nature. Although Dickens is simply acting as scribe in his 'On Strike' article, his own writings reveal a productive relationship with popular culture. The critic Sally Ledger claims that 'the popular author needs to establish a sense of "us" between himself and his readership', something that Dickens achieved very successfully. She continues: 'Dickens's "us" is a conception of "the People" that embraces the lower and middle classes of society' (Ledger, 2007, p. 4), a point that reminds us of Dickens's target readership for *Household Words*.

In looking at the Preston Lockout we have seen Dickens the journalist engaging in contemporary debates, and we have also been able to trace connections between some of his *Household Words* articles and aspects of *Hard Times*. These connections operate not only at the level of subject matter, but also in terms of language and literary technique. As we explore the interplay between fictional and non-fictional texts, you might be reminded of a point that emerged in Book 3 of this module in relation to creativity: 'It is the creative act that turns words and ideas into texts' (Book 3, Introduction, p. v). So the potential for creativity is embedded in language itself, however we use it, and is not simply a quality that can be roped off in the domain of fiction or, more broadly, 'the literary'. Some of the non-fictional examples we have looked at in this section, whether by Dickens or by the anonymous creators of the Preston Lockout's ephemeral literature, show that creativity in action.

So if both fictional and non-fictional texts share an element of linguistic creativity, and if there can be significant overlaps between the two kinds of writing in terms of subject matter as well as language, how much distance is there between the antonyms 'fiction' and 'non-fiction'? Ultimately, I would suggest, boundaries between the two forms of writing depend on our knowledge of the writers' intentions, and the kind of 'contract' they are entering into with their readers/audiences through their choice of genre. In the next section of this chapter we shall investigate a specific kind of fictional genre (it might be called a 'sub-genre' of the nineteenth-century novel) that Victorian readers were becoming quite familiar with by the time Dickens published *Hard Times*. But before we dig more deeply into the wider literary context for our discussion of *Hard Times*, the following activity provides another perspective on some of the topics we have considered so far.

Activity

You should allow about 15 minutes for this activity.

Now listen to the audio recording '*Hard Times, Household Words* and Dickens's Reputation', which you can find on the module website.

2.4 The Victorian 'social-problem' novel

In Chapter 1 of this book you looked at some of the evidence emerging during the 1830s and 1840s about the state of Britain's newly industrialised society. The 'condition of England', in Carlyle's famous phrase, was widely debated, but there was, it seems, something of an information gap about the actual living conditions of the poorest members of British society. As one literary historian notes:

> The middle and upper classes began to realise how little they knew about the lives of their less fortunate compatriots [...] As the appetite for knowledge about the condition of England was whetted, novelists found an audience interested in learning more about the plight of the working classes, and the novel became a method of teaching the middle and upper classes about the 'real' condition of England.
>
> (Simmons, 2002, p. 336)

There is a kind of paradox in 'evidence' about the dire state of newly industrialised society being circulated in the form of fiction, but the novel as a genre had always carried with it **didactic** possibilities. During the eighteenth century there was sometimes an overlap between the genres of 'conduct books', which advised young people (especially females) how to behave, and the newly emergent novel. In the nineteenth century religion came to the fore as an area where the novel could provide explicit teaching: most of these doctrinally driven novels are long forgotten, but they accounted for a large proportion of fiction published in the mid-nineteenth century. So perhaps it is not so surprising that writers should have used the novel form as a way of informing readers about current debates on factory regulations and child labour, for example. The novels' titles are often indicative: *The Life and Adventures of Michael Armstrong, the Factory Boy* (1840) by Frances Trollope, mother of the much more famous novelist Anthony, took a poor fatherless 10-year-old as its central character (Figure 2.3), while Elizabeth Stone's *William Langshawe the Cotton Lord* (1842) adopted a rather different perspective on the factory system.

These and other 'industrial' novels of the early 1840s are, like the mass of religious novels from this period, scarcely read at all now. But by the later 1840s another wave of novels concerned with the 'condition of

England' started appearing, and a number of these, having entered the canon of English literature, are still read and studied. *Hard Times* is often grouped with these 'social-problem' novels.

In the next activity you will look at one literary critic's introduction to this type of novel.

Figure 2.3 'Factory Children, or Love conquerd fear!', engraving in Frances Trollope (1840) *The Life and Adventures of Michael Armstrong, the Factory Boy*. Photo: © Private Collection/The Bridgeman Art Library

Activity

Reading 2.2 is a passage by Josephine M. Guy introducing the Victorian social-problem novel. Read this now, and make a note of the various ways in which Guy presents literature and history as being intertwined.

You should allow about 20 minutes for this activity.

Discussion

Guy talks about two different periods of history. The first is the period during which the major social-problem novels were written, the late 1840s and 1850s, when apparently there was a 'new kind of relationship between the novel and the social and political worlds which produced it'. The second period is the later twentieth century, when literary critics began to be interested in these social-problem novels (finding a new, cohesive label for them was part of this new literary interest). So we have the original engagement between Victorian fiction and society, discussed in terms of subject matter, authors' intentions and audience (you probably noticed, along the way, the reference to 'the moral authority often associated with Victorian fiction'), and then the critical perspective on this engagement, a century later. One of the most important points Guy makes in this passage, and in her book as a whole, is that literary history does not stand still: as new 'stories' of the past emerge, based on different kinds of evidence, or different historical principles, literary critics get busy alongside the historians, redefining and reinterpreting past literary works.

Besides *Hard Times*, Guy's list of principal social-problem novels includes two by Elizabeth Gaskell, *Mary Barton* (1848) and *North and South* (1855) – the latter took over the fiction-serial slot in *Household Words* once *Hard Times* was finished. The list also includes Benjamin Disraeli's *Sybil* (1845), Charles Kingsley's *Alton Locke* (1850) and George Eliot's much later *Felix Holt, the Radical* (1866) as part of the central cluster of texts. There is not space here to say much more about these social-problem novels, but the full title of Disraeli's *Sybil, or The Two Nations* encapsulates a common concern. For Disraeli the two nations are the rich and the poor. He notes the growing gap between them, not simply in economic terms but in every aspect of their lives, so that they are effectively

> Two nations between whom there is no intercourse and no
> sympathy; who are as ignorant of each other's habits, thoughts,

and feelings as if they were dwellers in different zones, or inhabitants of different planets.

(Disraeli, 1975 [1845], p. 67)

Of course, the gulf between rich and poor had always existed, and was more marked in the countryside than in the towns. However, traditional social systems did much to bridge the gap in the countryside. Local customs and practices inspired in part by Christian beliefs provided opportunities for communication between classes and ensured that local landowners took an interest in the well-being of their poorer neighbours. It was these networks of duty and deference that commentators felt were missing in the city. The sheer facts of inequality and lack of contact between the 'two nations' may have struck Disraeli as central issues in the changed Britain of which he was later to become prime minister, but twenty-first-century historians are likely to perceive growing antagonism between classes with clashing interests as the major problem of the period. What the social-problem novelists of the late 1840s and 1850s were looking for was some kind of equilibrium among all the social change and economic instability.

So how important is the separation between classes in *Hard Times*? It is perhaps not the driving force that it appears to be in earlier social-problem novels because of the parallels that Dickens sets up between the family and society. Both in the middle-class Gradgrind family and in the working world of Bounderby's mill, unequal, controlling relationships help to determine the movement of the plot. The relationship between Louisa Gradgrind and her father arguably mirrors that of Stephen with his employer, Bounderby, and because the stories of Louisa and Stephen actually become linked in the second half of the novel, our attention is directed towards the parallels.

In Reading 2.2 Guy points out that the main feature linking social-problem novels is 'the non-literary ambitions which certain authors were assumed to have held'. The novel as a genre served these non-literary ambitions in an appealing way, not least because novel-readers in the mid nineteenth century were accustomed to finding close connections between fiction and the realities of everyday social life. However, in some respects *Hard Times* stands apart from the literary conventions that tended to dominate the social-problem novel, and perhaps we can best begin to understand this distinctiveness by examining the concept of narrative voice in the novel.

the overall fictional fabric, and the real-life author stands outside this fictional whole, orchestrating the various voices within it. Sometimes the narrator-figure may express views and attitudes that we think correspond with those of the author, but this is by no means always the case. So in literary analysis we should always distinguish carefully between author and narrator, even when, as perhaps in this passage from *Mary Barton*, it would be very easy to conflate the two.

Very often, narrators who stand outside the action of the novel (not being directly involved as characters) appear to know everything that is going on, everywhere, even inside characters' heads – they are, in a technical sense, **omniscient**. The narrator of *Mary Barton* seems to be aiming more for the tone of a detached, real-life observer than an omniscient narrator, claiming, for example, to be unsure whether the crowds of people in Green Heys Fields are there because their employers have given them an official holiday or because they simply can't resist the appeal of the countryside on such a beautiful spring day. If we were able to read on beyond this short extract, however, we should find individual characters filling the foreground of the narrative and the narrator, having set the story in motion, fading into the background.

Gaskell's literary method involves what we now call **realism** (a term you encountered in relation to Art History in Book 2, Chapter 3). Of course, realist writing, which gives the impression of representing, as faithfully as mere words can, real-life actuality, existed well before the time of Gaskell and Dickens. But the nineteenth-century novel, especially in France and England, brought the practice of realism to the fore, establishing a set of conventions such as close attention to the physical details of everyday life, and language that aims for transparency rather than drawing attention to itself. We have seen from the opening of *Mary Barton* that Gaskell's narrative method certainly does involve detailed description of people and places, and when this technique is turned on the living conditions of the poorest inhabitants of Manchester's crowded streets, the effect is hard-hitting, as you can see from the following extract from Chapter 6 of the novel. In this passage, John Barton (Mary's father) and a fellow-worker visit one of the many cellar dwellings in Manchester's crowded streets, seeking out a sick colleague, Ben Davenport:

> [The street] was unpaved; and down the middle a gutter forced its way, every now and then forming pools in the holes with which

the street abounded. [...] As they passed, women from their doors tossed household slops of every description into the gutter; they ran into the next pool, which overflowed and stagnated. Heaps of ashes were the stepping-stones, on which the passer-by, who cared in the least for cleanliness, took care not to put his foot. [...] After the account I have given of the state of the street, no one can be surprised that on going into the cellar inhabited by Davenport, the smell was so foetid as almost to knock the two men down. Quickly recovering themselves, as those inured to such things do, they began to penetrate the thick darkness of the place, and to see three or four little children rolling on the damp, nay wet, brick floor, through which the stagnant, filthy moisture of the street oozed up; the fire-place was empty and black; the wife sat on her husband's chair and cried in the dank loneliness.

(Gaskell, 1970 [1848], p. 98)

Gaskell's depiction of the street and cellar where Davenport and his family live fulfils all the requirements of realist writing. The details are shockingly precise, conveying a sense of close, unflinching observation, and the language is, on the whole, factual rather than rhetorical. This passage also demonstrates a secondary meaning that is often attached to the term realism, one that is less to do with literary technique and more to do with attitude. Realism is often seen in opposition to **romance**, as it involves facing up to the actual problems of everyday life rather than retreating into fantasy, idealisation and escapism. In nineteenth-century novels we frequently find that romance, in its everyday sense in relation to love affairs, provides an important pivot for the plots, but the dominant mode is realism. And in certain passages, such as this extract from Chapter 6 of *Mary Barton*, we can see how closely the language of realist fiction is able to mimic non-fictional writing: you may well have noticed that Gaskell's account of the Manchester street is similar in many respects to Engels's description of the area of the city above Ducie Bridge in Reading 1.1 in the first chapter of this book.

I hope that examining these two extracts from Gaskell's writing will have given you the 'feel' of a certain kind of mid-nineteenth-century realism. Now we shall turn to *Hard Times* and ask ourselves whether this, too, can be classed as a realist novel. Again, we begin by looking at the narrative voice.

Activity

Re-read Book 1, Chapter 1 in our edition of Dickens's *Hard Times* (2003 [1854]), carrying on to the first three paragraphs of Chapter 2 (ending with '... to be stormed away'). We immediately notice a contrast with Gaskell's *Mary Barton* in that *Hard Times* begins with a speech by one of the characters rather than a gradual, narrator-led introduction to a particular time and place. But once the narrator's voice is heard, how would you say it differs from that of Gaskell's narrator?

After you have re-read the passage in *Hard Times*, I suggest you look back at Reading 2.3 and note any points of dissimilarity in the two narrative voices that strike you.

You should allow about 20 minutes for this activity.

Discussion

Dickens gives us a bare minimum of scene-setting (just 'The scene was a plain, bare, monotonous vault of a school-room'), before the narrator homes in on the speaker, as yet unnamed, but we discover in Chapter 2 that this is Mr Gradgrind. The strategy of describing a character before naming them is quite common, but the manner of Dickens's description certainly deserves comment. It is as emphatic and repetitive as Gradgrind's own speech, but the difference is that the narrator's language is also thick with imagery, that is to say, it is far from being purely factual. There are metaphors, such as 'square wall of a forehead', and one of them is even topped off with a further simile: 'the speaker's hair, which bristled on the skirts of his bald head, a plantation of firs to keep the wind from its shining surface, all covered with knobs, like the crust of a plum pie'. The effect of this imagery is, surely, comic. By comparing Gradgrind's bald head to a pie crust, Dickens creates a sense of incongruity that effectively punctures Gradgrind's self-importance. In the opening of the second chapter, we find the narrator acting as a kind of ventriloquist: although Gradgrind is not speaking directly, we seem to hear his voice as he describes, and dramatises, himself to an imaginary audience. The immediate effect of this strategy, it seems, is that the narrator is positioned alongside Gradgrind as a forceful presence in the narrative. So I should say that the narrative voice here is far more intrusive and dramatic than that of Gaskell's narrator.

You may have noted that the voice of the narrator in *Hard Times* is nothing like the voice of the 'conductor' of *Household Words* who addressed us in the journal's 'Preliminary Word', so there is probably even less temptation than in the case of *Mary Barton* to conflate the narrator's voice with that of the author. (But remembering that the conductor of *Household Words* was a role, too, we shouldn't assume that Dickens's own voice comes through in the 'Preliminary Word', either. The main point is that whether he is writing fiction or not, Dickens deploys a variety of voices.)

I mentioned that Gaskell's narrator retreats into the background once the story is underway. The narrator of *Hard Times*, however, is constantly reminding the reader of his presence. (I have so far avoided assigning a gender to the narrator, but I'll climb down from this particular fence now and say that the narrative voice sounds to me masculine. You may disagree – it is certainly possible to imagine a confident, assertive woman speaking the narrator's words – and this is not a major issue. My reason for thinking of the narrator as masculine is that many of his utterances have a semi-dramatic, public-speaking quality about them; in the mid-nineteenth century public speech was more often the prerogative of men than of women, and so the 'voices of authority' tended to be masculine.) At the beginning of Chapter 3, as we are introduced to the little Gradgrinds and their schoolroom, the narrator describes 'a large black board with a dry Ogre chalking ghastly white figures on it':

> Not that they knew, by name or nature, anything about an Ogre. Fact forbid! I only use the word to express a monster in a lecturing castle, with Heaven knows how many heads manipulated into one, taking childhood captive, and dragging it into gloomy statistical dens by the hair.
>
> (Dickens, 2003 [1854], p. 16)

Here the narrator explicitly calls on the resources of fantasy (or romance) to 'express' his meaning – and at the same time to show what an imaginatively impoverished upbringing the little Gradgrinds are having.

But the narrator adopts an entirely different stance, and tone, in this passage from Book 2, Chapter 6, after Stephen and Rachael have said goodbye to each other:

> It was but a hurried parting in the common street, yet it was a sacred remembrance to these two common people. Utilitarian economists, skeletons of schoolmasters, Commissioners of Fact,

genteel and used-up infidels, gabblers of many little dog's-eared creeds, the poor you will have always with you. Cultivate in them, while there is yet time, the utmost graces of the fancies and affections to adorn their lives so much in need of ornament; or, in the day of your triumph, when romance is utterly driven out of their souls, and they and a bare existence stand face to face, Reality will take a wolfish turn, and make an end of you!

(Dickens, 2003 [1854], p. 160)

Here we have a direct and uncomplimentary address to '**utilitarian economists**', etc., delivered in a prophetic tone (complete with biblical allusion in 'the poor you will have always with you') and culminating in an energetic threat. So Dickens's narrator not only keeps reminding us of his presence, but also speaks to us in a variety of moods. This is a far cry from Gaskell's consistent and understated narrative voice, and a major deviation from the norm of nineteenth-century realist technique. In fact, Dickens's handling of the novel's narrative voice alone (quite apart from any other non-realist elements in the novel) would make us pause before applying the label 'realist' to *Hard Times*.

2.6   The setting: Coketown

Perhaps nowhere in *Hard Times* are we more conscious of the narrator's voice than in Book 1, Chapter 5 ('The Key-note'), when Coketown, the setting for most of the novel's action, is described at length. Here again we find a distinct contrast with Gaskell's descriptive techniques in *Mary Barton*.

Activity

You should allow about 15 minutes for this activity.

Re-read the first four paragraphs of Chapter 5 (ending with '... world without end, Amen') and try to identify the non-realist elements.

Spend a few minutes, after your re-reading, jotting down particular words and phrases that would serve as good examples of non-realist writing.

Discussion

You may have noticed some similarities between the narrator's technique here and the description of Gradgrind in Chapter 1. The town is depicted using the same kind of repetitive syntax, and with similar emphasis on 'facts'. But here again (fanciful) imagery creeps in: there are 'serpents of smoke', and the piston of the steam-engine works up and down 'like the head of an elephant in a state of melancholy madness'. By the time we reach the end of the fourth paragraph, physical description has disappeared completely: the narrator slides from 'the material aspect of the town' to the 'immaterial', keeping up the same kind of linguistic patterns, but with a piling-up effect that culminates in 'was not, and never should be, world without end, Amen'. Fact, it seems, has become elevated to the status of a religion in Coketown, and the narrator conveys this idea by parodying the Christian *Book of Common Prayer*, whose phraseology would have been familiar to many of his readers. This kind of language use is not neutral or transparent, as realist writing often aims to be, but flamboyantly self-conscious and assertive.

Dickens's Coketown, of course, is a fictional creation: it is not Manchester or Preston, but a kind of caricature of an industrial town in the north of England (see Figure 2.5). So Dickens is not aiming for the kind of realism that Gaskell achieves: the dominant mode of *Hard Times* is **satire**, which involves exaggeration. Even so, we need to have some sense that the major setting for the novel, Coketown, has a serious resemblance to real places, otherwise the social criticism would not fully

Figure 2.5 Unknown artist, 'The Industrial North', wood engraving, *c*.1880. Photo: © INTERFOTO/Alamy

'bite'. So although the narrator keeps up the imagistic, sometimes impressionistic, descriptions of the town – see, for example, the opening of Book 1, Chapter 11 – there are also detailed close-ups that allow us to visualise people living and working in such a place.

Activity

Re-read the passage from Book 1, Chapter 10 which describes Stephen's return to his lodging at the end of the working day, from 'They had walked some distance …' (p. 68) to '… the room was clean' (p. 69).

You should allow about 10 minutes for this activity.

Spend a few minutes thinking about how the narrator's descriptive technique here differs from the opening of the 'Key-note' chapter.

Discussion

I expect you noticed the more specific attention to physical detail: for example, the jumble of objects in the shop window and the appearance of Stephen's room. We are, I think, less conscious here of the narrator pronouncing on things, and instead we are able to focus on factual-sounding observations such as the undertaker having a black ladder for sliding coffins out of the narrow houses' windows. I found myself able to visualise the streets and Stephen's room quite easily, certainly more easily than I could visualise the town as a whole from the description in the 'Key-note' chapter.

So we seem to be saying that the novel's approach to setting involves a mixture of realism and caricature. Is this just inconsistency? Well, if the effects were jarring and awkward, that probably would suggest lack of overall control. However, although *Hard Times* keeps readers on their toes with its combination of different styles, I'm not conscious of awkwardness but rather of concentration. In comparison with many other nineteenth-century novels, and certainly in comparison with some of Dickens's earlier novels, *Hard Times* feels tight – not overly schematic, but economical. Everything counts, including the setting and the way in which it is presented to the reader. The American critic Catherine Gallagher, analysing the description of Coketown in Book 1, Chapter 5, likens the repetitious sentence structure of the keynote paragraph ('[I]t was a town of red and black …') to a ledger book:

> Like much of the prose of *Hard Times*, this keynote paragraph carries the point stylistically. It's a melancholy piece of writing, and its melancholy is created by the labored tedium of the paragraph's rhythms. […] The prose doesn't just mime the monotony of the environment but also announces that the novel is both product and producer of the severe workfulness it seems to criticize. […] Workfulness is not just an attribute of people in this novel; it is a mode of representation and an angle of vision on the world in general.
>
> (Gallagher, 2006, p. 63)

Gallagher goes on to argue that *Hard Times* focuses not so much on the awful living and working conditions that people in newly industrialised towns had to endure, but rather on the fact of labour itself as the source of their unhappiness. Most importantly, she derives her argument from close attention to the language of the novel, demonstrating that style and meaning are interconnected. In terms of our present focus, Gallagher's reading demonstrates that 'setting' in the novel is more than a mere backdrop for the action. But, more generally, whenever we engage in literary analysis we need to remember that a text's form, content and meaning are bound up in each other.

2.7 Characters and plot

In his collection of articles, *The Art of Fiction*, the critic and novelist David Lodge suggests that 'Character is arguably the most important single component of the novel' (1992, p. 67), and for readers this is often the most immediately engaging component too. But just as fictional characters, or some of them, can assume an existence beyond their original surroundings, so discussion of a novel's characters can easily stray beyond its proper boundaries. One of the most common diversions is to start talking about fictional characters as though they were real people. We're tempted to do this, I think, not only because of perfectly sound interests in the workings of human nature, but also because there is not much in the way of appropriate terminology to steer our consideration of character towards literary analysis. However, some of the vocabulary we used in the previous section of this chapter, relating to realism, non-realism and satire, should help us to discuss character more easily. Also, our earlier focus on the role of the narrator foregrounded the overall narrative structure within which the novel's characters operate. In fact, what we are going to do now is not so much 'discuss character' as analyse the process of characterisation, or in other words we're going to consider the literary means by which Dickens constructs his fictional figures.

In Section 2.5 of this chapter we looked at the repetitive yet extravagant physical description of Mr Gradgrind on the opening page of the novel, but we haven't yet commented on the way his name, with its heavy alliteration and hard vowel sounds, also suggests the crushingly factual attitude towards life that he embodies. Dickens's strategy of nailing his characters through their names is well known, and *Hard Times* provides some good examples. Mr Bounderby turns out to be a 'bounder', or blackguard, Mrs Sparsit's claims to aristocratic connections and good breeding are 'sparse', and so on. When, in addition, such characters' physical appearances are described in ways that smack of caricature, the effects can be comically grotesque. In fact, in *Hard Times* many of the characters are presented in a deliberately stylised way: just as Dickens's depiction of Coketown shows some non-realist techniques in action, so does his characterisation (see Figure 2.6).

However, one of the most telling elements in Dickens's characterisation is the way that his characters speak. You will remember from Book 3 of the module how important speech is as a marker of identity, and some concepts from linguistics can help us with our literary analysis.

Activity

Here are two brief extracts from *Hard Times* in which different characters are speaking. Can you identify the speakers (out of context)?

Spend just a few minutes on this question.

1 Oh my friends, the down-trodden operatives of Coketown! Oh my friends and fellow countrymen, the slaves of an iron-handed and a grinding despotism! Oh my friends and fellow-sufferers, and fellow-workmen, and fellow-men! I tell you that the hour has come when we must rally round one another as One united power, and crumble into dust the oppressors that have too long battened upon the plunder of our families, upon the sweat of our brows, upon the labour of our hands [etc.]

2 Farewell, Thethilia! My latht wordth to you ith thith, Thtick to the termth of your engagement, be obedient to the Thquire, and forget uth. [...] People mutht be amuthed, Thquire, thomehow, [...] they can't be alwayth a working, not yet they can't be alwayth learning. Make the betht of uth; not the wortht.

Discussion

The first speech is by Slackbridge and the second by Sleary. If you found it easy to identify them, this is probably because, to borrow a term from linguistics, each character has a very distinctive 'idiolect', meaning a characteristic speech style. Slackbridge's speech is distinguished by bombastic rhetoric that is so generalised it sounds empty and insincere. Sleary's speech is distinguished in a different way, with more emphasis on phonetics, or how words sound.

Another character with a distinctive idiolect is Stephen. His speech is represented in such a way as to emphasise its oral qualities – we are meant to hear a northern accent and a working-class 'sociolect' (to borrow another term from linguistics, roughly equating to 'social dialect'). Interestingly, this working-class sociolect can also be recognised in the utterances of the circus folk (see, for example, young Kidderminster's contributions to the discussion in Book 1, Chapter 6, 'Sleary's Horsemanship'). Dickens chooses to depict the circus folk mainly 'off duty', so that we can hear their voices, and perhaps identify them, through their sociolect, with the workers of Coketown.

Besides the vocabulary and speech-sounds that help us to distinguish one character's voice from another's, we can also consider syntax, or the

Figure 2.6 The circus performers Andrew Ducrow and Louisa Woolford performing 'The Tyrolean Shepherd and Swiss Milkmaid', *c.*1830. (See *Hard Times*, Book 1, Chapter 3, pp. 17–18 and note 9, p. 305.) Photo: © V&A Images/Victoria and Albert Museum, London

way that their sentences are structured. The speech by Slackbridge that you have just looked at uses standard rhetorical ploys such as repetition (note all the 'friends' and 'fellows'), and long sentences with piled-up phrases (the last sentence in the extract goes on for several more lines). By contrast, Stephen generally speaks in short, simple sentences, but there is an interesting exception in the set-piece scene in Book 2, Chapter 5, 'Masters and Men'. Pressed by Bounderby to explain how he would set Coketown's industrial 'muddle' to rights (p. 148), Stephen's speech becomes more elaborate. For example:

> Sir, I canna, wi' my little learning an my common way, tell the genelman what will better aw this – though some working men o' this town could, above my powers – but I can tell him what I know will never do't. The strong hand will never do't. Victory and triumph will never do't. Agreeing fur to mak one side unnat'rally awlus and for ever right, and toother side unnat'rally awlus and for ever wrong, will never, never, do't. Nor yet letting alone will never do't.

> (Dickens, 2003 [1854], p. 149)

There are still enough markers of Stephen's idiolect to convince us that this is the same character speaking, but the syntax, with its repetitions and balanced sentences, is much more elaborate than usual. In fact, Stephen sounds like an orator. There are hints of this speech-potential in the previous chapter, when Stephen addresses his fellow-workers and Slackbridge, but you may still be wondering whether the presentation of Stephen's voice is consistent. This leads us on to questions about the function of characterisation in the novel as a whole.

It is clear that certain characters in *Hard Times* are associated with particular points of view, or perspectives on the issues that the novel debates. Moreover, these perspectives are arranged in a kind of pattern: Stephen's perspective contrasts with that of Slackbridge, Sleary provides a contrast with Gradgrind, and so on. However, the danger of over-stating this pattern or scheme is that we end up seeing characters as 'fixed'. One of the great strengths of longer narrative forms like the novel is that they provide space for showing how individual characters grow or develop. Of course, the question of whether or not any of the characters in *Hard Times* change during the course of the novel is intricately bound up with questions about how they are affected by the fictional events they are caught up in. And when we start to consider the novel's events, we are moving into another important area of analysis: plot.

In everyday usage, the term 'plot' implies covert, even criminal, scheming, as when Tom Gradgrind devises a scheme for robbing Bounderby's bank and framing Stephen for the crime. But in literary analysis the term is much more neutral. We use it to describe the interrelated events that comprise the 'action' of a novel (or play). It is tempting to call this the 'story', but in fact literary critics usually distinguish between the raw sequence of events (A followed by B, followed by C, etc.) that constitute a story, and the arrangement of these events as they will be presented to the reader (or audience, in the case of drama). This deliberate 'arrangement' is what we call the plot, and it can bring out patterns, or relationships between incidents, in a way that a story, being locked within a chronological sequence, cannot always do.

You are probably familiar with the idea that nineteenth-century novels, partly because of their length, involve a lot of plotting. As readers, we are especially conscious of this as we approach the end of a novel, because nineteenth-century conventions demanded some kind of final resolution, or 'tying together' of narrative strands. So plot-planning on the scale required for long nineteenth-century novels was an important part of the novelist's job. *Hard Times*, a relatively short novel by nineteenth-century standards, is more straightforward in this respect than many of Dickens's other novels, but even so there are some challenges. Dickens has to find a way of tying together the plot-lines involving the well-to-do characters (the Gradgrinds, Bounderby, Harthouse and Mrs Sparsit) with the events involving the working-class characters. Stephen's two visits to his employer Bounderby's house, his acquaintance with the mysterious 'Mrs Pegler' who turns out to be Bounderby's mother, and Tom's actions in laying the blame for the bank robbery at Stephen's door all help to knit together these two groups of characters. Sissy, too, acts as a link, initially between the circus folk and the Gradgrinds, but later she also becomes Rachael's friend and support in the search for Stephen. We can see from Dickens's 'memoranda', or working notes, for the novel that he planned the 20 instalments in varying degrees of detail, sometimes trying out possibilities that would tie together characters and themes with major plot developments.

Activity

Appendix I in our edition of *Hard Times* (2003 [1854]) reproduces Dickens's working notes for the novel. Study the 'memoranda' on p. 296, for 'Weekly No. 12, Chapter XXII', which corresponds to Book 2, Chapter 6 ('Fading Away'). Some of these notes are cryptic, but can you find any evidence of Dickens testing out ideas for the development of the novel's plot?

Spend just a few minutes on this question.

Discussion

Most obviously, we can see Dickens posing himself questions and answering them, for example 'Tom to rob Bounderby? Yes', or 'Sissy?

No'. But you may also have been struck by the fact that some of the ideas included in the notes for this chapter actually appear elsewhere. As well as working out the bank robbery plot, Dickens is clearly developing the plot-line of Louisa's near-seduction by Harthouse: 'Louisa's danger slowly drawn about her'. The last part of the notes, containing Louisa's words 'you have brought me to this, father. Now, save me!', will come in several chapters later, at the end of Book 2 (Chapter 12, 'Down'). Dickens was evidently planning a dramatic, cliffhanger moment for the end of Book 2, or Weekly No. 16. This was always a consideration for serialised novels: some element of suspense at the end of an instalment would sustain readers' interest across the intervening time and help to ensure that they bought the next issue.

It was only when *Hard Times* was published in volume form (at the same time as the serialised *Household Words* version came to an end) that Dickens added the notional division into three 'books'. The convention of publishing novels in three volumes had evolved from the eighteenth-century custom of printing some fictional works in several parts. The 'triple-decker' format became firmly established as part of the economics of nineteenth-century novel-publishing from the 1820s onwards, since it worked well for booksellers and commercial circulating libraries. A glance through the 'Dickens Chronology' at the front of our edition of *Hard Times* reveals that Dickens's novels were more often published in one volume after their initial appearance in serialised form, but with *Hard Times* he was clearly still thinking of the conventional architecture of the three-volume format when he divided the 20 weekly parts into three 'books' and added the titles: 'Sowing', 'Reaping', 'Garnering'. These book titles show Dickens superimposing a thematic structure on the week-by-week instalment structure, with strategically placed narrative turning points.

The sequence of processes implied in the book titles suggests not only the passage of time, but also the interdependence of these processes. The well-known saying 'You reap what you sow' emphasises the cause-and-effect possibilities of any train of events, and it is precisely the logic of cause and effect that determines much of the shape of literary plots. In *Hard Times* the agricultural metaphor of the book titles stands out against the industrial imagery that colours much of the novel, but perhaps one area where it seems most relevant is the growth of character. Starting the novel in a schoolroom implies that education is a form of 'sowing', and we shall see the effects of the Gradgrind education system in the development of Sissy and Bitzer, Louisa and Tom. These effects are mostly very bad, but Sissy is the exception here, maybe because, despite her sincere efforts, she regularly 'make[s] mistakes' at school (p. 59). In Book 1, Chapter 9 ('Sissy's Progress') she describes to Louisa her failure to grasp the significance of statistics, which she misnames 'stutterings' (p. 60), and admits, 'my poor father wished me so much to learn, and although I am so anxious to learn because he wished me to, I am afraid I don't like it' (p. 61). We see Sissy grow from a slightly bewildered child to a principled young woman who stays loyal to the Gradgrind family and supports them in adversity. Is this development a consequence of her resistance to the Gradgrind educational system? Even though she has evidently preserved from early childhood some of the values of Sleary's circus folk, such as fellow-feeling, I'm not sure that Sissy's positive qualities are seen to evolve in a thoroughly convincing way. But more plausible, to my mind, is the collapse of Mr Gradgrind, who is humbled and transformed when the disastrous effects of his child-rearing principles are borne in on him. Here I think we can see clear links between character and plot.

2.8   A polyphonic novel?

In Book 3, Chapter 2 of this module you were briefly introduced to the work of Mikhail Bakhtin, who, you may recall, was a literary critic as well as a philosopher. One particular strand of thought from his book *Problems of Dostoevsky's Poetics* (1984 [1929]) will help to round off our discussion of *Hard Times*. It involves the concept of 'polyphony' which, in music, suggests a combination of a number of different parts, or voices, without any one dominating. Bakhtin argues that the novel as a genre can also be polyphonic because it is able to render different voices in a well-mixed discourse; importantly, the author's point of view is simply another element in this mix rather than an overriding voice. Another way that Bakhtin describes the novel's capacity for slipping out from under the control of the authorial point of view is to suggest that novels can be dialogic (that is, they create dialogue between different points of view) rather than monological. So although the novel may present 'arguments' about social and/or political questions, and the principles underlying them, it differs from the kinds of argument offered by, for example, philosophers or political commentators, because it presents us with a variety of voices.

Activity

You should allow about 15 minutes for this activity.

Re-read the section of Kate Flint's introduction to *Hard Times* (2003 [1854]) from p. xxix ('*Hard Times*, ultimately, is not a programmatic book …') to the bottom of p. xxx ('… on which both didactic and imaginative writing are built'), and spend a few minutes thinking about how Bakhtin's concept of polyphony relates to the question of whether or not a text is didactic (that is, consciously instructive).

Discussion

Flint suggests that, unlike Gaskell and Kingsley, Dickens does not provide a clear overall message for his readers. In *Hard Times*, she claims, the novel's 'apparent certainties are continually, and deliberately, undercut'. One voice that stands out against any didactic purpose is Sleary's, with his insistence that people must be amused. Another complicating voice is that of the narrator, which, as we have seen, adopts a variety of shifting stances throughout the novel. I would consider these to be examples of polyphonic voices, keeping in play a range of possible meanings rather than subduing the novel's effect to one dominant line of argument.

You may have felt that in the final pages of her introduction Flint is simply trying to justify, or even explain away, inconsistencies in Dickens's novel. We glanced at the issue of inconsistency in Section 2.6, when we discussed the mixture of caricature and realism in Dickens's depiction of Coketown, and in Section 2.7, when we considered Stephen's surprising command of rhetoric. I leave you to come to your own judgement about these examples, but for myself I am inclined to side with Flint and look at what may appear to be ambiguity or instability in a positive light. Having several potential meanings in play within a literary text is rather like listening to different musical strands in a piece of polyphonic music. The reading experience, I would suggest, is more interesting – as readers, we have more to do, and are more aware of our role in making meanings out of what we read. Or, to come at ambiguity from a slightly different angle, we might say that it opens up possibilities of interpretation that are more subtle, possibly even more profound, than those lying on the surface of a text. It is these open possibilities that keep a novel, or any work of art, dynamic, and invite us to return to it.

Conclusion

In this chapter we have explored how Dickens's contemporary readers would have approached *Hard Times*, and we have also looked at some general features of novels, paying particular attention to mid-nineteenth-century conventions of realism that novelists such as Gaskell used so effectively. But our study of Dickens's novel has shown that realism can be mixed with other modes of writing, and that the novel as a genre offers considerable flexibility in terms of being able to keep different voices in play and resisting reductive interpretation.

As you have worked through the activities in this chapter, you have also been practising your skills in close reading of written texts, and I hope you have discovered that awareness of the contexts within which both fictional and non-fictional texts come into being actually enhances your attentiveness to their language and forms.

In the next chapter of Book 4 we resume the historian's perspective on our study of mid-Victorian Britain. But I hope your study of *Hard Times* has shown that novelists of the period were able to use fiction as a powerful way of examining contemporary society.

References

Bakhtin, M. (1984 [1929]) *Problems of Dostoevsky's Poetics* (trans. and ed. C. Emerson), Manchester, Manchester University Press.

Dickens, C. (2003 [1854]) *Hard Times* (ed. K. Flint), Penguin Classics, London, Penguin (set book).

Disraeli, B. (1975 [1845]) *Sybil, or The Two Nations*, Oxford, Oxford University Press.

Fielding, K.J. (ed.) (1960) *The Speeches of Charles Dickens*, London, Oxford University Press.

Gallagher, C. (2006) *The Body Economic: Life, Death, and Sensation in Political Economy and the Victorian Novel*, Princeton, NJ and Oxford, Princeton University Press.

Gaskell, E. (1970 [1848]) *Mary Barton: A Tale of Manchester Life*, Harmondsworth, Penguin.

Guy, J.M. (1996) *The Victorian Social-Problem Novel: The Market, the Individual and Communal Life*, Basingstoke, Macmillan.

Ledger, S. (2007) *Dickens and the Popular Radical Imagination*, Cambridge, Cambridge University Press.

Lodge, D. (1992) *The Art of Fiction*, Harmondsworth, Penguin.

Lohrli, A. (1973) *Household Words*, Toronto, University of Toronto Press.

Simmons, J.R. (2002) 'Industrial and "condition of England" novels' in Brantlinger, P. and Thesing, W.B. (eds) *A Companion to the Victorian Novel*, Oxford, Blackwell, pp. 336–52.

Slater, M. (ed.) (1996) *Dickens' Journalism, vol. 2: 'The Amusements of the People' and Other Papers: Reports, Essays and Reviews, 1834–51*, London, Dent.

Slater, M. (ed.) (1998) *Dickens' Journalism, vol. 3: 'Gone Astray' and Other Papers from Household Words, 1851–59*, London, Dent.

Further reading

If you are interested in exploring Dickens's social criticism more fully (and have time to tackle some bigger novels!), you will find that *Dombey and Son* (1848) or *Bleak House* (1853) offer even wider critiques of the underlying principles on which Victorian society was based.

Kate Flint's section on further reading in the set book (Dickens, 2003 [1854], pp. xxxiv–xxxvii) includes numerous useful suggestions, including a couple of Dickens websites.

If you would like to hear more about other aspects of Dickens's career, particularly his famous public readings, you can find five short audio recordings under 'Charles Dickens: Celebrity Author' on the OpenLearn website.

Reading 2.1 'On Strike'

Source: Dickens, C. (1854) 'On Strike', *Household Words*, 11 February, in Slater, M. (1998) *Dickens' Journalism, vol. 3: 'Gone Astray' and Other Papers from Household Words, 1851–59*, London, Dent, pp. 201–4.

When I got to Preston, it was four o'clock in the afternoon. The day being Saturday and market-day, a foreigner might have expected, from among so many idle and not over-fed people as the town contained, to find a turbulent, ill-conditioned crowd in the streets. But, except for the cold smokeless factory chimnies, the placards at the street corners, and the groups of working people attentively reading them, nor foreigner nor Englishman could have had the least suspicion that there existed any interruption to the usual labours of the place. The placards thus perused were not remarkable for their logic certainly, and did not make the case particularly clear; but, considering that they emanated from, and were addressed to, people who had been out of employment for three-and-twenty consecutive weeks, at least they had little passion in them, though they had not much reason. Take the worst I could find:

'FRIENDS AND FELLOW OPERATIVES,

'Accept the grateful thanks of twenty thousand struggling Operatives, for the help you have showered upon Preston since the present contest commenced.

'Your kindness and generosity, your patience and long-continued support deserve every praise, and are only equalled by the heroic and determined perseverance of the outraged and insulted factory workers of Preston, who have been struggling for some months, and are, at this inclement season of the year, bravely battling for the rights of themselves and the whole toiling community.

'For many years before the strike took place at Preston, the Operatives were the down trodden and insulted serfs of their Employers, who in times of good trade and general prosperity, wrung from their labour a California of gold, which is now being used to crush those who created it, still lower and lower in the scale of civilisation. This has been the result of our commercial prosperity! – *more wealth for the rich and more poverty for the Poor!* Because the workpeople of Preston protested against this state of things, - because they combined in a fair and legitimate way for the purpose of getting a reasonable share of the reward of their own labour, the *fair dealing* Employers of Preston, to their eternal shame and disgrace, *locked up* their Mills, and at one fell swoop deprived, as they thought, from twenty to thirty thousand human beings of the means of existence. Cruelty and tyranny always defeat their own object; it was so in this case, and to the honour and credit of the working classes of this country, we have to record, that, those whom the rich and wealthy sought to destroy, the poor and industrious have protected from harm. This love of justice and hatred of wrong, is a noble feature in the character and disposition of the working man, and gives us hope that in the future, this world will become what its great architect intended, not a place of sorrow, toil, oppression and wrong, but the dwelling place and the abode of peace, plenty, happiness and love, where avarice and all the evil passions engendered by the present system of fraud and injustice shall not have a place. …

'It may serve the manufacturers and all who run away with the lion's share of labour's produce, to say that the *impartial* God intended that there should be a *partial* distribution of his blessings. But we know that it is against nature to believe, that those who plant and reap all the grain, should not have enough to make a mess of porridge; and we know that those who weave all the cloth should not want a yard to cover their persons, whilst those who never wove an inch have more calico, silks and satins, than would serve the reasonable wants of a dozen working men and their families.

'This system of giving everything to the few, and nothing to the many, has lasted long enough, and we call upon the working people of this country to be determined to establish a new and improved system – a system that shall give to all who labour, a fair share of those blessings and comforts which their toil produce; in short, we wish to see that divine precept enforced, which says, "Those who will not work, shall not eat."

'The task is before you, working men; if you think the good which would result from its accomplishment, is worth struggling for, set to work and cease not, until you have obtained the *good time coming*, not only for the Preston Operatives, but for yourselves as well.

'By Order of the Committee

Murphy's Temperance Hotel, Chapel Walks,

Preston, January 24th, 1854.'

It is a melancholy thing that it should not occur to the Committee to consider what would become of themselves, their friends, and fellow operatives, if those calicoes, silks and satins, were *not* worn in very large quantities; but I shall not enter into that question. ... I found, even from this literature, however, that all masters were not indiscriminately unpopular. Witness the following verses from the New Song of the Preston Strike:

> 'There's Henry Hornby, of Blackburn, he is a jolly brick,
> He fits the Preston masters nobly, and is very bad to trick;
> He pays his hands a good price, and I hope he will never sever,
> So we'll sing success to Hornby and Blackburn for ever.

> 'There is another gentleman, I'm sure you'll all lament,
> In Blackburn for him they're raising a monument,
> You know his name, 'tis of great fame, it was late Eccles of
> honour,
> May Hopwood, and Sparrow, and Hornby live for ever.

> 'So now it is time to finish and end my rhyme,
> We warn these Preston Cotton Lords to mind for future time.
> With peace and order too I hope we shall be clever,
> We sing success to Stockport and Blackburn for ever.
> Now, lads, give your minds to it.'

The balance sheet of the receipts and expenditure of the twenty-third week of the strike was extensively posted. The income for that week was two thousand one hundred and forty pounds odd. Some of the contributors were poetical. As,

> 'Love to all and peace to the dead,
> May the poor now in need never want bread.

> three-and-sixpence.'...

Some of the subscribers veiled their names under encouraging sentiments, as Not tired yet, All in a mind, Win the day, Fraternity, and the like. Some took jocose appellations, as A stunning friend, Two to one Preston wins, Nibbling Joe, and The Donkey Driver. Some expressed themselves through their trades, as Cobbler Dick, sixpence, The tailor true, sixpence, Shoemaker, a shilling, The chirping blacksmith sixpence, and A few of Maskery's most feeling coachmakers, three and threepence. An old balance sheet for the fourteenth week of the Strike was headed with this quotation from MR CARLYLE. 'Adversity is sometimes hard upon a man; but for one man who can stand prosperity, there are a hundred that will stand adversity.' The Elton district prefaced its report with these lines:

> 'Oh! Ye who start a noble scheme,
>   For general good designed;
> Ye workers in a cause that tends
>   To benefit your kind!
> Mark out the path ye fain would tread,
>   The game ye mean to play;
> And if it be an honest one,
>   Keep stedfast in your way!
>
> 'Although you may not gain at once
>   The points ye most desire;
> Be patient – time can wonders work;
>   Plod on, and do not tire:
> Obstructions, too, may crowd your path,
>   In threatening, stern array;
> Yet flinch not! fear not! They may prove
>   Mere shadows in your way.
>
> 'Then, while there's work for you to do,
>   Stand not despairing by,
> Let 'forward' be the move ye make,
>   Let 'onward' be your cry;
> And when success has crowned your plans,
>   'Twill all your pains repay,
> To see the good your labour's done –
>   Then droop not on your way.'

In this list, 'Bear ye one another's burthens,' sent one Pound fifteen. 'We'll stand to our text, see that ye love one another,' sent nineteen shillings.

Reading 2.2 The Victorian Social-Problem Novel

Source: Guy, J.M. (1996) *The Victorian Social-Problem Novel: The Market, the Individual and Communal Life*, **Basingstoke, Macmillan, pp. 3–4**

The mid-nineteenth-century novels which we now call 'social-problem' or 'industrial' novels – principally *Hard Times, Mary Barton, North and South, Alton Locke, Sybil* and *Felix Holt* – were not described and identified as a group by their nineteenth-century readers or critics. In fact the label has a relatively recent origin for it dates only from the 1950s. [...]

The terms 'social-problem' or 'industrial' novel are generally used to refer to a body of English fiction written in the late 1840s and 1850s which allegedly takes as its subject-matter large-scale problems in contemporary British society, problems which in turn were the product of changing demographic patterns and changes in work practices associated with the accelerating industrialisation of the British economy. This literary engagement with contemporary affairs in turn depended upon what was claimed to be a new kind of relationship between the novel and the social and political worlds which produced it. Social-problem novels are typically distinguished from earlier novels, and from other works contemporary with them, by their attempt to comment on, and stimulate debate about, matters of general public and political concern. Thomas Carlyle's portmanteau phrase, the 'Condition-of-England question', is often used to describe these social matters; they centre on the perception that social order was under threat from conflicts between various interest groups in society, and particularly from the discontent of the increasingly impoverished and degraded working classes. The intentions of the writers who address these issues are assumed to be both serious and, more importantly, political. So social-problem novelists are commonly credited with the intention of trying to educate, and therefore by implication to change, the opinions and prejudices of their readers. In so doing, they are seen to be implying that the novel can, and should, have an important role to play in social and political life. As a consequence the moral authority often associated with Victorian fiction and the didactic function which proceeds from that authority are given a new dimension in the social-problem novel. The principal distinction of the sub-genre, then, exists not so much in any formal features or properties (the works in question are not formally innovative or experimental), but rather in the non-literary ambitions which certain authors were assumed to have held. Where critics have differed is in the various ways they have described and explained those ambitions. These descriptions and explanations have in turn depended upon the principles which have informed their historical research, and the kind of historical evidence which they have adduced as relevant to understanding literary works.

One way of accounting for both the number and variety of critical works which have been written about the social-problem novel is in terms of the changes which have taken place since the 1950s in the practice of literary history. As new ways of understanding the relationship between literature and history have been developed, and as new 'stories' of the past have been written, so historical sub-genres, such as that of the social-problem novel, have been redefined and reinterpreted.

Reading 2.3 *Mary Barton: A Tale of Manchester Life*

Source: Gaskell, E. (1970 [1848]) *Mary Barton: A Tale of Manchester Life*, **Harmondsworth, Penguin, pp. 39–41**

There are some fields near Manchester, well known to the inhabitants as 'Green Heys Fields', through which runs a public footpath to a little village about two miles distant. In spite of these fields being flat and low, nay, in spite of the want of wood (the great and usual recommendation of level tracts of land), there is a charm about them which strikes even the inhabitant of a mountainous district, who sees and feels the effect of contrast in these common-place but thoroughly rural fields, with the busy, bustling manufacturing town, he left but half an hour ago. Here and there an old black and white farm-house, with its rambling outbuildings, speaks of other times and other occupations than those which now absorb the population of the neighbourhood. Here in their seasons may be seen the country business of haymaking, ploughing, &c., which are such pleasant mysteries for townspeople to watch; and here the artisan deafened with noise of tongues and engines, may come to listen awhile to the delicious sounds of rural life: the lowing of cattle, the milkmaids' call, the clatter and cackle of poultry in the old farmyards. You cannot wonder, then, that these fields are popular places of resort at every holiday time; and you would not wonder, if you could see, or I properly describe, the charm of one particular stile, that it should be, on such occasions, a crowded halting-place. Close by it is a deep, clear pond, reflecting in its dark green depths the shadowy trees that bend over it to exclude the sun. The only place where its banks are shelving is on the side next to a rambling farm-yard, belonging to one of those old-world, gabled, black and white houses I named above, overlooking the field through which the public foot-path leads. […]

I do not know whether it was on a holiday granted by the masters, or a holiday seized in right of nature and her beautiful spring time by the workmen but one afternoon (now ten or a dozen years ago) these fields were much thronged. It was an early May evening – the April of the poets; for heavy showers had fallen all the morning, and the round, soft, white clouds which were blown by a west wind over the dark blue sky, were sometimes varied by one blacker and more threatening. The softness of the day tempted forth the young green leaves, which almost visibly fluttered into life; and the willows, which that morning had had only a brown reflection in the water below, were now of that tender gray-green which blends so delicately with the spring harmony of colours.

Groups of merry and somewhat loud-talking girls, whose ages might range from twelve to twenty, came by with a buoyant step. They were most of them factory girls, and wore the usual out-of-doors dress of that particular class of maidens; namely, a shawl, which at mid-day or in fine weather was allowed to be merely a shawl, but towards evening, or if the day were chilly, became a sort of Spanish mantilla or Scotch plaid, and was brought over the head and hung loosely down, or was pinned under the chin in no unpicturesque fashion.

Their faces were not remarkable for beauty; indeed, they were below the average, with one or two exceptions; they had dark hair, neatly and classically arranged, dark eyes, but sallow complexions and irregular features. The only thing to strike a passerby was an acuteness and intelligence of countenance, which has often been noticed in a manufacturing population.

There were also numbers of boys, or rather young men, rambling among these fields, ready to bandy jokes with any one, and particularly ready to enter into conversation with the girls, who, however, held themselves aloof, not in a shy, but rather in an independent way, assuming an indifferent manner to the noisy wit or obstreperous compliments of the lads. Here and there came a sober quiet couple, either whispering lovers, or husband and wife, as the case might be; and if the latter, they were seldom unencumbered by an infant, carried for the most part by the father, while occasionally even three or four little toddlers had been carried or dragged thus far, in order that the whole family might enjoy the delicious May afternoon together.

Chapter 3
Politics and the people

Donna Loftus

Contents

Aims

This chapter will:

- introduce a range of textual sources and develop your skills of analysis
- show how sources interrelate to produce an active exchange of ideas
- demonstrate how the study of language and culture contributes to the study of History as an academic discipline.

Materials you will need

In this chapter, you will need to watch the following film, which can be found on the module website:

- Public culture in an industrial city.

You will also be directed to the module website for an online activity.

Introduction

Activity

To begin this chapter, I'd like you to read the first paragraph of Reading 3.6. You will read this extract again in greater detail at the end of the chapter. For now, you need to do a fairly quick reading of the opening paragraph to establish the context and meaning of the source. To do this, you should ask the questions you encountered in the first activity in Chapter 1, followed by another, smaller set of questions aimed at addressing the issues we want to raise in this chapter.

You should allow about 10 minutes for this activity.

1   Some questions to place the document in its context:

    Who wrote it?

    When was it written?

    What type of document is it?

    Who was it written for?

2   What does this source tell you about Manchester in 1877? How is this account of Manchester different from those you encountered in Chapter 1?

Discussion

The first set of questions can be answered fairly quickly. We have no author for the extract but we do have a date: 17 September 1877. The extract is an eyewitness account of the trades procession organised to celebrate the opening of the new town hall in Manchester. It was written for readers of the *Manchester Guardian* newspaper.

The second set of questions requires a little more consideration. The extract describes the procession involving a large number of working men as a 'fitting conclusion [...] to the programme for celebrating the opening of the new Town Hall'. This suggests that the procession followed a number of other ceremonies and celebrations. This is a very different image of Manchester from those you encountered in Chapter 1. The extract describes working people joining with others, and turning up in large numbers to celebrate the opening of a civic institution. It suggests that Manchester has avoided the turmoil, class division and social unrest that Engels predicted and that the other social commentators of the 1830s and 1840s feared.

The years between 1852 and 1867 were famously referred to as the 'age of equipoise' by the historian William Laurence Burn in a book of 1964. It is a label that has remained virtually unchallenged. The mid nineteenth century is seen as a time of stability between periods of unrest and turmoil. During these years a strong civic culture and a vibrant public politics emerged. Burn also noted that he might have called his book 'the age of discussion': as the writer Walter Bagehot (1826–1877) argued, increased debate was a defining characteristic of the period (Burn, 1964, p. 18). There was public discussion of a greater range of issues and this included a more diverse range of the population. You might expect increased discussion to lead to a greater sense of disorder and disagreement, but in practice the reverse happened. For many social commentators, debate was seen as progress: it offered a way for the classes to know each other and a way of drawing the working classes into a liberal culture that promoted individualism, self-improvement and parliamentary-style politics which it was hoped would temper the radical politics of Chartism and socialism.

Newspaper reports on the opening of Manchester's town hall appear on the surface to demonstrate the success of this liberal vision of the industrial city. However, you will not be surprised to learn that this is only part of the story. If we take different voices and texts and explore them in different contexts, other perspectives emerge. This chapter takes up the history of Manchester and the surrounding districts that you began in Chapter 1. It asks you to think about how and why a greater confidence in the social order emerged after the 1840s, how pervasive it was and what this meant to contemporaries.

Section 3.1 introduces you to the civic culture that emerged in the industrial city in the mid nineteenth century which attempted to build shared values through a more inclusive culture and politics. Section 3.2 changes focus and asks you to consider the relationship between language, identity and politics. This section takes a different approach to the study of texts, in that you will be asked to think about how historians can study words in order to gain insight into the perception people had of themselves. How did working people describe themselves in relation to the people around them? Did the emphasis on shared interests override the ideas of 'class' that you encountered in Chapter 1? Section 3.3 asks you to think about what happened to consensus when the cotton famine threatened stability in Lancashire. Section 3.4 shifts the focus to consider the impact of civic culture and public politics on debates about the vote. The campaign for an extension of the franchise emerged with greater urgency in the 1860s, and questions about who had the right to a political voice were hotly debated. The final section (Section 3.5) brings the first three chapters of Book 4 to a close by asking you to think about how rituals are used to define communities and give certain voices the authority to represent the people. As you work through the chapter, think about who gets a 'voice', whether they are heard, and whether the reform of politics and political culture created or reflected a sense of 'equipoise'.

3.1 Civic improvement and social change

As you may recall from the introduction to Book 4, commentators 'strained the language' of the day in their attempt to describe the industrial city in the 1830s and 1840s (Gunn, 2000, p. 36). However, by the time Charles Dickens's novel *Hard Times* was published in 1854 there was more composure. Many of the concerns of the 1840s had not been resolved, but neither had any real threat to the social order been realised. In fact, despite revolutions across Europe in 1848 and widespread Chartist protests in the same year, by the 1850s there was a growing acceptance that factories and cities were permanent, and a growing confidence that they could produce prosperity and stability for all (see Figure 3.1).

Figure 3.1 Piccadilly Gardens, Manchester, 1889. Photo: © Francis Frith collection/akg-images

Activity

To get an overview of the changes that lay behind this new optimism, you should watch the film 'Public culture in an industrial city', which you can find on the module website. The film looks at the development of the city of Manchester in the mid nineteenth century. Watch the film and answer the following question:

How was Manchester transformed in the mid nineteenth century?

You should allow about 20 minutes for this activity.

Discussion

The accounts of Manchester written in the 1840s describe it as disorganised and chaotic. After 1838 a local council developed, and by the middle of the century the benefits of a more active local government and the impact of philanthropic projects were being seen. There was investment in schemes of social improvement and in spaces for shared politics and culture. A police force and fire service, sewers and roads made the city feel safer and more orderly. Buildings such as the Athenaeum and events such as the Arts Treasures Exhibition associated industrial capital with learning and culture.

These institutions and events comprised a 'public culture', which represented industry as benefiting all the people of Manchester. Spaces were created for social classes to mix, though you will have noted that the working classes accessed the Arts Treasures Exhibition with cheaper tickets available on separate days. The building of the Free Trade Hall on the site of the Peterloo Massacre represented a confidence in what Simon Gunn calls a 'new industrial civilisation' in which strong local ties bound radicalism and liberalism together against an older aristocracy. Later, the building of the new town hall symbolised the power of a civic spirit: it represented a collective responsibility for the city and its people. This is quite a contrast to the images of industry that were produced in the 1840s and that you encountered in Chapter 1. However, as Gunn reminds us at the end of the film, despite the public culture, with its emphasis on the collective identity of the people of Manchester, there were in fact many ways of understanding the city and, as you will see, there were many tensions below the surface.

You may like to refer back to Figure 1.4 in Chapter 1, which shows the locations of the Free Trade Hall and the new town hall in Manchester.

Manchester's emerging middle class played an important role in building this new industrial civilisation. The cotton masters were a diverse group. Some were paternalist employers who saw themselves as a new local wealthy elite taking up a long-established duty to ensure the welfare of their poorer neighbours, in this case their workers. Even those who subscribed to the 'Manchester school', characterised by Dickens as 'Gradgrinds', were aware that the legitimacy of political economy and utilitarianism would be established only if capitalism and the wealth it was generating for the new middle classes could be seen to benefit the wider community. A liberal consensus emerged in the 1850s which combined a belief in political economy with a collective commitment to the education of the working classes through schemes of social improvement. The result was a civic ethos in which self-help was encouraged through the building of libraries, and a culture of learning was promoted through investment in art, music and education. This ethos was reflected in events like the Manchester Art Treasures Exhibition of 1857 and in organisations such as the Hallé Orchestra.

Music and the Hallé Orchestra

Fiona Richards

On 5 May 1857 Prince Albert opened the Manchester Art Treasures Exhibition at Old Trafford, a lavish affair on the scale of similar events at Crystal Palace, London, as Figure 3.2 shows.

Figure 3.2 The Manchester Art Treasures Exhibition at Old Trafford, 1857. Photo © Illustrated London News Ltd/Mary Evans

Far in the background you may just be able to pick out an orchestra, assembled specially for this event. This gathering together of performers was a significant moment, as these musicians went on to form the new Hallé Orchestra, under the leadership of Charles Hallé (1819–1895; see Figure 3.3), who had emigrated from Germany and settled in Manchester in 1848. Their first official concert, which took place on 30 January 1858 in the recently built Free Trade Hall, was a much-publicised, eagerly awaited affair.

Activity

Below is the programme for this first concert. Relating this back to your work in Book 2, what are the striking features of this list of music?

Overture, *Der Freischütz*	Weber
Andante from Symphony in E flat	Mozart
Concertstück – pianoforte Mr. Hallé – in F minor, op. 79	Weber
First Symphony in C major, op. 21	Beethoven
Interval	
Overture, *La Sirène*	Auber
Ballet des Sylphes (Faust)	Berlioz
Selections, *Il Trovatore*	Verdi
Solo-pianoforte Mr. Hallé, *Three Songs Without Words*	Mendelssohn
Overture, *Le Siège de Corinthe*	Rossini

Discussion

While I'm sure some of these names and pieces will be unfamiliar, I hope you noticed some of the canonical genres you encountered in Book 2, Chapter 2, such as a Beethoven symphony and music by Mozart. Mr Hallé himself is prominent as piano soloist, and what is also noticeable is that four living composers are represented – Auber, Verdi, Rossini and Berlioz – reflecting the mid-nineteenth-century taste for romantic opera.

Two days later, the *Manchester Guardian*'s review of that first concert described it as 'quite an event in the musical history of Manchester', successful because 'no other town has so large a body of resident instrumental musicians' (1 February 1858, p. 3). So why was this such an important occasion, and what impact did it have? First, the Hallé went on to become one of the great orchestras of the world, still a

Figure 3.3 Sir Charles Hallé, *c*.1880. Photographed by Herbert Rose
Barraud. Private collection. Photo: The Bridgeman Art Library

thriving enterprise in its current home, the Bridgewater Hall. You've
even heard a recent recording of this orchestra as part of your study of
Chapter 2 in Book 2. But in the nineteenth century it had a particular
significance. Manchester at this time had an atmosphere that promoted

enterprise and free-thinking, traits that were reflected in the early days of the Hallé. The founder himself was renowned for his liberal attitudes towards programming and performers, fostering new works, and hiring and supporting young soloists. The availability of cheap seats and standing room at the Free Trade Hall meant that concerts were also open to a wide Manchester population, including millworkers (Figure 3.4). And, as with Beethoven, when Hallé died on 24 October 1895 his funeral was a grand affair, the streets lined with people as his coffin was taken from the suburbs of Greenheys to Salford.

Figure 3.4 Meeting of the Manchester and Salford Co-operative Society at the Free Trade Hall, Manchester, 1865. Photo: © Illustrated London News Ltd/Mary Evans Picture Library

Public libraries

Manchester's industrial and civic culture was intended to promote shared values across the classes. Often these values were those of the industrial middle class and they emphasised liberal principles of independence and self-improvement. There was some concern among the middle class that working people, if left to their own devices, might promote **socialist** forms of self-reliance. In the context of revolution abroad and uncertainty about the future of radicalism, the education of the workers in the 'true' meaning of independence was a political priority. In the 1850s and 1860s many industrialists actively promoted the building of public libraries and mechanics' institutes. In such spaces, the working classes were expected to discover 'truths'. To see what these truths were, let's examine reports on the opening of the Manchester Free Library in 1852 (Figure 3.5). The library replaced the Hall of Science, a space for lectures and public meetings built by a cooperative organisation inspired by the radical socialist ideas of Robert Owen (1771–1858).

OPENING OF THE MANCHESTER FREE LIBRARY.

Figure 3.5 The ceremonial opening of the Manchester Free Library, 1852.
Photo: © Illustrated London News Ltd/Mary Evans Picture Library

Activity

Read the three extracts below. They are taken from a series of speeches given by local notables and literary figures on the opening of Manchester Free Library and reported in the *Manchester Guardian* (4 September 1852, p. 8). Consider the language of the speakers carefully. What do the speakers think that the benefits of the library will be?

You should allow about 10 minutes for this activity.

The first speaker for you to consider is Charles Dickens:

Books [...] will cheer him [the working man] through many of the struggles and toils of his life, will raise him in his self-respect, will teach him that capital and labour are not opposed, but are mutually dependent and mutually supporting (hear, hear – applause), will enable him to tread down blinding prejudice, corrupt misrepresentation, and everything but the truth, into the dust.

The second is Sir Edward Bulwer Lytton (1807–1873), a writer and politician:

[Many] express an interest in the uses which may be made of this mighty arsenal. I call it an arsenal, for books are weapons either for war or for self-defence [...] To defend the weak, to resist the oppressor, to unite humility with courage.

The third speaker to consider is Richard Monckton Milnes (1809–1885), writer, MP and prominent campaigner for worker education, penny-banks and free public libraries:

Suppose a man, instead of some happy invention, to conceive a moral idea, or to get some notion in his head concerning the misery of his fellow creatures. Suppose that man to discover the evils of the society in which he lived, to ponder over his own wretchedness, and to contrast his own social being with the happier lot of others he saw around him [...] But let that man be guided to the books in this library, which would show him how far other people had thought and suffered before him, and how their feelings sympathised with his [...] the man [would begin] to understand himself, and [be] transformed into an intelligent, clear, and sensible philanthropist, instead of becoming a blind and ferocious fanatic. This is what books could do; and this was the difference between the present building being a Socialist Hall and a Free Public Library.

Discussion

The language that the speakers draw on is quite diverse, but all of them realise the power of knowledge. Lytton talks of books as 'weapons'. As such, the reading matter of the working people is a matter of some concern to the commentators. Dickens and Milnes argue that the right books will reveal a 'truth': that all people, regardless of class, share the same human concerns (Figure 3.6). Both Dickens and Milnes fear that 'working men' may be 'blinded' by their own ignorance and prevented from seeing this truth. In this way, the radical politics that led to the building of the Owenite Hall in 1840 were dismissed as irrational and based on false ideas. Milnes associates the 'right' outlook with philanthropy, or the love of humankind, and radical politics with hatred and fanaticism.

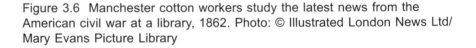

OPERATIVES READING THE LATEST NEWS FROM AMERICA—A SCENE IN CAMP-FIELD FREE LIBRARY, MANCHESTER.—SEE NEXT PAGE.

Figure 3.6   Manchester cotton workers study the latest news from the American civil war at a library, 1862. Photo: © Illustrated London News Ltd/Mary Evans Picture Library

The opening of the library shows the increasing role of print and literacy in community building, and the way certain kinds of knowledge and expression were claimed as 'true'. It also shows how reading was linked to rational and reasoned debate. The opening of the library was itself an occasion on which the power of informed opinion, correct expression and learning was demonstrated through the staging of a debate. Participants such as Dickens, as well as local notables and politicians, were invited to speak on resolutions. Debate was thus highly organised and contributions were regulated. The boundaries of debate were carefully policed by managing participation: working men were invited to attend a separate debate, which took place in the same room but later in the evening.

Activity

You should now complete the online activity 'Dickens's speech at the Free Trade Hall', which you can find on the Study Planner of the module website. Once you have done this, continue your reading below.

You should allow about 20 minutes for this activity.

Middle-class reformers were well aware of the power of education to inculcate the 'right' kind of values in the working classes. Joseph Brotherton (1783–1857), a Salford MP and retired cotton industrialist, called public libraries 'the cheapest form of police' (Howe, 1984, p. 286). But assessing the impact of such a strategy on the working classes is not straightforward. Evidence can be collected on who used the libraries, and some ideas can be gleaned about the kinds of reading matter working men and women chose. But it is difficult for historians to know how reading, no matter what it was, was interpreted and understood and whether it had any impact on working-class politics. Finding evidence of the impact of civic reforms such as libraries on working-class culture requires you to 'read against the grain'.

The next activity gives you the opportunity to look at some evidence gathered by Hippolyte Taine (1828–1893) in his *Notes on England* (1885 [1872]). Taine was a French philosopher and historian interested in the nature of society. His 'notes' were based on a tour of England undertaken between 1858 and 1871. They described England and English habits to French readers and they were published in French and English in 1872. Taine was at this time working towards a modern history of France and was interested in how England had managed to industrialise without the revolutions and unrest that took place in France in 1789, 1830, 1848 and 1852. The extracts you will read are based on Oldham, a cotton town close to Manchester.

Activity

Now read the extracts from Taine's *Notes on England* that are reproduced in Reading 3.1 and answer the following questions:

1 What 'voices' and 'texts' feature in the description of working people?

2 What do they tell us about working-class culture and politics in Oldham?

You should allow about 30 minutes for this activity.

Discussion

1   There is the voice of the 'manufacturers' attesting to the character of the working classes and reference to Elizabeth Gaskell's *North and South* as further evidence of the 'reason and fairness' of working men. The books and newspapers in the library are referred to as evidence of local people's desire for learning and their openness to new ideas. The richness of newspapers in particular is noted, for the range of perspectives they provide, and 'political economy' is mentioned as a body of knowledge that working men are acquainted with. Aside from the 'flags' (trade union banners), with their reference to justice, there are no working-class voices in the reading. The workers of Oldham are represented through Taine's observations and the opinions of his 'guides', figures of authority such as the manufacturer and the librarian.

2   Taine's notes show the importance of philanthropic schemes to the material well-being of locals in providing the library, a park and savings-banks. They suggest that local people make use of them. Taine's notes, however, do not indicate what these mean to people and, in particular, whether accessing these spaces and services has changed the way people feel about their lives. The lack of unrest might suggest that civic amenities have been successful in fostering consensus and shared interests between workers and masters. On the other hand, the notes also show the importance of work to social identity. The banners suggest that notions of justice and fairness at work are an important part of working-class politics and, despite the workers' education in political economy, that the threat of strike is an important strategic weapon in defence of wages. Despite the shared civic culture that is promoted here, workers still see themselves as having to defend their own interests in the workplace.

Taine's writing demonstrates the problems historians have in getting to the thoughts, feelings and experiences of the working classes and the poor. Descriptions of working-class life are often filtered through the narratives of others and made to serve the purposes of observers. Taine collected his evidence to explain the revolutions in France. He was interested in how the social order of the industrial towns in England had prevented widespread social upheaval; he was looking for consensus. The notes provide evidence of the importance of print culture and civic institutions in creating a sense of shared values, but they also reveal the existence of separate interests (see Figure 3.7). The library, philanthropy schemes and civic institutions, even knowledge of

Figure 3.7 Popular literacy on Mount Street, Manchester. Photo: ©
Manchester Archives and Local Studies, Central Library

political economy, had done little to shift a commitment among the
working class to 'justice', which, it would seem, was interpreted in
relation to wages. There may have been, as Taine suspected, no threat
of revolution from the working people of England, but the threat to
strike in defence of wages was all too clear. As you may have noticed, it
is also clear from Taine's writing that working men saw the masters as
their 'natural enemy'. As this analysis of Taine's notes shows, historians
need to be careful not to assume that working-class participation in
civic culture meant a wholesale acceptance of middle-class values.

Language and history

As you saw in Chapter 1, historians ask questions of a source in
order to determine its context and meaning. Historians are also a
product of their own time and some of the questions they bring to
a source (or questions they don't think to ask) are shaped by
current concerns and by debates between scholars.

The influence of a widespread interest in Marxism in the 1960s can be traced in the work of historians such as E.P. Thompson (whom you encountered in Chapter 1) who argued that a working-class identity emerged out of shared experiences of exploitation during industrialisation. With the declining influence of Marxism in the 1980s, scholars began to question whether class was a useful concept for understanding society and to challenge assumptions about the relationship between class, experience and politics.

An important study by the historian Gareth Stedman Jones has analysed the language used in Chartist campaigns. He argues that Chartists used ideas and concepts from an older radical tradition that pre-dated industrialisation. This allowed the Chartist movement to unite in one campaign a range of workers, from artisans to factory labourers, with a number of different experiences of work. Stedman Jones also argues (1983, p. 19) that Chartists wanted political rights so that they could defend a range of diverse social and economic interests; they were not necessarily interested in overthrowing capitalist society. In Stedman Jones's view, class was produced through politics; it was not a real thing resulting from the shared economic experience of exploitation but a device used to link people together in a political campaign. Other historians have taken this further, to argue that class is a story that people tell in making sense of their social relations, but it is only one story among many. People also see themselves as members of communities defined around, for example, gender, race, religion, family, or the nation (Joyce, 1991, p. 11).

These approaches provide new insights by showing how language and culture give meaning to experience. They do, however, pose methodological problems for historians. For a start, people use a shared language to communicate, but there may be subtle differences in its meaning; for example, 'self-help' can be interpreted as an individual or a collective quality. It is also difficult to deduce meaning from words on a page: sometimes words mean different things in different settings. However, the ability to give meaning to words, symbols and rituals is part of the process of power and politics. As the historian James Epstein has noted, 'the authority to give accent or meaning to such signs is an essential part of the exercise of political power. Struggles to enforce or destabilize such meanings often define the contested terrain of politics' (1989, p. 76). The study of language in history, then, requires a particular sensitivity to 'deconstructing' texts, to get below the surface and to see how different interpretations are used to make political claims. You will explore this further in Section 3.3, in relation to the cotton famine.

A careful and critical reading of sources such as Taine's notes in their political, social and cultural context can help you interrogate the meaning of the words on the page. Nevertheless, it is not always easy to see, for example, how terms such as 'self-help' or 'independence' are understood. The historian Patrick Joyce has extensively explored the relationship between language, identity, culture and politics. As he says, 'language use takes us to the heart of social identity, and ideas about language and culture were pregnant with ideas about society' (Joyce, 1991, p. 193). However, the fact that most of the sources left behind were produced by the middle classes makes our attempts to understand the past even more complicated. Sources that were produced by the working classes for the working classes are hard to come by. But there are some. Broadside ballads, like the ones you came across in the film about the Preston Lockout in Chapter 2, give historians rare insight into the ways the working classes understood their place in society.

3.2 Broadside ballads

Broadside ballads are verses or songs on popular themes that were sold in sheets, then circulated or posted on walls. They date back to the emergence of printing in the fifteenth century, and had, by the nineteenth century, moved beyond their rural origins to produce a 'distinctly metropolitan voice' (McWilliam, 2007, p. 214). They came to reflect the concerns and preoccupations of the common people and, as such, they are 'a valuable source for understanding the world of the working class who leave so few records behind' (McWilliam, 2007, p. 214). Nevertheless, they pose a problem for historians. A broadside was a commercial product, which means that it may say more about the attitude of the broadside producer than the audience. However, broadsides were produced to be sold, and it is unlikely that people would have bought them if they did not reflect their concerns.

What, then, can broadside ballads tell us about the social identities of the working classes in the Manchester factory districts? Take a quick look at Reading 3.2, 'The Working Men of England!' You will study this ballad in more detail in the next activity. You may notice that there is no date on the ballad and no author's name, and this makes it difficult to place the source. It also makes it difficult to work out the meaning of some of the words. For example, without a date the reference to 'reform' is uncertain. However, the printer's name appears on the broadside itself: T. Pearson of Oldham Road in Manchester. From this we can locate and date the source with some accuracy. Thomas Pearson was one of many broadside printers based in Ancoats in Manchester from around 1859 to 1866. The number of broadside printers in this area in the middle of the century and the number of broadsides that have been collected give some indication of the popularity of the form. An analysis of the themes that recur in Pearson's ballads highlights some of the preoccupations of the local population. Many were concerned with the experience of life and work in the new industrial districts, addressing topics such as the plight of the Irish in Manchester and the experience of factory work. Such concerns are not unexpected: as you know from 'Manchester and the factory: Quarry Bank Mill and Ancoats', the film you watched in your work in Chapter 1, Ancoats was dominated by cotton factories and populated by migrant workers, many from Ireland. Others, such as the ballad you will consider in the next activity, addressed a wider section of society.

Activity

Now turn to Reading 3.2 and read 'The Working Men of England!'. What sort of identity for working men is expressed in the ballad? To put it another way, what sorts of community are working men seen as being part of?

You should allow about 15 minutes for this activity.

Discussion

I was struck by the range of communities that this ballad refers to. It clearly addresses itself to working men; mention is made of workers in 'iron, wool and coal'. In fact, it sees working men as the basis of national prosperity. Despite this separate identity afforded to working men, little antagonism to employers is expressed in the ballad. Indeed, it honours 'masters and the founders of free trade'; it expresses support for queen and country, church and state. The ballad sees working men as separated from the upper classes by their everyday experiences of work, but nevertheless as a central part of the nation. References to 'good wages', 'plenty', 'freedom' and 'fair play' suggest a deeply held view that patriotism and mutuality are conditional on decent work and wages. You may also have noticed gender here; production and patriotism are presented as masculine pursuits.

Ballads such as 'The Working Men of England!' use traditional forms and traditional identities to express new concerns and new social roles. There is reference to the past, the land and labour's long history – an appeal that is used to express working men's natural claim to certain rights, such as 'fair play', which was used to refer to popular political slogans such as 'a fair day's wages for a fair day's work'. On the other hand, in the context of Ancoats and the surrounding factory districts, the ballad refers to new identities emerging out of new conditions of work. But no simple class identity is expressed. Indeed, the reference to the 'founders of free trade' suggests an affinity with liberal middle-class heroes such as Richard Cobden (1804–1865) and John Bright (1811–1889), who were renowned for their role in the Anti-Corn Law League, which, as you may remember from Chapter 1, was an important middle-class political movement. It is possible that 'reform' refers to the repeal of the Corn Laws.

Men, women and work

Ideas about gender and the family were central to the way the social order was understood and described in the nineteenth century. They also played a part in trade union and radical politics. The idea of a 'fair day's wages for a fair day's work' was increasingly associated with a breadwinner wage: a rate of pay that would enable a working man to support a family with a wife at home. Middle-class ideals of the family saw women's role as primarily domestic, concerned with the moral well-being of the family. By employing this domestic ideal, working men and trade unions were able to present a demand for increased wages as respectable and responsible. The breadwinner ideal linked masculine labour to paternal authority and independence. Men were the protectors of a household and providers for a family. Women were represented, along with children, as dependants. This fitted with dominant ideals of gender and the family. The Factory Acts, by intervening to limit hours of work for women and children, had also presented them as dependent on the state for protection, whereas male labour was free to look after itself. As work and independence were linked to political rights, women were marginalised from public political movements (Clark, 1995, pp. 266–9). Historians have argued that the breadwinner wage was a rhetorical device that did not reflect the reality of working-class lives: whatever the language of political campaigns, the working-class family in practice continued to function as an economic unit, with both men and women contributing (Rose, 1992, pp. 15–16). This was particularly the case in the Lancashire cotton industry, which depended on women's work in the mills. There were ballads that celebrated the dignity of female factory workers and unions that defended their pay and conditions. But, as claims to citizenship became associated with masculine labour, independence and respectability, women were marginalised in political campaigns.

Broadside ballads such as 'The Working Men of England!' presented working men as the 'motor of society' (McWilliam, 2007, p. 218). This idea of working men as the producers of wealth was, as you may recall from Reading 1.5 of Chapter 1, also a feature of Chartist politics. But this does not mean that ballads can be read as a simple expression of a separate working-class politics and identity. For a start, ballads are often patriotic, and present the nation as composed of employers and workers working together for the benefit of the wider community. Joyce's studies of broadside ballads have shown that, if a common enemy was identified in them, it was typically the idle rich rather than the employer (1991, p. 277). As the study of broadside ballads shows, the shared and separate interests of the middle and working classes were tightly balanced in the politics and culture of industrial towns and cities. As you will see, ideas of mutuality and community were easily threatened by events and crises such as the cotton famine of 1861–65.

3.3 The cotton famine of 1861–65

In the 1860s, restrictions on the supply of cotton as a result of the **American civil war** threatened the stability and prosperity of the cotton towns. The cotton famine, as it became known, put Lancashire, cotton and the factory system at the forefront of national political concerns as commentators feared the prolonged distress in the region would lead to social unrest. The cotton trade had, as you know from the film 'Manchester and the factory: Quarry Bank Mill and Ancoats' which you watched during your work on Chapter 1, suffered many fluctuations and crises since its mechanisation in the eighteenth century. One thing that made the cotton famine different was that it corresponded with the growth of public politics and the campaign to extend the franchise to working-class men. Public speaking and organised debates were ubiquitous in the 1860s and increasingly included working-class men (Hewitt, 2002, p. 1). A report in *The Times* from 1873 stated: 'In the course of these fifty years we have become a nation of public speakers […] We are now more than ever a debating, that is, a Parliamentary people' (quoted in Bevis, 2003, p. 577). Great orators, such as the **Liberal** MP John Bright (Figure 3.8), became renowned for their charismatic and engaging style of speaking. But, more importantly, men such as Bright opened up the appeal of liberalism to a broader spectrum of the population by taking up issues that directly concerned working-class men: issues such as the cotton famine and the American civil war.

Activity

You should allow about 20 minutes for this activity.

Turn to Reading 3.3, 'Address from Working Men to President Lincoln', and answer the following questions:

1   Where is the meeting held? Who has organised it? Why is this significant?

2   Whose voices are represented and how are they expressed?

3   What themes do you notice?

Discussion

1   The meeting is held in the Free Trade Hall, which, as you know from the film 'Public culture in an industrial city', was built on the site of the Peterloo Massacre. It has been organised by two working men. This suggests that the spontaneous and popular politics that fuelled the protest movements of the earlier nineteenth century have been

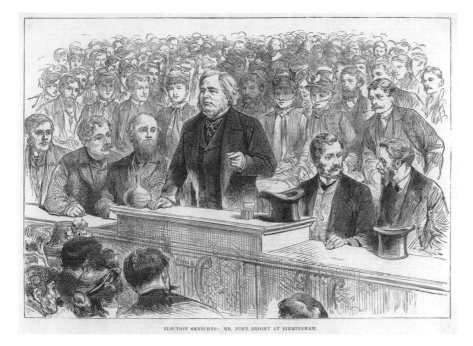

ELECTION SKETCHES: MR. JOHN BRIGHT AT BIRMINGHAM.

Figure 3.8 John Bright speaking at an election meeting in Birmingham.
Photo: © Illustrated London News Ltd/Mary Evans Picture Library

replaced by formal political meetings. However, in the context of the poverty and hardship caused by the cotton famine and of a revived campaign to extend the franchise to working men, the memory of Peterloo was not very far away.

2   Ritualistic forms of address give the event a structure and authority. The mayor chairs the meeting, though he makes clear the conditions in which he speaks: as a common man rather than a figure of authority. Resolutions are presented, debated and passed. Those who cannot be present give their opinion through their letters being read out. A sense of dialogue and exchange is reflected in the reporting, and acknowledgement is made of applause and affirmation from the audience. In this way, the report shows how different voices are brought into play in different ways. Most strikingly, the event presents working men, cotton masters, liberal politicians and intellectuals such as John Stuart Mill as sharing a political platform.

3   You may have picked up on the themes of freedom and an antipathy to slavery – both of which, as you've seen in the sources you have studied so far, had long been associated with radical politics. These are concerns that unite those present at the meeting. In the context of this debate, the freedom of British working men is shown in their ability to organise events such as this and speak at them.

Through the staging of debates like this, and the reporting of them in newspapers, the cotton famine became an important symbol of social and political progress. They helped promote sympathy and support for distressed cotton workers. The cotton famine put enormous stress on local charities, local ratepayers and Poor Law Boards, and special relief committees were set up in a number of cotton towns and cities to deal with the large numbers out of work. Employers, landowners, workpeople and trade societies contributed to special funds. Money came in from the colonies. Even people in the northern states of America contributed to relief funds (Henderson, 1969, p. 83). Accounts of the famine in Parliament and in the press emphasised the manner in which communities worked together to relieve the distress of cotton workers and the maturity and restraint of the unemployed. This was unlike the situation in the 1840s, when depressions in trade led to riots and unrest and the poor were regarded with little sympathy or understanding.

The image of whole committees working together and capital and labour united against slavery was powerful, but it was difficult to maintain as the famine progressed. By 1863 many of the unemployed were angry that levels of support were so meagre and that local cotton masters were not doing more. Unemployed workers in Stalybridge complained that relief was dealt out unfairly and used by manufacturers to get revenge on some workers for old trade disputes (Henderson, 1969, p. 108).

Activity

You should allow about 15 minutes for this activity.

Turn to Reading 3.4 and read 'The Riots in the North'. This is a newspaper report of the riots that took place in Ashton and Stalybridge during the cotton famine (Figure 3.9).

1   What do you notice about how this event was reported and how the working classes are described?

2   Think about the descriptions of the working classes and the social order that you have encountered so far. How is this account different?

Discussion

1   The eyewitness reporting creates the impression of the riot as it unfolds. The workers are represented as a 'mob', unthinking, irrational and violent, simply responding to hunger by following the crowd and attacking shops. You may also have noticed that women and children are present on the streets here. The image of the crowd, or 'rabble',

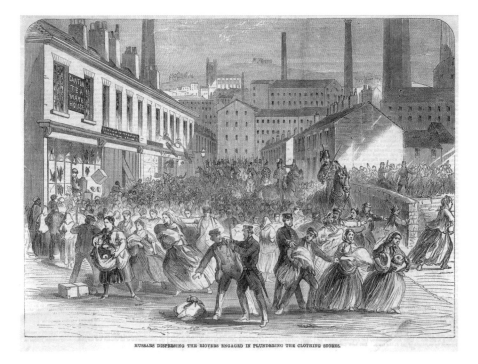

Figure 3.9 Riots at Stalybridge: the Hussars disperse rioters plundering the clothing stores, *Illustrated Times*, March 1863. Photo: © Mary Evans Picture Library

in a 'scramble' for bread and cheese suggests that it is not motivated by concerns about slavery and freedom but by anxiety about food. Established forms of authority are brought in, such as the Justice of the Peace (Hugh Mason, was, in fact, an employer known for his paternalism), the police and the military. The crowd, rather like children, is 'awed' and order is restored.

2 Many readers would have remembered the Plug Strikes that took place in the same area in 1842 (and which were mentioned in Chapter 1), and many would have feared a return to the social and political unrest of these times. As if to echo these fears, the report returns to some of the ways of describing the working classes and the social order that abounded in the 1840s. In describing the working classes as a 'mob' or a 'rabble', the report suggests that they act as a group rather than as individuals. The presence of women and children underlines the sense of chaos. The report suggests that the working classes are still inclined to violence and need strong direction and leadership from those in authority. You may remember a similar argument about the working classes from Thomas Carlyle in Chapter 1.

The riot brought into the foreground a number of different ways of seeing society, some of which drew on social commentary from the 1840s. These were used to counter claims that the industrial working classes were rational and responsible and to challenge the image of cotton manufacturers as enlightened representatives of a new industrial civilisation. Instead workers were a mob and, as a report in *The Times* from 24 March 1863 (p. 9) noted, the 'Cotton Lords' were an 'uneducated Plutocracy', using the famine to keep workers in a state of dependence so that they were forced to work for them for low wages when trade restarted. This is quite a different perspective from the ideas about the mutuality of capital and labour that had become a familiar part of civic culture in industrial towns and cities. In the long run, as you will see, the riot did not disrupt the image of Lancashire resolve, fortitude and independence. Nevertheless, as the reporting of the cotton famine and the Stalybridge riots shows, different visions of the social order coexisted and were drawn into debates to support arguments for and against parliamentary reform.

3.4 Parliamentary reform

Some of the ways of presenting the social order that circulated during the cotton famine were to have a direct bearing on the campaigns in the 1860s to extend the vote to working men. As you saw in Chapter 1, commentators such as Carlyle saw working-class protests as a way for 'dumb' creatures to express their need for middle-class leaders. Riots such as the one at Stalybridge were used to reassert this view. Others argued that they demonstrated the existence of separate and irreconcilable class interests, and the working-class propensity to think and act as a mass. Combined with the fear that an enfranchised working class would have a permanent majority in electoral terms, some commentators argued that giving working men the vote would make it impossible for Parliament to represent the nation. From a different perspective, the fact that the cotton famine, despite its pernicious effects in the north of England, had been borne without major unrest was used to argue that working men possessed the qualities that were associated with political rights: reason, intellect and independence.

The debate about the extension of the franchise used contrasting images of working men as 'tough' or 'respectable' to influence debate. In arguing against reform in a speech in the House of Commons on 13 March 1866, the Liberal MP Robert Lowe argued that 'If you want venality, if you want ignorance, if you want drunkenness, and the facility for being intimidated; or if […] you want impulsive, unreflecting and violent people, where do you look for them in the constituencies? Do you go to the top or to the bottom?' (quoted in Saunders, 2007, p. 582). On the other side of the debate, William Gladstone (1809–1898), as Liberal prime minister, referred to the success of self-help institutions, the growth of libraries, working men's institutes and savings banks as evidence of working men's fitness to vote (McClelland, 2000, p. 114). In a speech at the end of the second reading of the Reform Bill, on 27 April 1866, Gladstone referred directly to the cotton famine in his argument in support of reform. He argued that one word was enough to answer the opponents of reform: 'That word is Lancashire; Lancashire, associated with the sufferings of the last four years, so painful and bitter in themselves to contemplate, but so nobly and gloriously born' (Bassett, 1916, p. 375). Gladstone's words suggest he was persuaded to the cause for the extension of the vote by evidence of the improvement shown in civic culture and the resilience of the unemployed in Lancashire. This is not necessarily how the working-class campaigners saw it. For them, as for Chartists such as David Ross (whom you may recall from Reading 1.5 in Chapter 1), the vote was a right resulting from their role as the generators of the nation's wealth.

Gladstone's Liberal government was replaced by the Conservatives in June 1866 when the Reform Bill was defeated. A number of reform demonstrations were held over the summer. One such rally at Hyde Park in London that August resulted in a riot that was put down by police and troops. Those that took place in the north were extensively reported in *Reynolds's Weekly Newspaper*. In 1864 the price of *Reynolds's* was reduced after the abolition of the **stamp duty**, a tax on newspapers and documents. It soon became a bestselling radical newspaper, which was particularly popular in the manufacturing districts. It had been a supporter of Chartism and promoted the campaign for the vote vigorously.

Activity

You should allow about 20 minutes for this activity.

Turn to Reading 3.5 and read 'The Manchester Reform Demonstration and its Moral', an article which was published in *Reynolds's Weekly Newspaper* in 1866.

How is the social order described in this article? In what way is it the same as or different from some of the other sources you have read in this chapter?

Discussion

There is reference to groups that you will now be familiar with: 'Lancashire Lads' and 'Manchester men'. The reference to emancipation of 'white slaves' is used again. Similarly, the unity of interests between the 'down-trodden masses' and the 'friends of reform', liberal gentlemen such as Bright, is clear. The writing is more polemical. Resolve, stoicism and fortitude, qualities that had been seen as exemplary in helping working men withstand the privations of the cotton famine, and crucial in the public campaign for reform, are recast here as determination. It is made clear that working men and their liberal 'friends' will not give up the fight for the vote.

Like many of the extracts you have read, this account combines description and argument: it describes a demonstration and puts forward an argument in favour of parliamentary reform. There is the sense of dialogue and exchange that you are now familiar with, seen here in reference to the *Quarterly Review* and speeches in Parliament. Also, reference is made to the parliamentary-style politics of the reform campaign: the 'speeches, resolutions, petitions'. However, the report contrasts this with the violence with which protests have been met and hints that, if their demands are not met, the campaigners for reform might also be compelled to use force.

You may recall how riots such as the one in Stalybridge were used in some quarters as evidence that working men were still too ignorant and uncivilised for the vote. The report in *Reynolds's* twisted such logic round to present aristocratic privilege as stuck in the past – a remnant of pre-industrial England and, as such, not appropriate for modern industrial, parliamentary times. *Reynolds's* argued that a Parliament dominated by the aristocracy had little legitimacy and thus had no option other than the use of force to maintain its privileges and keep order. In contrast, the reform group presented its legitimacy through the reason and determination of the working man, who had allied himself with liberal figures to secure his right to vote. The latter argument won through and the Reform Act was passed in 1867.

3.5 Civic culture

To finish the chapter, and the first half of this book, I want you to return to an event which occurred ten years after the passing of the Reform Bill and which you considered briefly at the beginning of this chapter: the opening in 1877 of the new town hall in Manchester (Figure 3.10).

You began this chapter by examining a report of the procession of trade societies that passed through Manchester at that time. The procession was the final part of a series of celebrations organised over three days. As you may remember, our first reading of the first paragraph shows how this might be used as evidence of the 'age of equipoise': that the mid century was a period in which shared interests and values took precedence over conflict and class differences.

Figure 3.10 Manchester Town Hall, *c.*1885. Photo: © Francis Frith collection/ akg-images

Activity

You should allow about 30 minutes for this activity.

Now read all of Reading 3.6, 'Opening of the New Town Hall: the Trades Procession', and answer the following questions. We shall then think again about the 'age of equipoise'.

1   What impression of the social order do you think this report of the procession creates? How is order maintained?

2   Look at the way the workers and their banners are described. Why do you think they are described in this way?

3   What sort of workers are not mentioned?

Discussion

1   The first thing that may have struck you is the size of the procession: around 50,000 men took part. The report suggests that a good range of Manchester society was present: local administrators, the military, the police, the fire brigade and workers. Rituals are used to include others and three cheers are given for the queen, the mayor and mayoress, and Bright. Putting this all together, the report represents society as diverse but orderly. It also shows that the orderliness of the procession is the result of the high levels of organisation that have gone into the planning: delegates from the trade societies met the mayor and the chief constable, Captain Palin, to organise the event. The presence of the police and the military no doubt helped ensure order. However, as the report shows, the procession went well because the working men in it followed instructions.

2   The procession is a spectacle and the workers are on display. The scrutiny of their numbers, appearance, banners and behaviour is seen as important because the marchers represent their trades and the working classes in general. It is through work that these men have gained access to the streets of Manchester and it is through their trades that they are identified by the reporter. The banners are read as emblems of the trade societies' wealth and values. The banner of the Operative Cabinet Makers is greatly approved of because of its message of the separate roles but shared goals of capital and labour. On the other hand, the banner of the Carpenters and Joiners, with its confrontational message 'Deal with us on the "square", you have "chiselled" us long enough', is seen as a 'relic of olden time'.

3   Women and children are not mentioned despite being a significant part of the workforce. In fact, the industrial, factory-based labour on which Manchester's wealth was based is rather underrepresented. Instead, the representatives of the working class are male artisans or labourers who are members of trade societies.

Reading this extract 'against the grain' and in the context of broader debates about politics and society produces a more complex history of mid-century Manchester. The *Manchester Guardian*, which originally published this article, is not passively describing the procession. The newspaper was closely associated with the local political elite and keen to represent the city and its politics in a positive light to broader audiences. The detailed description suggests that this is an eyewitness account – a statement of fact – however, the repetition of certain themes such as orderliness and independence makes clear that certain ways of behaving are being promoted as acceptable. We can see this in moments of discord – for example, when the account attempts to fit the Carpenters and Joiners into its narrative. The absence of references to women speaks volumes about who is included as part of the local political community and who is not. It is clear that only certain groups are able to represent the population in the new public spaces that are emerging in the city. With a careful reading of events like this, we can see how descriptive accounts are often, perhaps unwittingly, presenting recommendations for an ideal society. As such, we have to be careful not to accept them uncritically as fact.

In the mid nineteenth century and into the 1870s, being visible, being seen in these public rituals, accorded people a certain authority: a right to a public political voice. One of the most important changes we can trace from the evidence presented in this chapter is the emergence of a public political sphere composed of working men. The Reform Act of 1867 gave the vote to adult male householders in borough constituencies, along with lodgers who paid a rent of at least £10 a year for unfurnished lodgings. The Act did not bring in full democracy, but it did increase the number of working-class electors. The Reform Act, together with the establishment of the Trades Union Congress in 1868, represented the successful extension of the public political platform to include many working men. These reforms, in associating citizenship with perceived masculine attributes such as work and independence, demonstrate a tension in the history of politics: greater democracy is based on honest and open debate, but this is made possible only by regulating access to the public platform (Vernon, 1993, p. 7).

Conclusion

This chapter has shown how a sense of equipoise was reflected and created in descriptions of society that emphasised connections between 'the people' and shared interests rather than class differences. Civic spaces and ritualistic forms of communication and address created social bonds and provided ways for a range of people of different classes to communicate. Social tensions still existed beneath the rhetoric of shared interests, but there was a greater confidence that these could be resolved. This confidence was a reflection of a public culture that emphasised shared interests while at the same time regulating and managing debate. Issues relating to work and wages, and questions about the fundamental legitimacy of capitalism, were still matters of concern and were taken up in earnest by the trade union movement. However, they were rarely heard in local civic politics.

This chapter has also developed your skills in analysis and interpretation. It has shown how a greater attention to language and culture allows historians to dig deeper into questions of class, identity and politics. Old forms of expression are given new meanings in changed contexts. For example, you saw how broadside ballads used a traditional form to express the new experience of work in industrial towns and cities. You have also seen that the form in which ideas are expressed helps create new identities. The public platform of mid-nineteenth century England, the act of debating itself, helped define working men as a political constituency. Speaking at public meetings with well-known liberal figures, and marching in civic processions, enabled working men to express themselves as free and equal citizens. It is clear, too, that the social identities expressed in debates are also fluid. Working men might regularly participate in civic culture, attend the local library, read political economy and still defend their rights as workers. Similarly, a shared language does not imply a shared meaning. Categories such as independence and respectability could be interpreted in different ways.

All the chapters in the first half of Book 4 have demonstrated that voices and texts are dynamic and changing. Understanding these changes requires an awareness of the way a debate develops through dialogue in different contexts. In the second half of this book, you will explore context in another way by considering how meanings change when people and objects move.

References

Anonymous (n.d.) 'The Working Men of England!' in *Bodleian Library Broadside Ballads*, Bodleian Library, University of Oxford; also available online at http://ballads.bodleian.ox.ac.uk/ (Accessed 23 September 2014).

Bassett, A.T. (1916) *Gladstone's Speeches*, London, Methuen.

Bevis, M. (2003) 'Volumes of noise', *Victorian Literature and Culture*, vol. 31, no. 2, pp. 577–91.

Burn, W.L. (1964) *The Age of Equipoise: A Study of the Mid-Victorian Generation*, London, Allen and Unwin.

Clark, A. (1995) *The Struggle for the Breeches: Gender and the Making of the British Working Class*, Berkeley, CA, University of California Press.

Epstein, J. (1989) 'Understanding the cap of liberty; symbolic practice and social conflict in early nineteenth-century England', *Past and Present*, vol. 122, no. 1, pp. 75–118.

Gunn, S. (2000) *The Public Culture of the Victorian Middle Class*, Manchester, Manchester University Press.

Henderson, W.O. (1969) *The Lancashire Cotton Famine, 1861–1865*, 2nd edn, Manchester, Manchester University Press.

Hewitt, M. (2002) 'Aspects of platform culture in nineteenth-century Britain', *Nineteenth-Century Prose*, vol. 29, no. 1, pp. 1–32.

Howe, A. (1984) *The Cotton Masters, 1830–1869*, Oxford, Clarendon Press.

Joyce, P. (1991) *Visions of the People: Industrial England and the Question of Class*, Cambridge, Cambridge University Press.

McClelland, K. (2000) 'England's greatness, the working man', in Hall, C., McClelland, K. and Rendall, J. *Defining the Victorian Nation: Class, Race, Gender and the Reform Act of 1867*, Cambridge, Cambridge University Press.

McWilliam, R. (2007) *The Tichborne Claimant: A Victorian Sensation*, London, Hambledon.

Rose, S. (1992) *Limited Livelihoods: Class and Gender in Nineteenth-Century England*, London, Routledge.

Saunders, R. (2007) 'The politics of reform and the making of the Second Reform Acts, 1848–1867', *Historical Journal*, vol. 50, no. 3, pp. 571–91.

Stedman Jones, G. (1983) *Languages of Class: Studies in English Working-Class History*, Cambridge, Cambridge University Press.

Taine, H. (1885 [1872]) *Notes on England*, New York, Henry Holt and Co.

Vernon, J. (1993) *Politics and the People: A Study in English Political Culture 1815–1867*, Cambridge, Cambridge University Press.

Further reading

For a good overview of civic and public culture, see Gunn (2000). There is a considerable literature on post-Chartist politics; for an overview of this that explains the rise of popular liberalism, see McWilliam (1998). On the extension of the franchise, see Hall, McClelland and Rendall (2000), in particular the chapter by McClelland, 'England's greatness, the working man'. A good place to explore the Hallé orchestra can be found here: http://www.halle.co.uk/conductors. aspx

Gunn, S. (2000) *The Public Culture of the Victorian Middle Class*, Manchester, Manchester University Press.

Hall, C., McClelland, K. and Rendall, J. (2000) *Defining the Victorian Nation: Class, Race, Gender and the Reform Act of 1867*, Cambridge, Cambridge University Press.

McWilliam, R. (1998) *Popular Politics in Nineteenth-Century England*, London, Routledge.

Reading 3.1   *Notes on England*

Source: Taine, H. (1885 [1872]) *Notes on England*, New York, Henry Holt and Co., pp. 291–9.

Visiting Oldham, we found the working men keeping holiday in honour of the society to which they belong. They walked in procession, carrying flags – on one flag, that of the brickmakers, were the portraits of the founders; in the centre was a luminous eye surrounded with mottoes, to the effect that they asked for justice and nothing but justice. [...]

... They have no other aim than the increase of wages, they never think of attacking the Government, as they would assuredly do in France. They are not political; they are not even social; they entertain no Utopian schemes, never dream about reconstituting society, suppressing interest, abolishing inheritance, equalising incomes, making the State a joint-stock company, in which every individual is a shareholder. Manufacturers tell me here that in this country there is nothing of that sort: 'Our working men do not generalise like yours; besides, they have a smattering of political economy; above all, they have too much common sense to pursue chimeras. A strike is what we have to fear, and not a socialistic movement.' I have just read a very fine novel written by a person who lived here, and who was an acute observer, 'North and South', by the late Mrs. Gaskell, in which the character of a working man is depicted and the history of a strike is narrated. If the portrait is as faithful as I believe it to be, then the men of that class are possessed of a large store of reason and fairness. They are perpetually at variance with the masters, but the struggle is restricted to the question of supply and demand. [...]

... Nevertheless the situation has had its effect, and it cannot be denied that the workman regards his master as his natural enemy. The masters make very great and very praiseworthy efforts with a view to lessen this feeling of hostility. They found or become trustees of savings-banks and of penny banks, in which the workman may deposit his smallest saving. [...]

We visited several establishments for instruction and public recreation. We first went to Peel's Park, a sort of large English garden, situated in the heart of the city, where the poor may seat themselves amid trees and flowers. It was founded by means of a private subscription amounting to £35,000, and includes in addition a museum and a library. [...]

Thence we proceeded to the free library, also established by private subscription, and chiefly used by working men. It contains 25,000 volumes. The librarian said that there are 10,000 readers a month; newspapers are to be found there also. Whoever is introduced by two respectable persons may borrow books; from 1,200 to 1,400 persons are regular borrowers. I learn from the register that the lives of Nelson and Wellington are chiefly in request, and that even theological works find readers. According to our guide, many of these working men are well informed, and make collections; one was mentioned who knew the names and appearance of 900 species of beetles. Natural history and the natural sciences in general are greatly to their liking; they are fond of facts, and of proofs established by experiment, and are often led far beyond the Bible to the very depths of Positivism; the Secularists get many recruits from among their number. On the other hand, they read treatises on political economy, and newspapers; now English newspapers, even those of a small town, are instructive, filled with correspondence, with circumstantial and accurate information. […]

… Self-help is always the watchword, and is one little understood in France; from the same interior source issue forth the societies, the institutions which abound here, among others the municipal institutions; Manchester administers her own affairs, pays and appoints her police, governs herself almost without the intervention of the Government. Consequently the social edifice rests upon thousands of independent columns, and not like ours, upon a single one; accidents, catastrophes, like our revolutions of 1830, of 1848, of 1852, are impossible here.

Reading 3.2 'The Working Men of England!'

Source: Anonymous (n.d.) 'The Working Men of England!' in *Bodleian Library Broadside Ballads*, **Bodleian Library, University of Oxford; also available online at http://ballads.bodleian.ox.ac.uk/ search/roud/V13793 [accessed 20 November 2014].**

Oh, the working men of England, we labour for the great.
We toil away both night and day to keep the Church and state.
In every part, in every clime, our commerce and our toil,
Adds lustre to the genius of Great Britian's [*sic*] native isle;
On every fort, on every tower, the British flag's unfurl'd,
Which tells the strength of Britian's power in all parts of the world.
Our hardy tars that plough the deep our glory to expand,
With the produce of our labouring men, the pride of Britian's land.

Chorus:

Oh, the working men of England will never cease to be,
The prop of this great nation and they ever should be free;
They tell without a murmur when good wages they command
And bring, honour, glory and renown to Britian's happy land.

Oh, the working men of England when they got reform,
What merry joy without alloy their happy brows adorn,
They care not for Whig or Tory, but labour and be paid,
With honour to free masters and the founders of free trade.
And should a foreign foe ere threat to tread upon our shore,
Our working men would fly to arms as they have done before.
There's not a britian in this isle, but boldly forth would stand,
In defence of wife and kindred, his Queen and native land.

Oh, the working men of England, what progress they have made,
In iron, wool and coal, the staple of our trade;
The morning bells being rung, for toil it fills them with delight,
In hopes of joyous plenty on a glorious Saturday night;
And may kind providence divine their humble efforts aid,
And freedom's sons for ever shine on commerce and free trade.
Contentment is the workman's lot, he'll toil by night or day,
But give him plenty in his cot, with freedom and fair play.

Reading 3.3 'Address from Working Men to President Lincoln'

Source: *Manchester Guardian*, **1 January 1863, p. 3.**

Last evening, a public meeting was held in the Free-trade Hall, which was crowded, in order to pass resolutions in favour of the cause of the United States, and to adopt an address to President Lincoln. The meeting had been called by an advertisement, signed by J.C. Edwards and E. Hoosons, two working men. [...]

J.C. Edwards said that the promoters of the meeting were not prepared with a chairman; but he saw that the Mayor of Manchester was in the room, and, considering His Worship's connection with the working classes in the past, and their esteem for him, he thought the Mayor was entitled to the position of chairman of the meeting. He made a motion to that effect [...] The Mayor said: Before I take the chair, I wish you to understand that I do not take it as Mayor of Manchester, but simply as Abel Heywood.– (Hear, Hear.) [...] J.C. Edwards, the secretary, read the following extract from a letter from Mr. J. Stuart Mill:

> Dear Sir, – I thank you very sincerely for your two letters, and for the important and most gratifying information which they contain. Hardly anything could do more good at present than such a demonstration from the suffering operatives of Lancashire, while there is in the fact itself, and in the state of mind which prompts it, a moral greatness which is at once a just rebuke to the mean feeling of so great a proportion of the public, and a source of unqualified happiness to those whose hopes and fears for the great interests of humanity are, as mine are, inseparably bound up in the moral and intellectual prospects of the working classes. [...]

J.C. Edwards moved the following resolution:

> That this meeting, recognising the common brotherhood of mankind and the sacred and inalienable right of every human being to personal freedom and equal protection, records its detestation of negro slavery in America, and of the attempt of the rebellious Southern slaveholders to organise on the great American Continent a nation having slavery as its basis. [...]

The reading of the address was frequently applauded.

Reading 3.4 'The Riots in the North'

Source: *Observer*, 30 March 1863, p. 3.

On Monday morning, between nine and ten o'clock, a police-officer, who had been sent to Staleybridge [*sic*] by Mr Dalgleish, the chief constable, to watch the progress of events in that borough, arrived at the town hall in Ashton, with the alarming intelligence that a vast mob of persons had left Staleybridge for the purpose of riot in Ashton. Mr Dalgleish thereupon called in all the public officers, and shortly afterwards Mr Hugh Mason, J.P., arrived, and, with Mr Dalgleish, decided upon calling out a troop of the 14th Hussars, stationed in the Ashton Barracks […] With Mr Mason at their head, they then went towards Stamford-street, with the view of preventing the mob from entering the town. They were too late, however, for before this could be done the mob had attacked the bread shop of Mr Handforth, baker, in Old-street, and the inmates, through fear, at once threw out loaves of bread, which led to a general scramble among the rabble. From this shop they proceeded to Joshua Taylor's, a corn dealer and cheese factor, and here again both bread and cheese were thrown to them. […] The mob from this place went towards the gas works, whither they were followed by the police, and soon after […] a shower of stones was hurled at them, one of the missiles striking Mr Mason, but not heavily. The moment the stones were thrown the police turned face about and confronted the mob, which must now have numbered some 3,000 men, women and children. The Hussars, who had been stationed in Henry's-square, at this moment came up, or the result might have been serious. At any rate their appearance, and the bold front shown by the police, had the effect of awing the mob, who, on the former making a charge with drawn sabres, now broke up into gangs, and the streets were cleared.

Reading 3.5 'The Manchester Reform Demonstration and its Moral'

Source: *Reynolds's Weekly Newspaper*, 30 September 1866, p. 1.

Adversity is the test of devotion; and it is just possible that one of the reasons why the weather was so wet, cheerless, and depressing, on Monday last, was to test the earnestness of the 'Lancashire Lads' in the great struggle now going on for the political emancipation of the white slaves of England. [...]

The Manchester men stood the rain; from this, then, the Tories may learn that, if need be, they are prepared to stand fire. In the cause of reform, the Manchester men did not flinch from the cold wet which soaked their clothes through to the very skin. [...]

The Tories, or aristocracy, on the one hand, anticipate an appeal to the sword, or civil war, for the preservation of their privileges. Of this we have abundant proof in the Hyde-park display of police and Household Guards, to massacre the men of London; in the contributions of 'persons of quality' to the pages of the 'Quarterly Review'; in the leading articles of the recognized Tory journals; in the speeches of the Tory members of parliament – General Peel, for instance – who looks forward to the day when the Thames will run red with the blood shed in defence of the throne and the aristocracy [...]

On the other hand, the friends of reform are becoming apprehensive that something very different from speeches, resolutions, petitions, and peaceful demonstrations will have to be resorted to before the people of England are delivered from the galling yoke of aristocratic domination. Even Mr Bright, one of the most constitutional agitators that ever stood on a platform – a gentleman who, in the opinion of some of his best friends and most ardent admirers, has been in the habit of placing an excessive emphasis on the importance of purely moral means of deliverance of oppression – even Mr Bright has at length come to contemplate a contingent appeal to the muscular and military might of the insulted and down-trodden masses, for the overthrow of aristocratic usurpation under which the wealth-creating people of England, Ireland, and Scotland have groaned for hundreds of years.

Reading 3.6 'Opening of the New Town Hall: the Trades Procession'

Source: *Manchester Guardian*, **17 September 1877, p. 6.**

A procession of working men belonging to the various trade societies of Manchester and Salford formed a fitting conclusion on Saturday to the programme for celebrating the opening of the new Town Hall. Such a demonstration in point of numbers could be got up only in a manufacturing centre, and in regard to the variety of trades represented it was especially characteristic of Manchester and the neighbourhood. The success with which it was carried out may be ascribed in great measure to the exceptionally fine weather, but without the admirable police arrangements, the services of the military, the strict observance of the instructions issued by the Chief Constable, and last, though not least, the hearty spirit with which the working men themselves entered into the day's proceedings, the assembly of such an immense number of men must have been attended with some considerable risk. As there is no place in Manchester with space enough for 50,000 men, the Committee to whom the arrangements were entrusted determined for the convenience of mustering to divide the societies into three sections, distinguished respectively as A, B, and C. A section, numbering over 14,500, was instructed to meet in Piccadilly, Portland-street, and the adjacent thoroughfares; the B division, consisting of 14,020 men, in Stevenson Square, Oldham-street, Ancoats-street, and neighbouring thoroughfares; and the C division, of 14,380 men, in Oldham Road and other streets branching off both sides of it up to Lloyd street on one side and Reather-street on the other. A constable, accompanied by a marshal bearing a board with the number of his society, marked the spot where the head of each society was to be formed. […]

The idea of enabling the working classes to take part in the opening proceedings originated several months ago with some of the leading members of the trade societies. It was warmly taken up by the City Council, by none more warmly than the Mayor himself; and the sub-committee to whom the arrangements were entrusted accordingly made the working men's demonstration one of the main features of the programme. Delegates were appointed from the respective trade societies to meet the Mayor and Captain Palin, and the details of the programme were discussed and arranged at meetings held every Tuesday evening in the Town Hall. […]

When the societies commenced to arrive the Mayor, at the request of his friends, donned his scarlet robe of office, in order that the processionists might the more easily distinguish him from the rest of the Corporation by whom he was surrounded. The Mayoress remained seated by the side of her husband until the square became gradually filled, when in the presence and hearing of the assembled thousands the bands played the National Anthem. The music was followed by three cheers for the Queen, three cheers for the Mayor and Mayoress, and three cheers for Mr. John Bright. The Town Hall bells then began to play, and the procession marched past the Mayor in the order given in the programme. [...]

... The Manchester branch of the Amalgamated Society of Journeyman Tailors, who came next, were more strongly represented. The men were most of them fashionably dressed, and nearly all wore flowers, real or artificial, grouped with excellent taste in the button-hole of their coats. The tailors boast the possession of a heraldry, and the coat of arms of the Tailors' Guild is prominently emblazoned on the obverse of their banner. A picture of our first parents on the reverse of the banner exhibited by contrast the force of the motto of the Guild – 'From small beginnings great things arise,' the small beginnings in this case being, of course, the covering of fig leaves. The members of the local branch of the Amalgamated Society of Bootmakers, some 250 strong, succeeded the tailors. 'May the manufactures of the sons of Crispin be trod upon by all the world' is the aspiration to which the Society gives vent by its banner. The axiom 'Union is strength,' with the addendum 'Beware of differences,' is laid down as that which should be the guiding rule of the members of the Society. The Manchester Branch of the Operative Cabinet Makers of Great Britain and Ireland, a wealthy body, were distinguished by a costly banner, the most splendid by far of all the banners in the procession. It took four men to carry it. The front of the banner is occupied by a representation of 'Capital and Labour.' An elderly man, seated in a gorgeous apartment, is the embodiment of 'Capital,' while several workmen, holding in their hands specimens of highly finished cabinet work, uphold the dignity of 'Labour.' The figures are in medieval dress, and the surroundings are in perfect harmony. The reverse of the banner is divided into six panels, illustrative of the objects of the Society, from which we gather that it supports a member when out of employment, when suffering from sickness and in old age, that it insures his furniture from fire, helps him if he desires to emigrate, and finally inters him decently when death overtakes him.

Altogether the banner is highly satisfactory as a work of art, and does infinite credit to the taste of the members of the Society. [...]

The societies forming the C division, which came next, numbered 25 [...] First in order came the Amalgamated Society of Carpenters and Joiners, and the General Union of Carpenters and Joiners, headed by the district banner of the General Union. Prominent among the flags which these bodies displayed was one which may be regarded as a relic of olden time. It was a plain flag, and had on in large letters the words 'Those who assert that politics will ruin trade unions have yet something to learn.' On the reverse side were the words: 'Deal with us on the "square", you have "chiselled" us long enough.' It was said that this banner was made during the agitation for the Reform Bill of 1832, and has been in the possession of the Carpenters' Society since.

Chapter 4
The tourist gaze and religious objects

Paul-François Tremlett

Aims

This chapter will:

- introduce you to the study of tourism, religion and material culture
- develop your skills and understanding of key concepts in the study of tourism
- explore the idea of context in relation to the afterlives of objects
- develop your critical and analytical skills
- develop your observational and listening skills.

Materials you will need

In this chapter, you will need to watch the following films, which can be found on the module website:

- Religious tourism.
- Touristification.

You will also be directed online to visit an Indonesian tourism website.

Introduction

The aim of this chapter is to introduce you to some religious objects and to examine what happens to them when they become part of what we shall be calling the **tourist gaze**. To anticipate our conclusions somewhat, we shall see that the **touristification** of religious objects adds new layers of significance and meaning to those objects. This will be understood as an ambivalent process. Some commentators have argued that touristic relationships diminish the sacrality, or 'religiousness', of religious objects, or (to put it another way), because of tourism, religious objects lose their **authenticity** as religious objects and instead become **commodities**. Others have claimed that tourism in a certain sense resurrects religious objects and gives them new biographies and afterlives, in the process revitalising religious traditions. This chapter will introduce you to these debates and will equip you with the critical skills you need to participate in them for yourself.

As we have seen in Book 1 of this module, anthropological approaches to material culture, in common with the approach taken here, tend to be object-driven and focus not on an object in isolation but rather on an object in context. But what is 'context'? Context can refer to the ways in which an object has been put to use, the possible association of an object with a specific function, or aesthetic, or the cultural, social or religious meaning and significance of an object. When we talk about context it is typically a kind of shorthand for time and space – that is, objects exist in time and in socially and culturally constituted places. When we talk about historical context or social or cultural context, then, we assume that history, society and culture somehow condition, or (to put it more strongly) determine the ways in which we think about objects, the meanings we ascribe to them, the uses we put them to, how we encounter them, and so on and so forth. It is a perspective that typically sees in objects – and the ways that they are put to use in different historical, social and cultural situations – clues about social relationships. The focus throughout this chapter will be on the processes through which religious objects change their meaning or acquire additional meanings because of tourism.

4.1 Shifting contexts

In this section we are going to use the idea of contexts as a tool for thinking about how religion and tourism constitute overlapping arenas in which religious objects can be encountered and used. Intuitively, we may feel that the kinds of object we associate with religion and the kinds of object we associate with tourism inhabit different worlds, and we might expect them to have very different lives and move through very different chains of function and use. For example, we might formulate, for ourselves and without much prompting, the idea that religious objects belong to the realm of the **sacred** while tourist objects belong to the realm of the **profane** or secular. This kind of logic has indeed been central to western thinking about religion in the Humanities and the Social Sciences. Emile Durkheim (1858–1917) was one of the founders of modern Sociology and a pioneer of the sociological study of Religion. He developed the following definition of religion:

> All known religious beliefs, whether simple or complex, present one common characteristic: they presuppose a classification of all the things, real or ideal, of which men [*sic*] think, into two classes […] generally designated by two distinct terms which are translated well enough by the words *profane* and *sacred* […] This division of the world into two domains, the one containing all that is sacred, the other all that is profane, is the distinctive trait of religious thought; the beliefs, myths, dogmas and legends are either representations or systems of representations which express the nature of sacred things, the virtues and powers which are attributed to them, or their relations with each other and with profane things … [Religion is] *a unified set of beliefs and practices relative to sacred things, that is to say, things set apart and forbidden – beliefs and practices which unite into one single moral community called a Church, all those who adhere to them.*
>
> (Durkheim, 1971 [1912], pp. 37–47; original emphasis)

This definition arose from Durkheim's reflections on fieldwork conducted among Australian Aboriginal peoples at the end of the nineteenth century (though not by Durkheim himself). By studying what many people then believed were representatives of humanity's earliest forebears, Durkheim reasoned that it would be possible to discern the origins of religion. This assumption rendered Australia's Aboriginal peoples as living fossils – 'relics' of a long-distant past – and was linked to an evolutionary conceptualisation of human development that has since been abandoned as evidentially unsound by most sociologists and anthropologists.

Despite the problematic assumptions on which Durkheim's research on religion was based, his definition has proved influential. For Durkheim, 'sacred things' were 'things set apart'. What he meant is that religion invests certain objects with special meanings and significances, and these special meanings and significances generally pertain to moral restrictions on how or when these objects can be used, who can handle them and such like. In other words, religion sacralises certain objects, and this sacralisation means that the objects that are recognised as sacred by a particular community or tradition are to be treated differently from other, otherwise similar objects. Importantly, Durkheim did not think that the sacredness of an object lay in some special quality inherent in the object itself. Rather, he believed that the sacred quality of an object was a social or cultural construction. From Durkheim's point of view, what made an object sacred was the socially constituted and, as such, arbitrary system of rules and prohibitions that surrounded it and set it apart – not the object itself. But the question we have set ourselves is: what happens to religious objects when they are no longer simply 'set apart'? Indeed, what happens to a religious object when it falls under the tourist gaze?

Activity

Can you think of a sacred or religious object that is no longer, as Durkheim says, 'set apart'?

Discussion

There is potentially a long list of objects that may be included in such a discussion. One example of such a class of objects might be religious paintings of, for example, fifteenth- and sixteenth-century Christian Europe, such as those you encountered in Book 2, Chapters 3 and 4. The religious significance of such works has been significantly de-centred by secular, aesthetic values. This genre of painting is just as likely today to be encountered set apart in a museum or gallery space that carries its own aura of secular sacrality. Even where such works are still encountered in a church or Christian religious building, they are seen as works of art rather than as vehicles for the transmission of particular religious practices and mental or bodily dispositions.

Today, objects, sites and events associated with religion often inhabit dual spaces that carry both 'sacred' and 'profane' meanings, or 'religious' and 'touristic' meanings. Before moving on to explore this phenomenon in greater detail, let us begin with some questions about tourism.

4.2 Tourism

What is tourism? Perhaps this seems like a foolish question. I have been on holiday. It is more than likely that you have been on holiday, too. Most people we know have been on holiday. Almost all of us, at one time or another, have been tourists. We do not really think about going on holiday or being a tourist as something novel or odd or unusual. We expect it. We are at ease with it. We enjoy it and derive pleasure from planning it, doing it and reminiscing about it. We display our tourist souvenirs in our homes for others to see. A hundred and fifty years ago, however, most people did not go on holiday and most places were not equipped to receive tourists. Museums, nature trails, public memorials, leisure facilities, art galleries, hotels and the complex transport infrastructures necessary for people to be able to actually get from location A to location B simply did not exist. So, is tourism something new? Furthermore, can we distinguish between different kinds of tourism, or between tourism and travel? We shall address these questions shortly. In what follows we are going to work through some differing aspects of tourism, beginning with the idea that tourism is a kind of religion for modern, secular societies, before moving on to examine the question of the historical novelty of tourism and then the idea of the tourist gaze.

From pilgrimage to tourism?

Here we are going to briefly consider the idea that tourism is a modern form of religion. The idea rests on an analogy between tourism and **pilgrimage** – a journey that might be undertaken for devotional or penitential reasons. Consider the following:

- Tourism involves travel to places outside the normal spaces of home and work.

- Tourism involves the suspension of the norms of ordinary social life. This means that when people are on holiday, they tend not to behave in the same way as when they are at home or at work. Their behaviour changes.

- Tourism involves the expectation of new, possibly life-changing experiences. So, like the pilgrim, the tourist leaves his or her normal place of residence and the familiar of the everyday in order to seek out the extraordinary.

These points establish a contrast between work and tourism – between the quotidian and the extraordinary. The tourist emerges as someone seeking to escape the routines of everyday life, as someone on a quest for some kind of special experience. This is why some scholars have made a connection between tourists and pilgrims: both are on journeys that take them away from ordinary life towards an encounter with something radically out of the ordinary. In this view, there is nothing particularly new about tourism. Rather, tourism merely re-expresses human nature's need for the new.

Is tourism really pilgrimage by other means? If the tourist is a kind of modern-day pilgrim, then perhaps tourist sites like museums are the 'shrines' of the contemporary world. The secularisation of western societies and the steady diminution in the significance of religion could be said to have created a void that is filled up by tourism, such that some have argued that tourism has become the religion of modern, secularising societies.

Tourism and the modern world

Some scholars claim that tourism is an activity that is a very special marker of modern society. However, if pilgrimage is one possible predecessor of tourism, then the so-called Grand Tour is also a significant precursor (Stausberg, 2011, p. 3; Urry, 2002, pp. 4–5; Towner, 1985). Between its establishment during the seventeenth century and the emergence of mass tourism in the middle of the nineteenth century, the Grand Tour was a circuit of European travel undertaken by British travellers that took at least two forms. During the seventeenth century the circuit focused for the most part on urban sites in France, Italy, Switzerland, the Netherlands and Germany (Towner, 1985, p. 302) and was primarily undertaken by the British aristocracy for reasons of personal, intellectual and emotional cultivation, as well as by amateur scientists interested in collecting natural specimens of various kinds. However, by the beginning of the nineteenth century the Tour had changed. Although the principal routes remained the same, the ranks of those undertaking the Tour had grown to include the middle classes. While the motives for undertaking the Tour continued to include education and health (such as visits to spa towns like Baden in Switzerland), middle-class Tour-ists were also interested in mountain landscapes, which were said to evoke powerful experiences. However, it should be understood that the numbers of people who actually went on the Tour were tiny. In the 1830s it is estimated that approximately

50,000 British people were abroad in any one year, a figure that represents about 0.3 per cent of the population at the time. The advent of the railways, steamships and, of course (in the early twentieth century), cars rapidly changed this state of affairs. In fact, we can actually date quite precisely the founding of modern tourism to 1841, when Thomas Cook (see box and Figure 4.1) organised his first 'package tour' – and it is significant that this coincided with the development of photography:

> [T]ourism and photography came to be welded together and the development of each cannot be separated from the other. Both sets of practices remake each other in an irreversible and momentous double helix. From then we can say a 'tourist gaze' enters and makes the mobile, modern world.
>
> (Urry, 2002, p. 149)

Clearly, entrepreneurs such as Cook played an important role in the development of tourism, and it is ironic – at least in the context of this chapter – that Cook's forays into the business of tourism were motivated by his religious convictions. However, the development of tourism cannot be reduced to the activities or motivations of one individual. Other, much wider processes were at work in the world at large – changes in technology (as indicated above) and changes in the organisation and structure of the world economy, for example. An additional and compelling factor in the development of tourism was **nationalism**, which in turn was linked to changes in the organisation of political institutions during the nineteenth century.

Thomas Cook (1808–1892)

Born in Melbourne, Derbyshire, Cook was raised a Baptist. He later became a minister, touring local villages preaching and advocating temperance (abstinence from alcohol). The first excursions Cook organised were for Temperance Society members. Later, with his son John Mason Cook, he began offering package tours to European and non-European destinations, including Paris, Egypt and the USA. He also organised tours to the Holy Land (Palestine), believing that they conferred moral benefit. These trips were marketed even though they generated financial losses. His son

Figure 4.1 Thomas Cook, undated photograph. Photographer unknown.
Photo: © Bettmann/CORBIS

did not share his father's religious convictions. When Thomas
Cook retired, his son took over the business and loss-making tours
were ended. The first Cook's round-the-world tour was in 1872.

What is nationalism? It can be described as an ensemble of discourses and social practices through which national histories are written, displayed, taught and learned, and integral to this process is the construction of places like museums, monuments and heritage sites:

> Nation formation produced great enthusiasms for nationalism [...] and [...] the new spectacles of nation: the capital cities; the 19th-century Exhibitions designed to showcase national industry and art; new national parks to showcase national natures and geographies; the new national monuments to symbolize national achievements (the Eiffel Tower, the Statue of Liberty, Nelson's Column); new museums to house a nation's historical objects and/or its imperial collections and showcase its international power and influence. In a powerful way then, nations and nationalisms determined what was relevant, what was interesting, what was exciting in the modern age.
>
> (Franklin, 2004, p. 289)

When tourists visit the UK today they typically go to see sites like Trafalgar Square and Nelson's Column, the British Museum and Stonehenge. However, before the nineteenth century these sites either did not exist or were not considered to be places of special aesthetic or historic interest in the ways they are today. Their development as places of interest was part of a general shift, in the mid nineteenth century, in the way people looked at their world and conceived of their relationship to it. Tourism cannot be understood to be separate from the profound political, economic and technological changes that have reshaped the world from the mid nineteenth century onwards.

The tourist gaze

In a book called *Society of the Spectacle*, the French thinker Guy Debord (1931–1994) claimed that life in modern societies is dominated by images and performances or, in his terminology, 'spectacles'. Debord said that 'in societies where modern conditions of production prevail, all of life presents itself as an immense accumulation of *spectacles*. Everything that was directly lived has moved away into a representation' (1983 [1967], p. 1; original emphasis). He went further to suggest that 'the spectacle is not a collection of images, but a social relation among people, mediated by images' (Debord, 1983 [1967], p. 4).

What was it that he was trying to tell us? Debord was a revolutionary Marxist, involved in the 1968 student uprisings in Paris. Although not always cited by scholars, his ideas have been very influential in studies of tourism and museums. Debord's use of the term 'spectacle' focused attention on how vision is organised in modern societies. And when we look at the scholarly literature on tourism we find that vision, sight and seeing – sightseeing – are a consistent focus of debate among scholars. All the way through scholarly articles and books on tourism we find references to 'sight sacralisation' (MacCannell, 1999, pp. 44–5) and 'the tourist gaze' (Urry, 2002). We might legitimately wonder what all the fuss is about. After all, seeing is hardly new; we do it all the time! But the trouble with seeing is precisely that it feels so natural and so ordinary. The point is that these scholars are suggesting that *how* we see what we see is not natural. Our senses have been trained in particular ways by the societies that we live in. In other words, seeing is not a neutral or matter-of-fact or natural activity. Rather, it is a learned activity and tourism is a particular social practice that teaches us to see in a particular way. This is one way to understand the tourist gaze: it is a particular, historically specific way of seeing or envisioning the world.

Photography and, increasingly, video are regarded by many scholars as integral to the tourist gaze and to the tourist experience in general. Accordingly, we can conceive the tourist gaze as a collection or ensemble of visual practices and techniques for apprehending the world around us (Figure 4.2). However, tourism is not just about training people to see places and objects in particular ways such that they become 'good' tourists. It is also about preparing places and objects to be seen by tourists such that they become 'good' tourist sites and spectacles. A useful definition of tourism might therefore run something like this: tourism is 'the preparation of people to see other places as objects of tourism, and the preparation of those people and places to be seen' (Franklin and Crang, 2001, p. 10). According to this definition, tourism is a way of seeing or perceiving people, places and objects. In addition, people, places and objects are themselves changed in order to make them attractive to the tourist gaze.

One implication of this definition is that tourism changes us and the world around us. With regard to this latter point, consider the following: 'we should begin to view modern tourism [...] *as an ordering*, a way of making the world different, a way of ordering the objects of the world in a new way' (Franklin, 2004, pp. 278–9; original emphasis). Tourism is shaping the world in which we live, the way things, people

Figure 4.2 Audience wearing 3-D glasses during the opening night screening of *Bwana Devil*, Paramount Theater, Hollywood, 1952. Photographed by J.R. Eyerman/Time Life Pictures/Getty Images. Photo: © Time & Life Pictures/ Getty Images

and places are seen, and the ways they are presented to us to be seen. This is what is meant by 'ordering'. We are, then, being asked to think very carefully about the world we see as tourists. What kind of a world is it? What happens when even entire villages become objects of the tourist gaze? And what happens to us when we become tourists, when we point our cameras at this or that and take a picture?

Earlier, I posed the question of whether it is possible to distinguish between different kinds of tourism. We have already noted that the tourist gaze refers to a specific way of seeing the world and for preparing certain objects in the world to be seen. But there is not just one tourist gaze; rather, there are different tourist gazes that correspond in a general way with particular types of tourist activity. For example, we can describe a 'romantic gaze', 'in which the emphasis is on solitude, privacy and a personal, semi-spiritual relationship with the object of the gaze', and a 'collective gaze' that 'necessitates the presence of large numbers of other people [...] Other people give atmosphere or a sense of carnival to a place' (Urry, 2002, p. 43). Whereas the former might be associated with the nature-lover on a country walk or hike, gazing at a beautiful sunrise or mountain peak or waterfall, the latter might refer to mass excursions to what used to be called 'holiday camps', or the seaside, or a trip to Ibiza or New Orleans. Thus we can acknowledge that there are different kinds of tourism (and therefore different kinds of tourist) and these can be linked to different kinds of sight and seeing.

Activity

Take a few minutes to think about tourism and travel. What would you say is distinctive about 'tourism'? What sets it apart from 'travel'? Jot down some of your ideas.

Discussion

Addressing this question helps us to build up our understanding of what tourism is. Travel implies movement from one location to another. I 'travel' to work every day – and it is very unlikely that I shall ever confuse travelling to work with going on holiday. There is a critical element to the latter that simply is not present when I am travelling to and from work, and that is the element of leisure.

Slowly but surely we have been getting to grips with tourism. It can be compared with pilgrimage; but, despite the Grand Tours of the eighteenth century experienced by a tiny minority, tourism is something new in human history that emerged in the mid nineteenth century alongside fundamental changes to the political, economic and technological infrastructures across the globe. It involves our senses, particularly our sense of sight (the tourist gaze), and actually enables us to see the material world in new ways, even changing that world to make it attractive and transforming it into an object for seeing. There are different kinds of tourism and, correspondingly, different kinds of tourist gaze. Finally, tourism is an activity or social practice distinct from mere travel because it involves leisure.

4.3 Tourism and religion

Given that we are studying religion and tourism, the crucial areas for us to focus on will be 'the interfaces between tourism and religion(s) – i.e. the ways and places where these two "systems" meet and interact' (Stausberg, 2011, p. 31). If we follow this eminently sensible advice we shall, first, recognise that religion impacts on tourism. Examples of this are the increasing numbers of travel firms and agencies organising trips and excursions for religious individuals and groups to visit religious sites and places, and the increasing numbers of religious organisations developing sites for religious tourists to visit. Second, however, we shall also see that tourism impacts on religion too, turning it into a 'spectacle', or a sight, or a performance to be photographed or filmed. We shall see that tourism is an activity that actively re-contextualises religious objects, in the process assigning those objects new meanings. Let me reiterate this key point: tourism draws in objects and assigns them new meanings. In what follows we shall examine some examples of:

- religious tourism
- the transformation of religious objects by tourism.

Religious tourism

When we talk about religious tourism, we mean religiously motivated journeys or outings to visit particular religiously significant places. However, while the motives for travel may be religious, the activities – among other things visiting sites, taking photographs and purchasing souvenirs – are recognisably 'touristic' behaviours. With this in mind, we are now going to watch a short piece of film about contemporary Buddhist pilgrimage to Bodh Gaya in Bihar, northern India.

Activity

You should now watch the film 'Religious tourism', which you can find on the module website. This film was originally made for Open University students taking a course introducing them to various aspects of religious life in the modern world. It formed part of an introduction to Buddhism and concerns pilgrimage to Bodh Gaya. (Bodh Gaya is the place where the Buddha, the founder of Buddhism, is said to have attained enlightenment while meditating under a tree.)

You should allow about 15 minutes for this activity.

In the film, the voice-over and interview questions impose a religious narrative on what you will be watching, but if you observe carefully you may spot behaviour that is more recognisably touristic. In other words, even when religious motivations propel individuals and groups to visit religious sites, those individuals and groups will often behave in such a way that religious behaviour seems hard to separate from touristic behaviour. Furthermore, you may find it difficult to say what it is that is specifically 'religious' about Bodh Gaya.

Watch the film a couple of times and note down what you see. Then answer the following questions:

- How many people did you see in the film carrying or using a camera or a video recorder?
- How many different types of souvenir were on sale?
- Could you visually differentiate the pilgrims from the tourists?
- On balance, did Bodh Gaya look like a religious site or a tourist site?

Discussion

Like me, you probably could not tell, just by looking, who were the pilgrims and who were the tourists. In addition, Bodh Gaya seemed to be both a religious site and a tourist site at the same time. Bodh Gaya is clearly a site of religious significance but it also has historical, architectural, aesthetic, artistic and heritage significance that draws visitors interested in these other meanings and values (it is worth noting that the Mahabodhi Temple Complex at Bodh Gaya is listed by UNESCO – the United Nations Educational, Scientific and Cultural Organization – as a 'world heritage site'). Finally, although the interviews establish that many visitors travel to Bodh Gaya because of their religious convictions, the behaviour that pilgrims engage in while they are there appears to overlap with the kinds of behaviour we might expect from tourists – the taking of photographs and the purchasing of souvenirs.

We are now going to start to think more concretely about what happens to religious objects when they become drawn into the tourist gaze. To do this, we shall be looking at examples from the south of France and the island of Flores in Indonesia. We focus first on the shrine of St Sara, the patron saint of the **Romani**, and the different contexts in which the shrine is today being given meaning and significance. We shall see in the course of our discussion that the icon of St Sara has, over time, taken on meanings that seem to exceed its religious significance to the Romani.

The shrine of St Sara

Figure 4.3 Saint Sara, Saintes-Maries-de-la-Mer, France. Photographed by Phil Wahlbrink. Photo: © Phil Wahlbrink/WahlbrinkPHOTO/Alamy

Every year in May, from the 18th to the 25th, thousands of Romani gather at Les-Saintes-Maries-de-la-Mer, a small village located in the region of the Camargue in southern France. They come for the festival of their patron saint, St Sara, represented by a dark-skinned statue housed in the crypt of the local church (see Figure 4.3). On 24 May a procession takes place and the statue is carried out of the church to the sea and back again. The theatre historian Eric Wiley (2005) describes the procession for us in evocative terms:

> The procession forms on the village's acropolis in front of the [...] 10th-century church [...] From there it moves on narrow,

spectator-lined streets down to the waterfront and to a stretch of beach where about 15 thousand people have gathered, standing on a pair of rock jetties that border the beach on each side, on several boats at sea, and on the strand itself. From these vantage points they watch the boisterous procession cross over the sand and enter the shallows of the Mediterranean Sea. Leading the way is a 16-member, mounted cadre of local men called *les gardians*, who wear the traditional black hats of the region's bull breeders and carry old-fashioned, trident-tipped bull prods. The procession is comprised of perhaps two dozen Romanies, several of whom carry the statue of Sara on a platform above their shoulders, while others play music and sing or carry brilliant, flower-covered crosses and banners; a thick Bible; or iconographic objects of Romani culture, such as a miniature model of a caravan and horse. They shout 'Vive Sainte Sara!' as they process, and Romanies in the crowd shout it back. A number of clergymen also participate, walking in full-length, white vestments, and pronouncing 'Vive Sainte Sara!' into handheld, electric bullhorns. In the seawater, one of the clergymen performs a symbolic cleansing of Sara's statue while journalists and tourists swarm around him. Following this brief service, *les gardians* escort the procession back through the multitude on the beach and then to the doors of the church.

(2005, pp. 135–6)

Activity

You should allow about 15 minutes for this activity.

You should now watch the film 'Touristification', which you can find on the module website (the title will become clearer as you read on). This film is an extract from a documentary, *We Have No War Songs*, produced for Dutch television in 1996. It shows the procession of St Sara from the church in Les-Saintes-Maries-de-la-Mer to the sea. The voice-over and interviews are in English and French (with subtitles). The film will give you a flavour of the procession itself, but be sure to listen carefully to the voice-over and the interviews. Write down any points you think are significant, and consider these questions:

• What do the people interviewed in the film have to say about the Romani and the pilgrimage to Les-Saintes-Maries-de-la-Mer?

• Do you think what you have seen is a religious pilgrimage or a cultural spectacle?

You may decide that you need to watch the film more than once.

Discussion

There is no straightforward answer to these questions. Certainly, there is a vital religious dimension to the pilgrimage, but that religious dimension is interwoven with cultural elements such as the presence of the famous horse riders of the Camargue, music, and cultural and historical issues surrounding the Romani – including a history of discrimination as well as the Romani assertion of a distinct cultural identity in which St Sara is embedded (recall the claim, by one Romani interviewed in the film, that St Sara herself was Romani). In other words, it seems impossible to plausibly or unequivocally describe this as a religious pilgrimage motivated by religious sentiments and values, or as a cultural spectacle implicated in the values of tourism.

Religious pilgrimage or cultural spectacle?

Romani pilgrimage to Les-Saintes-Maries-de-la-Mer was apparently well established by 1855, but the procession of St Sara was established much later (in 1935) by the Marquis Folco de Baroncelli as part of his more general efforts to promote local culture. The efforts of Baroncelli put the Camargue and the Romani at Les Saintes-Maries-de-la-Mer on the tourist map. St Sara is a major symbol of Romani religiosity and many Romani attend the festival for religious reasons. Romani pilgrims claim that St Sara protects them against illness and misfortune and helps them in their times of need. During the festivities, they touch and embrace the statue. In addition, water is lifted from the well in the church, which is said to have healing properties, while candles purchased during the pilgrimage are kept and then lit at times of need, or are given as gifts to those who, for one reason or another, could not attend the pilgrimage. In short, St Sara is involved in a complex web of relationships between and among Romani pilgrims and the otherwise dispersed Romani populations that come together for the pilgrimage.

But many others come to Les-Saintes-Maries-de-la-Mer as tourists seeking an encounter with 'authentic' Romani culture and tradition; to experience the natural beauty of the Camargue landscape with its world-famous wetlands and flamingos, and the Camarguais culture of horses and bulls; or to sample the architectural and artistic history of the region, such as the spectacular Roman ruins in the nearby town of Arles, or indeed the association of Arles with artists such as Vincent Van Gogh, as well as other examples of regional Provençal culture. And the local tourist offices promote the pilgrimage not as a religious event but as a cultural spectacle, arranging for Romani to wear traditional clothing and to pose for photographs during the week-long festivities. The Romani who carry the icon from the church to the sea dress 'in costume', presenting journalists and tourists alike with numerous photo opportunities. In short, the religious procession has become a tourist spectacle – a chance for the village and the region to sell itself and profit from the thousands of tourists who visit every year.

However, there is another, more recent aspect to the pilgrimage that the anthropologist Ellen Badone (2008) wants to draw our attention to. This is the fact that tourists are now going to Les-Saintes-Maries-de-la-Mer because of claims made about St Sara by Dan Brown in his novel *The Da Vinci Code*, which was published in 2003. Official Roman Catholic narratives about St Sara's identity are inconclusive. Some Romani scholars, by contrast, have suggested that St Sara is evidence of the Indian origins of the Romani and that she is, in fact, the Hindu goddess Durga or Kali, the consort of Shiva. But *Da Vinci Code* tourists come because in Brown's novel a new theory as to St Sara's identity is postulated, namely that she is the daughter of Mary Magdalene:

> [Since 2003] Les-Saintes-Maries-de-la-Mer has attracted literary tourists who want to visit the sites associated with the book [*The Da Vinci Code*]. The novel is structured around the theme of the continuity of the bloodline of Jesus, a fact apparently concealed for centuries by the Catholic Church to maintain its political and social power. Brown combines fiction with legend and historical evidence, suggesting in the novel that, after the Crucifixion, Mary Magdalene, who was pregnant with Christ's child, fled Palestine for Gaul [France], where she gave birth to a girl named Sarah. Given that some versions of the legend of the shrine's foundation at Les-Saintes-Maries-de-la-Mer recount that Mary Magdalene was among the persecuted Christians who accompanied the two Saint Maries on their voyage across the Mediterranean, and given the lack of certainty about St Sara's identity, it is not surprising that some readers of *The Da Vinci code* believe that the statue of St Sara in the church is a representation of the daughter of Christ and Mary Magdalene.
>
> (Badone, 2008, p. 36)

Let us now try to analyse what is going on at Les-Saintes-Maries-de-la-Mer around the statue of St Sara. It is obvious that this religious object has what we can recognise as religious significance, particularly for the Romani. This is the first context within which our statue is embedded. However, beyond the religious importance of St Sara there is also the fact that this religious object has been transformed into a cultural object that, according to Romani scholars, indicates the origins of the Romani people in India. St Sara is a symbol not only of Romani religiosity but also of Romani culture, identity and self-understanding. In addition, the local tourist offices appropriate St Sara in order to successfully market the Romani pilgrimage as a cultural spectacle. In other words, St Sara moves not only within religious but also within tourist contexts. She symbolises not merely a spiritual or sacred presence for the Romani but also the vitality and authenticity of Romani and wider regional culture. Moreover, the presence of *Da Vinci Code* tourists at the festival adds further layers of meaning to St Sara, meanings associated with 'new age' and feminist interpretations of Christianity. These latter interpretations emphasise experience of the sacred over official church doctrine or belief, and furthermore the importance of a feminine principle to the Christian conception of God.

If you now take a moment to recall Durkheim's definition of religion and his claim that '*sacred things*' are '*things set apart*', you can see that tourism has drawn St Sara into a context that is not obviously or purely religious but is, rather, concerned with 'selling' her as a marker of Romani culture and, more recently, as a marker of a new age and a feminist perspective on Christian theology. St Sara is now no longer 'set apart' but has become drawn into the tourist gaze. In the process she has taken on new meanings, values and significances that exceed her religious valuation by Romani pilgrims. These complex layers of meaning indicate that 'the shrine is a busy intersection […] or […] a screen on which multiple, overlapping groups of stakeholders project their own pictures of spiritual and social reality' (Badone, 2008, p. 42).

Badone's likening of St Sara to an 'intersection' is evocative. The word suggests movement, travel and connection. If St Sara is an intersection, then we can imagine her as a meeting place where different meanings meet or collide. In the meeting or collision of Romani religious devotion to St Sara, the packaging of Romani culture as a spectacle to be seen by tourists and the arrival of tourists inspired by *The Da Vinci Code*, we can say that tourism has transformed a local religious shrine. However, we need to be careful how we understand this process. Does it reduce the religiousness of St Sara? Has she been changed from an authentic marker of Romani religiosity or, for that matter, of Romani culture, into a commodity that is (metaphorically) sold to tourists?

Before we move on to our next example, remember that here tourism is not simply a question of the arrival of tourists – outsiders – in Les-Saintes-Maries-de-la-Mer, whose presence transforms the meaning, value and significance of St Sara. We need to acknowledge that St Sara is actually being prepared for display to tourists by the Romani themselves. Scholars call this process 'touristification'. According to this point of view, 'far from being an external force striking a local society from without, tourism – or, rather, what I am inclined to call the *touristification* of a society – proceeds from within' (Picard, 1997, p. 183; original emphasis).

The megaliths of Flores

Our final stop on our brief survey of tourism and religion is in southeast Asia; specifically, the island of Flores in Indonesia. Indonesia is the most populous Muslim country in the world, a former colony of the Dutch and, today, an immensely popular tourist destination.

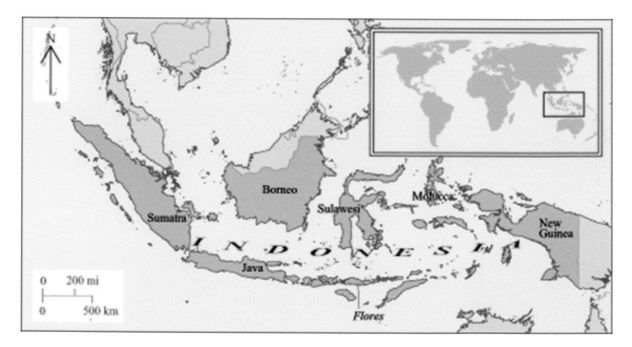

Figure 4.4 Map of Indonesia, showing the island of Flores

A significant legacy of the Dutch colonial period is that the villagers in the part of Flores we are interested in converted to Catholicism in the 1920s. In our trip to the south of France, we focused on how tourism changed the meaning of the icon of St Sara. In our trip to Flores in Indonesia, we are going to follow the same steps in our analysis to examine the clash of meanings between the Indonesian tourist board, tourists and locals. But before we begin, take a look at the map of Indonesia (Figure 4.4). As you can see, it is a large country made up of numerous islands. Flores is a small island towards the eastern end of the archipelago. The sheer number of islands presented the Dutch colonists and later independent administrations with problems of development and governance. On the island of Flores, which is quite remote and relatively impoverished in terms of natural resources, the Indonesian government has promoted tourism not only as a way of stimulating the local economy but also as a way of promoting nationalism and as a means of integrating cultural minorities more effectively into the state.

Now imagine you are a tourist looking at some of the standing stones shown in Figure 4.5. Imagine that you have come to see them on the advice of the tourist guidebook you are carrying with you. You have perhaps already seen standing stones in different parts of the British Isles or in continental Europe, you may associate them with 'Stone Age'

Figure 4.5 Megaliths, Bena, Flores, Indonesia, 2008. Photographed by M@rcel. Photo: © M@rcel/Alamy

culture, and you may assume that they possibly had a ritual or religious function that is now long forgotten. How you see the Indonesian standing stones is framed in advance by previous images, sights and/or experiences of apparently similar stones elsewhere in the world, and the associations they have in your mind with religion and a long-dead past. Your encounter with the Indonesian standing stones is also framed in advance by their presentation in the tourist literature you have with you, and by the Indonesian government's tourist board, which has taken steps to 'develop' the villages where these stones are located into tourist destinations. Your encounter with the Indonesian standing stones has been framed – or, to use the kind of language we find in the scholarly literature, 'mediated' – by a whole collection of images and ideas.

Activity

You should allow about 10 minutes for this activity.

This activity is in two parts. To begin with, look at the photograph of the standing stones in Figure 4.5 and write down some of your thoughts and impressions.

Then follow the link, which you can find on the Study Planner of the module website, to an Indonesian tourism website. You will be directed to some alluring pictures of a 'traditional' village (Bena), including images of some standing stones or megaliths, and a short piece of text which states (when I visited the website in September 2014):

> Bena Village is located in the Ngada district in the center of the island of Flores. If you have a chance you should certainly try to visit this secluded idyllic village.
>
> The architecture of Bena is very traditional and it still has many ancient rites and customs that are remnants of the megalithic era.
>
> (Lavalon Bar & Hostel, n.d.)

Note down the words and phrases in this passage that you think are most likely to entice tourists to Bena village. State why you think these words and phrases are important.

Discussion

At first glance, I was reminded of standing stones I have seen at Avebury in the UK and at Carnac in France. However, although it may be tempting to assume that standing stones in Europe and standing stones in southeast Asia may have something in common, if I really want to understand the megaliths in Flores in Indonesia then I shall need to adopt an anthropological perspective, which would mean visiting the villages where they are located and talking to the villagers to try to ascertain how local people understand them, use them, interact with them, and so on. It is important to remember that our initial thoughts and impressions might be very much at odds with the thoughts and impressions of the Indonesian villagers themselves. Tourists and locals may have very different ideas about the significance, meaning or importance of a particular place or object.

Let us now look at the words and phrases that are being used by the Indonesian tourism website: 'secluded idyllic village', 'traditional', 'ancient rites and customs', 'remnants of the megalithic era'. What kinds of images and feelings do these words and phrases suggest to you? Perhaps you are more of a beach person, in which case Bena village might not attract your interest. Fair enough. But if your interest is indeed piqued by the idea of an encounter with a village full of abundant references to ancient culture and religion, then Bena is for you. But are these representations of the megaliths accurate? What impact does the tourist gaze have on a village like Bena? Is it the villagers who decide what is or what is not 'traditional', or does the Indonesian government's tourist board decide?

Tourist boards, tourists and locals

According to the tourist geographer Stroma Cole, there is a significant difference in the way the megaliths are understood by villagers and by the Indonesian tourist board and by the tourists who come to visit. For the Indonesian government, traditional culture was typically viewed as an obstacle to economic development. However, that view has given way to the realisation that such culture can become a tourist spectacle that can generate significant revenues, and therefore aspects of so-called traditional culture have been selected by the government for 'preservation'. We can see, if we refer back to our quote from the tourism website, that the megaliths are deliberately associated with an ancient past and tourists may well conclude that the megaliths of Flores *are* rather like the standing stones that can be seen in places like Avebury or Carnac – markers of an ancient past. But, as Cole points out, in Flores the megaliths are potent symbols of the villagers' ancestors and of the relationship between the living and the dead, and they have retained this meaning for the villagers despite their conversion to Catholicism. The villagers still engage in ritual practices that periodically renew the relationship between themselves and their ancestors. According to Cole, this creates confusion for the tourists:

> Tourists are faced with cultural confusion: the megaliths in the hamlets are found alongside Catholic graves with cement headstones and wooden crosses. To the casual observer megaliths are part of a culture that was a relic of the villagers' past; if the villagers are now Catholics then the megaliths belong to past beliefs. [...]
>
> Tourists sometimes use local children to find the site and these children frequently climb and play on the stones. Tourists often equate this with children showing a disregard for the megaliths and therefore conclude that these relics have no contemporary importance for the villagers.

(2003, pp. 147–8)

So Cole is suggesting that the megaliths are not relics at all, even though this is broadly how they are marketed by the Indonesian tourist board. Moreover, the fact that children play on and around them points not to the irrelevance of the megaliths for the villagers, but rather to the fact that in this culture the boundaries between sacred and profane are quite different from those that western tourists may expect. In fact, the megaliths are markers of the ancestors and of the importance of maintaining bonds of memory and reciprocity between the living and the dead through ritual exchange. For Cole, the different and even contradictory layers of meaning, value and significance that have attached to the megaliths have potentially negative consequences:

> The transformation of contemporary symbols into heritage, worthy of preservation, may have the function of attracting tourists and bringing revenue into the area. However, it also has a number of other consequences. Assigning megaliths to the past by bestowing heritage status on them is another indirect yet potentially powerful way of severing the villager–ancestor relationship. Furthermore, the new symbolic meaning of the stones is of a 'primitive and unchanged society'. This meaning may be controversial, the villagers may wish to contest 'primitive' and 'unchanged' labels after 30 years of 'being developed'. Furthermore, tourists view the

megaliths as historic relics rather than contemporary symbols of the villager–ancestor relationship. Tourists inadvertently have a state sponsored view of the megaliths and their significance: a tourist attraction that relates to the villagers' past. Over time, the newly appropriated meaning of the megaliths, as a relic of the past, may eclipse their contemporary cultural significance.

(2003, p. 148)

Cole's concerns are important. The emphasis she places on the local or indigenous understanding of the megaliths – a point of view that is not represented in the tourist literature – is important. But what about the role of the villagers, albeit under the direction of the state, in the preparation of themselves, their village and their megaliths to be seen by tourists? Does touristification – the involvement of the villagers themselves in the display of the megaliths – create possibilities for the villagers to have at least some autonomy in the presentation of their religion to the wider world?

Across our three examples from Bodh Gaya in India, Les Saintes-Maries-de-la-Mer in France and Flores in Indonesia, we have been examining what happens to religious objects when they fall under the tourist gaze. In the activities we have been developing our observational, listening and analytical skills – which, incidentally, are vital anthropological skills – to see if we can distinguish pilgrims from tourists and tourist sites from religious sites, to try to make sense of a religious pilgrimage that is also promoted as a spectacle of culture and identity, and to try to make sense of the different perspectives of different groups (tourists, locals, government) and how those perspectives constitute or frame objects in different ways. This means that when studying objects such as the shrine of St Sara or the megaliths of Flores, we have been studying not the objects themselves but the ways in which they stand in for other things – for Romani culture and identity, and for primitive culture and relations between the living and the dead. It is the symbolic power of objects to stand in for experiences, feelings and ideas that makes them so interesting and so rich for study.

4.4 Tourism, authenticity and commodification

One question that we have asked but as yet not addressed is the extent to which tourism reduces the religiousness or sacrality of religious objects. Two important concepts in the study of tourism are authenticity and **commodification**. The first thing we need to understand is that these two words are not neutral; in fact, they imply certain values that we may hold, whether consciously or unconsciously, about tourism. In particular, authenticity and commodification suggest that there is something 'shallow' about tourists and tourism and that the things and places that tourists visit are not the 'real thing'. The idea is that tourism packages something – to use our own examples, a pilgrimage shrine or standing stones in a village – into commodities that are then sold to tourists. This process of commodification transforms the shrine and the megaliths into spectacles devoid of their original or genuine or authentic meaning. Cole registers this dimension of the scholarly literature on tourism as follows: 'tourism turns culture into a commodity, packaged and sold to tourists, resulting in a loss of authenticity' (2007, p. 945). Anthropologist Erik Cohen describes the trajectory of the literature on tourism in the same terms:

> Much of the literature on the nature of modern tourism and its impact upon host societies relies on several important assumptions. […]
>
> First, tourism is said to lead to 'commoditization' […] In particular, 'colorful' local costumes and customs, rituals and feasts, and folk and ethnic arts become touristic services or commodities, as they come to be performed or produced for touristic consumption […] The critical issue is that commoditization allegedly changes the meaning of cultural products and of human relations, making them eventually meaningless.
>
> (1988, pp. 371–2)

When Guy Debord – whom we encountered earlier in this chapter – was writing about 'the society of the spectacle', he was describing exactly this kind of process, except that for Debord commodification and loss of authenticity were processes that were not limited to tourism but, rather, had come to condition the entirety of modern life. As we think about this, we might pause to reflect on what we do as tourists; typically, we look, we take photographs and we purchase souvenirs to remember by (in French, *souvenir* means 'to remember'). But are our photographs and souvenirs neutral carriers of our memories of this or that holiday? Perhaps they – like the places we have been and the sites we have seen – are primarily commodities that condition how we encounter the world around us. According to critics of tourism, 'commoditization, engendered by tourism […] destroys not only the meaning of cultural products for the locals but, paradoxically, also for the tourists' (Cohen, 1988, p. 373), because commoditisation 'is a process by which things (and activities) come to be evaluated primarily in terms of their exchange value' (Cohen, 1988, p. 380). Accordingly, tourism is a social practice for which the only significant values are monetary values. If we follow the logic of this critique of tourism, we see that behind it lies a particular definition of authenticity as a 'quality of pre-modern life, and of cultural products produced prior to the penetration of modern […] influences' (Cohen, 1988, p. 375). In this view, on our journeys to Bodh Gaya, Les-Saintes-Maries-de-la-Mer and Flores we encountered not the 'real' or authentic world but the world as a commodity produced *for* the tourist gaze – in other words, a world manufactured for the gaze of tourists. To go a step further, we could argue that the religious objects we encountered are no longer religious objects at all. Rather, their sacrality and religiousness have been replaced by their value as commodities that attract tourists on a quest for the authentic – a quality which, paradoxically, has been destroyed by the very processes that attract the tourists to see them in the first place.

I confess to finding this argument compelling. But it is not the whole story.

Activity

Looking back over the account of commodification given here, would you agree that tourism devalues religion? If you disagree, can you come up with an argument to support your view? What would you say are the main issues in arguing for or against this proposition?

You should allow about 10 minutes for this activity.

Discussion

If you agree that tourism devalues religion, you are probably seeing tourism as something that happens to communities from the outside. Tourists turn up somewhere, and that somewhere slowly but surely disappears under a slew of roads, hotels, bars, museums, cultural performances and what have you, until it ends up looking just like everywhere else. If you disagree, you might have argued, like the anthropologist Michel Picard, that 'far from being an external force striking a local society from without, tourism – or, rather, what I am inclined to call the *touristification* of a society – proceeds from within' (1997, p. 183; original emphasis). In other words – and this is a point that is also stressed by Cohen (1988) and Cole (2007) – tourism may actually provide locals with a degree of autonomy and agency in how their megaliths (for example) are seen and experienced by outsiders. As such, tourism may not destroy the meaning of religious objects. Instead it may create 'afterlives' for them, and new trajectories through which they can be encountered and interpreted. Rather than simply becoming symbols of commodification, they may also become symbols of revitalisation and of the renewal of religious traditions that might otherwise have lacked the resources necessary to maintain them.

Let me add one further point: it is not the case that we need to decide once and for all that tourism is either (a) destructive or (b) empowering, but rather that we need to recognise the ambivalence of tourism and the competing meanings and pressures it brings into play. To return to Badone and a quote cited earlier in this chapter, we can say that tourism is 'a busy intersection [...] a screen on which multiple, overlapping groups of stakeholders project their own pictures of [...] reality' (Badone, 2008, p. 42).

Conclusion

In this chapter we began by thinking about religion and tourism. We started with the notion of context and the idea that contexts can change or shift. We considered Durkheim's sociological definition of religion and of sacred objects as things 'set apart'. Then we looked at tourism: first, at its similarities with pilgrimage and as a replacement for religion in modern societies; second, as a social practice that is a key marker of the modern world; and, finally, at the tourist gaze. The point was made that tourism involves a certain way of seeing objects and a certain way of preparing objects to be seen. Through reference to textual and visual resources we considered case studies from Bodh Gaya in India, Les-Saintes-Maries-de-la-Mer in France and Flores in Indonesia. We asked whether it is possible to distinguish tourists from pilgrims, a religious pilgrimage from a regional, cultural festival, and the perspectives of locals, tourists and a government tourist board. Finally, we asked whether tourism simply transforms religious objects such as statues and megaliths into commodities, thereby destroying their authentic, original or real religious meaning, or whether tourism might empower locals to revitalise local religions. However, this chapter has not merely encouraged us to think, as it were, 'at a distance' about tourism, as if it were something separate from or outside us. Rather, we have consistently asked ourselves what it is to be a tourist, given the significance that the tourist gaze has not only for how we as tourists see the material world, but also for how that world is presented to us as tourists to be seen. It is important that we reflect on how we see what we as tourists see, and on how objects are prepared in advance to be seen by us in a certain way.

Further reading

The resources below provide further ethnographic materials on complexes of tourism, religion and culture in Indonesia, Cuba, Spain and Ethiopia. The Appadurai volume of collected essays (1986) provides a more general introduction to the study of material culture. Students should consult Appadurai's introductory essay and conduct further reading in line with their own personal interests.

Allerton, C. (2003) 'Authentic housing, authentic culture? Transforming a village into a "tourist site" in Manggaral, eastern Indonesia', *Indonesia and the Malay World*, vol. 31, no. 89, pp. 119–28.

Appadurai, A. (ed.) (1986) *The Social Life of Things: Commodities in Cultural Perspective*, Cambridge, Cambridge University Press.

Argyriadis, K. (2008) 'Speculators and santuristas: the development of Afro-Cuban cultural tourism and the accusation of religious commercialism', *Tourist Studies*, vol. 8, no. 2, pp. 249–65.

Crain, M.M. (1997) 'The remaking of an Andalusian pilgrimage tradition: debates regarding visual (re)presentation and the meanings of "locality" in a global era' in Gupta, A. and Ferguson, J. (eds) *Culture, Power, Place: Explorations in Critical Anthropology*, Durham, NC and London, Duke University Press, pp. 291–311.

Turton, D. (2004) 'Lip-plates and "the people who take photographs": uneasy encounters between Mursi and tourists in southern Ethiopia', *Anthropology Today*, vol. 20, no. 3, pp. 3–8.

Chapter 5

Exhibiting absence: museums and memorials of the Shoah

Tim Benton

Contents

Aims

This chapter will:

- explore how and why objects are selected and presented by museum professionals to represent people's experience and ideas
- show how to interpret objects, and the way they are presented, in museums and memorials, using photographs and video
- investigate how architectural space and form, in the absence of objects, can be used to stimulate emotions and memories among visitors
- interrogate the way museums and memorials employ objects and architectural space to meet the demands of visitors' interests and the political agendas of funding authorities
- help you to reflect on some of the ways in which personal and collective memories of the murder of European Jews are managed in museums and memorials to the 'Holocaust' or 'Shoah'
- develop your understanding of context through reflection on the importance of history to the study of material culture.

Materials you will need

In this chapter, you will need to watch the following films, which can be found on the module website:

- Memorial of the Shoah, Paris
- The Jewish Museum, Berlin.

You will also be directed to the website to view a video clip of people visiting Micha Ullman's Bibliothek monument in Berlin.

Introduction

The contemporary museum developed out of early modern cabinets of curiosity and private collections, and found their present form in attempts to order archaeological and ethnographic artefacts in the late nineteenth and early twentieth centuries. (You will recall that some of the origins of collecting and display were explored in 'Getting started: key concepts' at the beginning of the module.) These precursors of the contemporary museum were interested in displaying objects which referred to people, cultures and historical events that were temporally, geographically or culturally distant. In this sense, many museums are 'archaeological': they display fragments of lost civilisations in such a way that we can not only wonder at the skills of craftsmanship involved or the strange and beautiful forms of the objects produced, but also, through juxtaposition with other objects and with the help of explanatory information, attempt to reconstruct something of the human experience in these cultures. Attempts to commemorate the murder of around 6 million Jews by the Nazis (the National Socialists in Germany) within living memory present this generic issue in a particularly poignant form. Whole communities of Jewish people, their possessions, places of worship and culture, were wiped out. How can museums represent this tragedy? What objects can be found or created to represent this loss? The large number of **Holocaust** museums which have sprung up around the world in recent years offer a wide range of strategies for representing this absence, of people, things and culture. These strategies are influenced by the immediate context of time and place where the displays are located. Sometimes, either because the emotions triggered by objects are too strong or because it is considered best to allow the visitor's imagination to fill the gaps, other means are deployed, without objects, to stimulate emotions. In this chapter we shall see that many museums and memorials dispense with objects in their attempt to convey the horror of the **Shoah**.

Shoah

The term Shoah (from the Hebrew for 'catastrophe') is preferred by many Europeans to the term Holocaust (from the Greek 'consumed by fire'), which has connotations of sacrifice about it. The Yiddish word *khurban*, meaning destruction, is used to denote both the Holocaust and the destruction of the temple in Jerusalem (by the Babylonians in the sixth century BCE, and by the Romans in 70 CE) and the **diaspora** (the forced exile of the Jews from the land of Israel over the centuries). In this chapter I use the words 'Holocaust' and 'Shoah' as appropriate for different countries. It should be noted that Jews were not the only targets of Nazi violence. Trade unionists, homosexuals, **Roma**, **Sinti** and people with mental or physical disabilities were treated in equally appalling ways. This chapter, however, concentrates on the different strategies that have been developed by curators, artists and architects to memorialise Jewish victims of the Nazis.

Objects in museums can be said to have many different kinds of value. Their value can be measured in various ways: according to their 'authenticity' (proof that the object is really what it is claimed to be); their rarity or uniqueness; their 'beauty in themselves' (we shall need to qualify this); their 'explanatory value' (what they tell us about the past); and their 'contextual value' (how they fit into a museum display). Whether artefacts can be said to be 'beautiful in themselves' is doubtful. Our taste, the predisposition to like some things more than others, is culturally acquired, although many commentators have claimed that certain proportions, colours, textures and shapes have a similar effect on everyone. In general, we learn to distinguish what is considered 'good' or 'beautiful' from what is held to be 'bad' or 'ugly', although we can make an effort to separate ourselves from this cultural predisposition. Within a culture, however, many people will tend to like the same kinds of things, and museums play a crucial role in reinforcing this tendency by presenting selected objects for our admiration.

Museums

Museum curators have to struggle to satisfy three main purposes: (1) the responsibility to conserve and preserve objects in their care; (2) the political aims of those who fund the museum (often, in the end, government); and (3) the need to attract the public to attend in large numbers. These aims often conflict.

Among the aims of government which influence museum policy are the reinforcement of social cohesion, the celebration of national history and myths, and the desire to increase tourism. Curators have their own professional values, based on their training as archaeologists or art historians, for example, that tend to privilege criteria based on personal aesthetic judgement and the perceived rarity value of objects. But some of the most prized objects in a collection (from a curator's point of view) may fail to attract a wide public, or may throw embarrassing light on a country's 'national record'. Under pressure from the visiting public, curators sometimes set aside their interest in 'authenticity' and rarity in order to 'tell a story', using objects and displays which have been created anew, like a film set. And in almost every museum display there is a mixture of 'authentic' objects and storytelling display techniques.

Museums play an important role in confirming the confidence of people who believe that they are 'cultivated' and that this culture gives them 'distinction', which can be almost as important as wealth or class in terms of defining the social elite. Most museum curators see it as part of their job to educate all visitors into this culture and enable them to share this sense of distinction.

Like other forms of heritage, museum objects may also have 'relic value'; that is, they may be appreciated or venerated for their association with a set of beliefs. Without these beliefs, most relics would tell us very little – they may be nothing much to look at. Many archaeological remains are also like this: it may be possible to prove their great antiquity and importance as witness to great moments in history, but they may be incomprehensible to the viewer without being accompanied by considerable explanation. It has also been suggested that a respect for the special value of art may constitute a belief system, and that without this 'aura' most people would find it difficult to take pleasure in art. Curators try to provide such celebratory support for artworks in the way they are displayed and explained. By contrast, some objects may have no authentic value at all – they may be modern reconstructions or reproductions – but have great value in terms of explaining things. Models, diagrams, reconstructions and re-enactments are of this kind.

Another factor which is extremely important in considering the way in which objects can be used to communicate ideas is context. An object in one location might be incomprehensible or strike a false note, whereas in another location it might take on quite new meanings. The way in which objects are shown together is also very important.

Figure 5.1 Gyula Pauer and Can Togay, 'Shoes on the Danube promenade', Budapest, 2005. Photographed by Travel Ink. Photo: Getty Images

In 2005 the sculptor Gyula Pauer and film director Can Togay created 60 pairs of shoes in bronze and placed them on the banks of the River Danube, 300 metres from the Hungarian parliament building in Budapest (see Figure 5.1). This memorial commemorates the shooting of people from the Jewish ghetto in Budapest in the last year of the Second World War, following the invasion of Hungary by Germany in March 1944. The people were lined up on the banks of the Danube and shot by members of the Arrow Cross Hungarian fascist militia, their bodies falling into the river. Around 10,000 people are thought to have perished in this terror. Figure 5.2 represents some of the shoes confiscated from murdered prisoners (mostly Jewish) at the Majdanek concentration camp as part of the Nazi policy of genocide.

Figure 5.2 Shoes confiscated from Jewish prisoners at the Majdanek concentration camp in 1942–45, on display at the United States Holocaust Memorial Museum, Washington, DC. Used with the permission of the State Museum at Majdanek. Photo: USHMM, Washington

The photograph is exhibited in the United States Holocaust Memorial Museum in Washington, DC. Figure 5.3 illustrates shoes collected to send to German troops on the Russian front during the terrible winter of 1941.

Activity

Look carefully at the three images of shoes in Figures 5.1–5.3. Jot down your thoughts about the stories these images tell. For each image, make some notes about its authenticity, context and emotional impact.

Discussion

These images tell their stories very differently. The bronze shoes on the banks of the Danube (Figure 5.1) are constructed: they have no 'authenticity' as such. But the context of the 'Shoes on the Danube

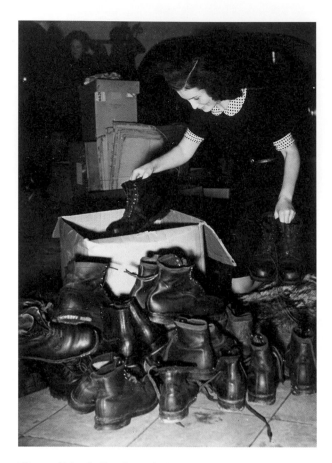

Figure 5.3 Collection of shoes donated by Berlin citizens for soldiers on the Russian front, December 1941. Topography of Terror Exhibition, Berlin. Photo: Bavarian State Library, Munich

promenade' monument is all-important. Hungarian people are well acquainted with the history of the Arrow Cross atrocities and the monument is sited on the spot where this particular atrocity occurred. The monument is highly emotive; the shoes look as if they have just been worn, and we can intuit a range of identities associated with them, of gender and of social and professional categories.

By contrast, the shoes in Figure 5.2 have become shrivelled with age and give a disturbing impression of decay. We are told that these are authentic – real shoes confiscated from prisoners before they were murdered. The context is important. This photograph in another location would be less powerful, but here, displayed in a large colour print in a museum dedicated to the murder of 6 million European Jews, it carries a powerful punch. These are discarded shoes – one might be tempted to say dead shoes – and it is impossible to ignore the allusion here to the mass of people rejected and discarded by Nazi ideology.

Figure 5.3 is a documentary photograph with little particularly to say about either the donors or the future recipients of the shoes, except that each pair of shoes has a lived-in identity. You feel that if these were your shoes, you could identify them. The photograph, of course, represents a single moment in time and is true (authentic) to that moment. As presented here, the context is neutral. If you had seen the photograph in a propaganda context, glorifying the heroism of German troops, it would have affected you differently. As it is, the photograph makes little emotional impact.

Largely protected in western society from the sight of dead bodies, most people today tend to turn away from images of the dead, unable to accept the transformation of living people into corpses. So the suggestion that the display in the Holocaust Museum in Washington might incorporate some of the human hair shorn from Jewish prisoners on their arrival at the concentration camps, and used for industrial purposes by the Germans, was rejected by the exhibition committee. Although ethnographic museums have often included body parts in their displays – a practice that is increasingly challenged by ethnic groups – it is rightly considered unacceptable to show embalmed corpses of victims of genocide, and by extension any parts of their bodies. The shoes illustrated in Figures 5.1–5.3 therefore perform an important role in providing a stimulus for reflection without breaking codes of conduct. (The challenge presented to museums by certain ethnic groups, with regard to body parts or artefacts with spiritual importance, is discussed in Chapter 6.)

5.1 Objects and memory

Building a display

Museums use different kinds of object in order to reinforce each other. The case of an important 'relic' of the Warsaw Ghetto uprising and its brutal suppression (described below) demonstrates how value can be given to an authentic object of great significance.

The rusted milk-churn (illustrated in Figure 5.4) buried by Emanuel Ringelblum (1900–1944) in the Warsaw Ghetto during the uprising in 1943, containing some of the diaries, documents, posters and papers documenting life there, is described in the official book of the Washington Holocaust Memorial Museum as 'perhaps the Museum's most important historic artefact' (Weinberg and Elieli, 1995, p. 109). Part of its importance lies in the scale of the tragedy of the Warsaw Ghetto. Before the Second World War, the city of Warsaw had been home to 375,000 Jews: roughly 30 per cent of its population. Soon after the Nazi occupation of Poland in 1940, the Germans began to force Jewish people from the countryside and in the towns to live in ghettos in the big cities. The Warsaw Ghetto swelled in numbers and was sealed off from the rest of the city, leading to the death by starvation of around 10 per cent of its inhabitants. A rebellion against the increasing maltreatment of the Jews, which included mass deportations to the Treblinka extermination camp in July–September 1942, was launched in January 1943. After fierce fighting, resistance was crushed in April 1943 by the systematic firing of the ghetto. Almost all the buildings there were then razed to the ground and the area turned into a concentration camp for the survivors, who were almost all subsequently deported to Treblinka and murdered.

Ringelblum, a university professor and historian, put together a team of people to document life in the ghetto. When its destruction became inevitable, Ringelblum buried the archive in several milk-churns and metal boxes. Two of these were subsequently discovered, in 1946 and on 1 December 1950 (the latter is the one in the Holocaust Memorial Museum in Washington). In the Holocaust Museum, the milk-churn is displayed in front of a fibreglass facsimile of a section of wall from the Warsaw Ghetto which survived.

Figure 5.4 Milk-churn used for storing the Ringelblum Archive in the Warsaw Ghetto, 1943. United States Holocaust Memorial Museum, Washington, DC. Permission granted by the Emanuel Ringelblum Jewish Historical Institute, Warsaw. Photo: USHMM, Washington

Activity

Look at Figures 5.4 and 5.5. How does the display of Ringelblum's milk-churn in the museum create meaning and emotional impact?

Figure 5.5   Presentation at the United States Holocaust Memorial Museum, Washington, DC, showing photographs of the Lódź and Warsaw Ghetto murals (to left and right) and, at the end, the Ringelblum milk-churn in front of the facsimile wall of the Warsaw Ghetto. Photographed by Edward Owen. Photo: USHMM, Washington

Discussion

The churn is presented with traces of the sand and earth adhering to it after several years buried underground. This creates a certain wonder, similar to that produced by very old archaeological remains. It is also displayed on its own, like a work of art or a religious relic. The object itself does not explain its meaning. This meaning is supplied by the museum presentation – captions, audio guide, catalogue information – which makes its unique value comprehensible. But the museum display also provides meaning, with the facsimile segment of wall creating an urban context. Moving wider (Figure 5.5), the churn and the reproduction of the ghetto wall are, in turn, framed by two huge photographs. The one on the right is of the ghetto in Lódź, showing one of the bridges which, as in the case of the Warsaw Ghetto, allowed Jews to pass from one section of the sealed-in ghetto to another. The effect of the display is to produce a strong impression of 'being there', as a witness of the forced separation of a people. Furthermore, the threatening sense of being

Figure 5.6 Reproduction cast of the gate to the main camp at Auschwitz, United States Holocaust Memorial Museum, Washington, DC. This shows the sign 'Arbeit Macht Frei' ('Work Makes One Free'). Photographed by Edward Owen. Photo: USHMM, Washington

channelled into a narrow corridor has a visceral effect, creating a physical sense of anxiety. Context and display may work directly on the emotions to support the message conveyed more rationally by the objects.

The founding director of the Holocaust Museum, Jeshajahu Weinberg, explains the importance of 'authentic' objects in the museum thus: 'Authentic three-dimensional artifacts provide the strongest historical evidence, stronger even than documentary photographs. They constitute a direct link to the events, which are embedded in them, as it were. Having been there, they have become silent witnesses' (quoted in Weinberg and Elieli, 1995, p. 67).

In other cases, reconstructions, such as that of the gate to the main camp at Auschwitz (Figure 5.6), have little 'authentic' value, but make up for this as chilling stage props which put the visitor into the shoes of the victims of the Holocaust.

Commemorative objects

The most obvious kind of object commemorating an absent person is the tomb. Whether the departed person is represented by a photograph or in a textual inscription, the reverential display of a slab, perhaps a religious symbol, and some kind of marker is enough to evoke the missing person. But tombs require human nourishment. Without the attentions of relatives and friends to keep the site clean and replenish flowers, tombs lapse quickly into sad neglect. The same goes for all kinds of memorial, which require regular ceremonies and the participation of people for whom the object of the memorial remains important, if they are to retain meaning. This seems to be true of memories themselves. All lived experience seems to leave some traces in the brain, but these need to be assembled into 'stories' if they are to be remembered (Winter and Sivan, 1999, pp. 12–16). Furthermore, even these structured memories will fade unless rehearsed, typically with the help of others. Those times of the year when families pull out the photo albums, or tell stories about shared memories, are important in the maintenance of memories. The sociologist Maurice Halbwachs, in an important but contested book, argues that all memories – including 'personal memories' – are social, because without the opportunities for exchange and rehearsal they will quickly fade away (Halbwachs, 1980).

Activity

You might like to take a few minutes to think about this. In your experience, is it true that memories are social? Can you summon up a memory that you have never shared with anyone? Have you ever discovered that a memory turns out to be untrue, or to depend on what someone told you?

Discussion

One of the reasons that memories are often unreliable (when tested against the 'facts') is that we often construct memories around what we think should have happened as much as what we think we heard and saw. This is personal, and each of us manages our memories in different ways. I do believe that I have many memories which are truly 'personal' and have not been shared with anyone else. Reflecting on this, however, these are all memories which I rehearse from time to time, either because they made a particular impact on me or because they deal with situations which recur. Memories are often attached to objects. A well-known technique for memorising large quantities of text is to break it down and attach short segments to objects or places in our imagination. When museum curators use objects associated with historical information, a similar process is triggered. Once you know the stories associated with the shoes by the Danube or the Ringelblum churn, a sight of the objects alone will bring the information back to mind.

It has been persuasively argued that processes of forgetting are very necessary if people are to 'move on' after painful experiences (Forty and Kuchler, 1999). For most of us this happens naturally, and memories of the departed transmute from the cemetery to the photo album, from reflection on loss to celebration of happier times. In the case of collective memory, however, there are tensions which make this process of forgetting difficult. This is particularly true of acts of war and genocide. Relatives of the victims of genocide can never forget, and questions of guilt and blame, not to mention issues of compensation and criminal proceedings, remain long after most of the perpetrators have passed away. It has taken a long time for the explicit and widespread memorialisation of the Shoah to develop, but in the last 20 years or so there has been an increase in the number of monuments and museums dedicated to documenting and explaining the genocide of the Nazi period. For example, in 2010, in central Berlin alone, there were 312 memorials to the period of the Nazi dictatorship, ranging from simple plaques to full-scale museums.

Collective memory

We need to consider the term 'social' or 'collective' memory. Can a group of people share a memory? In a literal sense, probably not. But it has long been recognised that, just as personal memories may in many cases be determined by social interaction, communities may share collective myths or stories, of which each individual may have some direct experience but which go beyond the personal memories of any one person. Memories of war and other catastrophes are usually like that. In the west it is often claimed that anyone aged 60 or over would be able to tell you where they were when they heard of US President Kennedy's assassination in 1963, but the memory of that event is largely composed of information and images gleaned from the media or recounted by friends. Objects, museum displays, photographs, films, novels and memorials, with their associated ceremonies, can all play a role in preserving and rehearsing collective memory.

It has been argued, for example by the French historian Pierre Nora, that the oral traditions in rural communities used to keep social memory alive, but that the effect of mass migration to cities has left a vacuum (Nora and Kritzman, 1996). Nora founded a project to encourage historians to write about 'places of memory' as a kind of substitute for the social memory of traditional communities. It does seem that the enormous increase in memorials, heritage sites and museums since the 1960s fills a need for collective memory which also serves to maintain identity. This is linked with the rise of the modern nation-state which, especially after the Treaty of Versailles (1919) following the First World War, has associated national boundaries as far as possible with ethnic and linguistic groupings. Most people have a strong sense of national identity, although it may be hard to pin down what this depends on. Many people feel a sense of belonging to more than one nation, because of migration, circumstances of birth or religious allegiances. Wars and sporting events serve to place the sense of national identity under stress, which is compounded in the face of racist ideologies and their definitions of ethnicity.

The individual and the mass

The absence of living people is often referred to by using representations, photographic or otherwise. A particular problem is created when very large numbers of people are concerned. As the American Professor of Religion and Culture Eduard Linenthal explains, commenting on the design of the Holocaust Museum in Washington, DC:

> Museum planners worried that the millions of individual deaths that made up the Holocaust would be lost in a story of mass death and a fascination with the technique of destruction. The design team was determined to personalize the Holocaust, since it wanted visitors to eschew forever the role of bystander. This, they believed, could best be accomplished through a painful link with the faces of Holocaust victims.

> (1994, p. 410)

The Tower of Faces display (Figure 5.7) in one of the three-storey towers in the Holocaust Museum in Washington includes around 1000 photographs from the Yaffa Eliach Shtetl Collection, taken between

Figure 5.7 The Tower of Faces (the Yaffa Eliach Shtetl Collection) in the Permanent Exhibition at the United States Holocaust Memorial Museum, Washington, DC. Photographed by Edward Owen. Photo: © USHMM, Washington

1890 and 1941. The history behind it is as follows. The well-established Jewish community in Ejszyszki, Lithuania, was wiped out by an SS death squad on 25–26 September 1941. Of 4000 Jews living in the town, only 29 were left alive. One of the survivors of this horror, Dr Yaffa Eliach (b.1937), became one of the trustees of the Holocaust Memorial Council and began collecting thousands of photographs of Jews who had lived in Ejszyszki between 1900 and 1944. The Tower of Faces, comprising images from his collection, combines individual identity with large numbers, in a vertical space which creates a feeling of awe and unease. These images are presented with all the scratches and dust marks transmitted through the processes of copying and enlarging personal photographs. Similar displays, commemorating murdered children at the Yad Vashem centre in Jerusalem (designed by the architect Moshe Safdie (b.1938)) and in the Mémorial de la Shoah in Paris, achieve a comparable effect in different architectural contexts. Displays of this kind cause us to pause and reflect on the importance of juxtaposition. Clearly, the display as a whole has a quite different meaning from that of the multiplication of individual representations.

5.2 The Shoah

Having considered various ways in which museums use objects, we must now turn to the particular case of the Shoah, or Holocaust. For here we are talking about a kind of absence which is almost impossible to comprehend fully. There are many towns and villages in central Europe that had thriving Jewish communities in 1930 and were virtually wiped out between 1933 and 1945. Of the 520,000 Jews living in Germany in 1933, roughly half had left or been interned by 1939 and all but 10 per cent of these were murdered in the systematic extermination programme – the 'final solution' – which was put into effect throughout the German-occupied territories after 1942. Persecution of Jews continued in the Soviet bloc after 1945; survivors of Nazi persecution in occupied Poland and Ukraine found themselves accused of unpatriotic **cosmopolitanism** and harassed into forced assimilation or exile. Hundreds of thousands of Russian Jews emigrated to West Germany, North and South America and Palestine. Of the 115,000 Jews living in Germany in 2010, around 100,000 were immigrants from Russia, as most of the surviving German Jews had emigrated, chiefly to Israel or the United States.

The Yiddish culture of the **shtetls** (small villages with a predominantly Jewish population), towns and urban communities in central Europe, with its music, literature and traditions, has virtually disappeared. Yiddish, a language that evolved in the late medieval period in largely German-speaking communities, was spoken by around 11 million people in central Europe in 1933 (Guillemoles, 2010, p. 15). It has been replaced by Hebrew as the preferred language in Israel and in most Jewish communities in Europe, although it survives in some traditional groups and among certain intellectuals. Thus museums and memorials in European cities wishing to commemorate the tragedy of the Shoah do so in a context in which a recent cultural and human history has been completely restructured.

Visitors to a monument or museum commemorating the Holocaust located anywhere which came under Nazi domination in the war are almost bound to be divided into two groups: those for whom the victims are 'us', and those for whom the victims are 'them'. This is because active or passive acceptance of Nazi race laws (see below) was imposed universally, and it is not easy to reconcile this with postwar democratic attitudes. The aim of most genocide memorials is to try to bridge this gap, by showing how 'we' could easily have become the victims, just as 'we' could easily have become the perpetrators of the crimes.

We need to be careful about definitions of 'Jewishness'. In Judaic law and tradition, Jewish identity is passed down through the female line, although it is also possible to convert to Judaism. After centuries of anti-Semitic legislation (throughout Europe) that enforced the separation and discrimination of people of Jewish descent, liberalising legislation in the nineteenth century in most European countries enabled Jews to join the professions, serve in the army and marry Christians. Prejudice remained, however, and the very success of Jewish men and women in business, the arts and politics created strong undercurrents of hatred which were fuelled by antagonism to the leadership roles held by Jews in some socialist and communist movements. Most European Jews considered themselves patriotic citizens. Around 100,000 German Jews served in the army in the First World War and many were decorated for bravery. Hitler received a medal at the hands of a Jewish officer. But however far some Jews may have felt assimilated into their countries, the racist policies of the National Socialists in Germany and the Fascist parties in many other countries targeted Jews on purely ethnic grounds.

The Nazi Nuremberg race laws of 1935 defined Jews as those who had three or four grandparents of Jewish descent. Those with one or two Jewish grandparents were classified as being of 'mixed blood'. Throughout the area dominated by Germany just before and during the war, the classification and documentation of racial origin were systematically carried out. In a sense, classification, of a different kind, has been perpetuated after the war by cultural organisations such as the Yad Vashem centre in Jerusalem and similar bodies in many other countries concerned to build reliable statistics of Jews murdered or exiled during the Shoah. Most museums have large archives and libraries which are required to authenticate the objects in their collections. Memorials and museums of the Holocaust have a particular attitude to documentation, however, since this is a basic defence against the attacks of sceptics who claim that the facts of the extermination of Jews have been exaggerated. Created in 1953 by a unanimous vote in the Knesset (parliament) in Jerusalem, the Yad Vashem was conceived as the single authoritative centre for the documentation of the mass murder of Jews between 1933 and 1945. Every Jewish victim of the Shoah was given posthumous Israeli citizenship 'as a sign that they have been reunited with their people' (Wieviorka, 2004, p. 31). Definition of Jewishness was thus an essential part of the undertaking, whatever the people concerned may have thought about their identity. The Shoah has made ethnic identity an inescapable part of our perception of the history of the twentieth century.

An attempt was made by the Yad Vashem to prevent other organisations dedicated to documenting and commemorating Jewish victims of the Shoah from collecting donations and publicising their work (Wieviorka, 2004, pp. 31–2). For example, the Centre de documentation juive contemporaine (CDJC) was set up in 1942 by the French rabbi and industrialist Isaac Schneersohn (*c.*1879–1969) in Grenoble, at the time under Italian occupation, and later moved to Paris, where it was eventually incorporated in to the Mémorial de la Shoah museum. Top-level negotiations were required in the 1950s to obtain permission from the Yad Vashem for the CDJC to continue its work.

Mémorial de la Shoah, Paris

The Memorial to the Unknown Jewish Martyr was opened on 30 October 1956 in a street near the Marais, in Paris, where many Jews had traditionally lived and worked. At first the memorial consisted of a walled-in courtyard in which was located a giant bronze urn, bearing the names of the extermination camps where so many French Jews died (Figure 5.8). Underneath this urn is a crypt and the memorial to the unknown Jewish martyr, with a Star of David and a perpetual flame (Figure 5.9). Ashes from murdered Jews from the camps and from the Warsaw Ghetto, mixed with earth from the land of Israel, are interred here. This is a memorial to the whole Shoah, not just to the French deportees. The specifically Jewish environment is accentuated by an inscription in Hebrew which reads: 'Look and see if there is any suffering equal to my suffering. Young and old, our daughters and our sons cut down by the sword.'

Following the inauguration of this tomb, negotiations proceeded to install a library, museum and archive here, to house the CDJC archive founded by Schneersohn. As we have seen, one of the obstacles at first was the wish of the Yad Vashem in Jerusalem to concentrate offerings from the Jewish faithful on its own, definitive archive of Jewish suffering.

The Memorial of the Shoah Museum finally opened in January 2005. It is a private foundation, funded in part by Jewish organisations in France. The museum includes a permanent display, exhibitions, a library

Figure 5.8 Mémorial de la Shoah, Paris, outside view. Used with the permission of the Mémorial de la Shoah, Paris. Photo: © Tim Benton

Figure 5.9 Memorial to the Unknown Jewish Martyr. Mémorial de la Shoah, Paris. Used with the permission of the Mémorial de la Shoah, Paris. Photo: © Tim Benton

Figure 5.10 Engraved names of Jews deported from France to German-run concentration camps. Mémorial de la Shoah, Paris. Used with the permission of the Mémorial de la Shoah, Paris. Photo: © Tim Benton

and an archive for all visitors, but it identifies itself clearly as a Jewish foundation. The Star of David is not only inscribed on the façade in stone, but woven into the structure of the window grilles.

Just as many war memorials include long lists of the names of fallen soldiers, the Memorial of the Shoah Museum includes a space where the names of 76,000 Jews deported from France to German-run concentration camps are recorded (Figure 5.10). These names are continually checked and updated, based on research in the museum's archive, which is cross-referenced to the Yad Vashem database in Jerusalem. Some of the names inscribed on the stone walls have been erased and others added, as this process of verification continues. Some of the boxes of card indexes compiled by the French authorities under the **Vichy regime** (the French government of 1940–44 which collaborated with the Nazis) are displayed in the museum (Figure 5.11). The recording of names, whether carved in stone or preserved in books or index cards, is one of the fundamental prompts for collective memory. As in the case of collected photographs, a list of victims of military action or genocide allows for both a representation of the scale of the tragedy and the opportunity for relatives or friends to find 'their' name. It is common in these sites to see people touching a name, or leaving flowers or a note nearby.

Figure 5.11 Room displaying part of the card indexes of Jewish people collected by the Vichy regime. Mémorial de la Shoah, Paris. Used with the permission of the Mémorial de la Shoah, Paris. Photo: © Tim Benton

In the museum, detailed information and photographic records demonstrate the role of the many hundred French internment camps and the *rafles* (round-ups) – when French police snatched Jews from their homes in the middle of the night and sent them, eventually, to their deaths in Auschwitz after internment at the housing estate of Drancy, a suburb of Paris (see Figure 5.12). In 1995 the then French president, Jacques Chirac, apologised to the Jewish people for the complicity of French policemen and civil servants in these events.

A long list of names of *les Justes* (the Just) is inscribed on the outside wall of the compound of the Mémorial de la Shoah. These are people recognised by the Yad Vashem in Jerusalem as having helped Jews during the Vichy period, putting their own lives at risk in doing so.

Figure 5.12 Drancy internment camp during the Second World War.
Photographed by Pool Bassignac/Turpin/Contributor. Photo: © Gamma-Rapho
via Getty Images

All this makes the memorial a place designed for the Jewish people. But
for non-Jewish visitors, the permanent collection gives a painstaking and
meticulous description of what happened under German occupation
and Vichy rule in France during the war.

Activity

You should now watch the film 'Memorial of the Shoah, Paris', which you
can find on the module website. As you watch, make notes on how the
museum serves the purpose of commemoration. How is evidence used in
the displays?

You should allow about
20 minutes for this
activity.

Discussion

The first point is that the memorial presents itself clearly as a Jewish
private institution. Its primary function is for Jewish people to mourn and
reflect on the fate of the 76,000 men, women and children deported from
France and killed during the German occupation. The wall of names and
the design of the crypt reinforce this message. The long list of names of
the 'Just' – people who put their lives at risk by helping Jews in France –
is recorded on a wall outside the enclosure of the museum. A second
function of commemoration, however, is to explain to the visitor what
happened in these terrible years. The role of French *gendarmes* and

Figure 5.13 Hut 6 from the Beaune-la-Rolande internment camp. Mémorial de la Shoah, Paris. Used with the permission of the Mémorial de la Shoah, Paris. Photo: © Tim Benton

officials in carrying out Nazi policy is stressed, providing uncomfortable viewing for French visitors. There are some shocking objects, such as the door of hut 6 from the Beaune-la-Rolande internment camp (see Figure 5.13) and the machine used by the camp guards to grind down the bones of victims in the last moments before the arrival of Allied troops. Focus on individuals brings the story home. As its third function, the museum includes an important archival resource, allowing anyone who is interested to search for information about victims of the Shoah, and this archival function is represented in the display, with an exhibition of samples of the index cards compiled by the authorities under the Vichy regime.

Evidence is in the main used 'objectively', to record events, legislation and statistics. Much of the display uses traditional methods – photographs,

Figure 5.14 Mémorial de la Shoah, Paris: offerings left by relatives at the wall of remembrance. Used with the permission of the Mémorial de la Shoah, Paris. Photo: © Tim Benton

film and documents – to tell the story. Mini-histories of individuals, supported by objects such as a spoon or a garment, reach out for a more personal response. An assemblage of portraits of 2500 children combines the poignancy of individual existence with something of the scale of the tragedy.

Where a list of names of murdered Jews is displayed, the traditional form of recognition and remembrance is to leave a small stone or lamp in front of it (see Figure 5.14). This tradition derives from the Book of Genesis in the Bible, where the first monument was a *Sa'adutha*, or witness-pile of stones. This motif has been used at many of the memorial sites of concentration camps. The Treblinka Memorial in Poland, for example, designed by Adam Haupt, Franciszek Duszenko and Franciszek Stryniewicz and built in 1959–64, employs around 17,000 roughly shaped stones leading to a massive granite structure, consisting of two blocks of granite masonry framing a narrow crack and capped by a sculpted cross-piece (see Figure 5.15).

Figure 5.15 Adam Haupt, Franciszek Duszenko and Franciszek Stryniewicz, Holocaust memorial, Treblinka, Poland, built between 1959 and 1964. Photographed by Justin Leighton. Photo: © Justin Leighton/Alamy

Treblinka I was a forced labour concentration camp, while Treblinka II was one of the deadliest of the purpose-built extermination camps. Around 300,000 people from the Warsaw Ghetto were gassed there between June and October 1942. In all, a total of perhaps 900,000 people (including 1000 Sinti and Roma) were detained in Treblinka I and II, most of whom died. After the revolt in the summer of 1943, when some Jews managed to escape, Treblinka II was dismantled and the remaining Jews there shot. The site was ploughed over, leaving almost no trace of it. The strategy of trying to hide every sign of industrial genocide meant that many concentration camps had been destroyed before the Allied armies arrived in 1945. The Treblinka Memorial, therefore, represents absence at two levels: that of the murdered people and that of the site itself.

A similar motif of commemorative stones was used in the Mauthausen concentration camp memorial in Austria, where a carpet of rough stones represents the Jewish victims. In this case the stones have a double significance, since Mauthausen was a forced labour camp near a granite quarry and many of the prisoners there died from exhaustion and malnutrition while being made to carry the heavy stones from the quarry. Mauthausen was just one of a number of camps in Austria providing slave labour. Many of the prisoners at Mauthausen were intellectuals and political opponents from countries such as Greece, Yugoslavia and Italy which were overrun by the Germans in the later stages of the war. Only a proportion of the detainees were Jews. But towards the end of the war the number of Jewish prisoners there mounted rapidly, as the concentration camp at Auschwitz-Birkenau was emptied prior to the arrival of Russian troops. Twenty-eight monuments and plaques commemorate the different communities represented among the victims at Mauthausen.

Genocide

Genocide is a crime which has been defined in various ways. Not all cases of the systematic murder of civilians are accepted as belonging to the category of genocide. For example, an American historian, Rudolph Joseph Rummel, has estimated at 262 million the civilian ('innocent') victims in the twentieth century, coining the term 'democide' to describe the deliberate killing of civilians in times of war and peace. Although Rummel's figures have been contested and are hard to verify, being largely based on comparing statistics before and after wars or other disasters, his books are a reminder of the scale of destruction of human life in the twentieth century. Genocide, or ethnic cleansing (the deliberate killing of civilians on the basis of ethnicity), is a subset of democide. In this context, the killing of over 1 million ethnic Armenians in Anatolia by the Ottoman regime in 1915, the deaths of 5 million Ukrainians in a famine created by the seizure of crops and seed in 1932–33 by the Soviet government, and the attempt to liquidate all ethnic

Jews, Roma and Sinti in Europe between 1941 and 1945 have a particular status, being clearly identifiable as attempts to kill or remove all people of a particular ethnic origin from a territory. Denial of the intentional killing of ethnic groups is still widespread; at the time of writing (2014), the Turkish government has not accepted that the atrocities of 1915 were part of a deliberate policy. But, of course, relatives of the millions of other civilians who suffered in the Second World War, subject to bombing, starvation, forced migration and disease, may feel that their memories need to be addressed as well. This explains part of the significant expansion of memorials and monuments in recent years.

5.3 Memorialising absence

The Shoah created unique issues for the memorialisation of loss which could not be managed solely by conventional museographic means. A recent spate of Holocaust memorial foundations all over the world attests to the need to come to terms with what happened, in a context in which many of the issues of racism have not been fully resolved. In this context, 'authentic' objects have often been seen as problematic, and more abstract means of communication have been sought.

The Jewish Museum in Berlin

The Jewish Museum in Berlin was planned as an extension to the Berlin Museum. A Jewish Museum had been opened in 1933, but was closed by the National Socialist government in 1938. After a long process of lobbying by the Association for a Jewish Museum, an eighteenth-century building – formerly a courthouse – was allocated to the project and an international competition launched in 1988 to find an architect to enlarge it. The winner of this competition, Daniel Libeskind (b.1946), had a reputation as an intellectual and teacher, but had built very little before this. The fragility of the political consensus over the project was exposed in 1991 when the Berlin Senate voted to scrap the museum. Following international pressure, the project was reinstated and the shell of the building was opened to the public in 1999, when over 350,000 people visited the extraordinary zigzag concrete labyrinth, with its echoing spaces, jagged slashes of windows and open voids. Three floors of museographic display were then installed and the museum opened in September 2001.

Activity

You should now watch the film 'The Jewish Museum, Berlin', which you can find on the module website. How did Daniel Libeskind use architectural means to convey a message about the Holocaust? Compare this with what you have seen of the Holocaust Museum in Washington, DC and the Mémorial de la Shoah in Paris.

You should allow about 20 minutes for this activity.

Discussion

Both Libeskind in Berlin and James Ingo Freed (1930–2005; then senior partner of I.M. Pei Associates), the architect of the Holocaust Museum in Washington, aimed to create a sense of disturbance in the visitor,

Figure 5.16   View of the staircase and the 'You are My Witnesses' wall in the Hall of Witness, United States Holocaust Memorial Museum, Washington, DC. Photographed by Carl Cox Photography. Photo: USHMM, Washington

suggesting something of the feeling of being cut off from normal society and losing a sense of identity. Freed achieved this by the use of intimidating scale in the Hall of Witness (Figure 5.16) and by the use of brutal materials in the elevators. The towers, evoking the guard towers of concentration camps, also inject anxiety-making vertical spaces in between the main gallery spaces. Martin Smith, the first Exhibition Department director of the Holocaust Museum, was a film director and conceived his task as that of 'telling a story'. The display developed from 'documentary' to increasingly visceral techniques, in which the visitor shares the experience of victims: entering a ghetto (Figure 5.5), and passing through a Polish cattle truck and under the gateway of Auschwitz (Figure 5.6). We also saw how a selected number of 'authentic' objects (we have already discussed Ringelblum's milk-churn; see Figure 5.4) were mixed with reconstructions.

At the Jewish Museum in Berlin, Libeskind adopted a highly violent attitude to the relationship of his building and its context. Even from the outside, the building presents a tortured image. The brutal concrete form of the tower of the Holocaust and the inclined piers of the garden of exile, coupled with the jagged lines of the windows, create a strong

Figure 5.17 Daniel Libeskind, extension to the Jewish Museum, Berlin; designed 1988, completed 2001. This image shows (left) the tower of reconciliation and (right) the garden of exile. Used with the permission of the Jewish Museum, Berlin. Photo: © Tim Benton

sense of disturbance (Figure 5.17). In the interior, the basement forms an introduction to the museum, using architectural means to destabilise visitors and lead them to the experiences of exile or extermination (Figure 5.18). The floor slopes, the walls lean inwards and stark choices are presented to the visitors: to follow an 'axis of continuity', an 'axis of exile', or an 'axis of Holocaust'. The latter leads to a grim, enclosed and dark tower with a thin opening at the top which lets in a little light, the cold air and noises from the outside world. The axis of exile leads to a 'garden' where the vegetation is out of reach, on the top of a cluster of leaning piers, on a sharply inclined surface. Nothing in this world seems safe. A few, highly selective, authentic objects are displayed along the 'axes' of continuity, exile and Holocaust. The tragic story of individuals is told by single objects – a violin, a parcel, a letter. The four-storey staircase also re-creates symbolically the toil of forced labour. In the

Figure 5.18 Daniel Libeskind, basement of the extension to the Jewish Museum, Berlin; designed 1988, completed 2001. This image shows (left) the axis of continuity leading to the stairs to the museum, and (right) the axis of exile leading to the garden of exile; across these runs the axis of the Holocaust. Used with the permission of the Jewish Museum, Berlin. Photo: © Tim Benton

museum proper, on the upper floors, authentic objects are displayed in traditional fashion to document Jewish culture over ten centuries in Berlin. Here the approach is specifically educational.

By contrast, the Memorial of the Shoah in Paris is not constructed to create a disturbing space. The crypt is reverential. In the museum, the effects of shock and dismay are produced by the objects rather than the architectural treatment.

At a conventional war memorial, members of a community can gather to commemorate the dead. But most Jewish communities in Europe were simply wiped out by Nazi persecution. Only in some European cities has a substantial Jewish community survived, but in the others commemoration is shared by absent Jews and present non-Jews. As a consequence, many Holocaust memorials and museums are almost as much about the guilt of the perpetrators as the suffering of the victims. This has made every Holocaust memorial in Germany, France and the other formerly occupied countries intensely controversial. It has even been stated that the real memorial of the Shoah lies in public controversy, in political assemblies, in the legislature, in the media and in the engagement of local communities – which has taken various forms, including graffiti and destruction. In other words, the potential of a new monument to create controversy assures the rehearsing of myriad issues in the media and among communities.

The German 'counter-monuments'

The commemoration of absence has given rise to a number of monuments which have been called **counter-monuments** by the American historian James E. Young (2000; 1993). His argument has been succinctly summarised in a review by the historian Jay Winter:

> Whereas national political leaders, especially but not only in Germany, still seek symbols of healing and closure, artists undermine that enterprise. They offer 'countermonuments,' in which the key space consists not in the design or object but the space between the object and the viewer. Memory then always remains in the eye of the beholder, and the members of each generation must interrogate themselves about what memory is and what they are doing when they gaze at an object or a monument.
>
> (2001, p. 357)

Young was anxious that Holocaust memorials should not allow the German people to safely lock up their collective memories in monuments and ceremonies which would let brief cathartic moments of pity and shame obscure the continuing issue of racial prejudice. In an article recounting his involvement in the debate around and the eventual selection of the architect for the national Holocaust memorial in Berlin, he expresses himself delighted that the first competition to choose an artist to build this monument led to fierce controversy and a stalemate:

> Good, I wrote at the time. Better a thousand years of Holocaust memorial competitions and exhibitions in Germany than any single 'final solution' to Germany's memorial problem. This way, I reasoned, instead of a fixed icon for Holocaust memory in Germany, the debate itself – perpetually unresolved amid

ever-changing conditions – might now be enshrined. Of course, this was also a position that only an academic bystander could afford to take, someone whose primary interest lay in perpetuating the process itself.

(Young, 2002, p. 68)

Young notes that in the 15-strong jury set up to judge the 528 designs in the first competition, regular disagreements broke out between the intellectuals, who seemed to be interested primarily in ideas and the sophistication of the artistic ideas presented, while 'the intellectuals sniffed at the lay-jurors' middle-brow eye for kitsch and monumental figuration [and] their philistine emotionalism' (2002, p. 67). Young believes that the most thought-provoking and rigorous memorials are the 'counter-monuments' which refuse to play the game of emotional release. We can see here a reflection of a long-standing suspicion of representative images – iconoclasm – when referring to sacred subjects. But the debates also reflect the suspicion of abstraction and conceptual art among many people outside the circle of art connoisseurs.

Esther Shalev-Gerz and Jochen Gerz's 'Monument against Fascism' in Harburg, a central district of Hamburg, consisting of a 12-metre-high square section column covered in lead, was inaugurated in 1983. Located in a busy shopping area, the monument invited visitors (in several languages) to inscribe their names as a commitment not to forget the murder of Hamburg's Jews. As the surface within reach became covered with names, the column was lowered into the ground, so that in 1993 only its top remained. With the monument gone, the artists claimed: 'Each time you pass the spot, in the absence of the image, there is a betrayal' (quoted in Grynberg, 2003, p. 166). The monument, which had attracted considerable protest, had been covered by a scrawl of names and graffiti, which the artists considered to be a fair reflection of current attitudes. The artists maintained: 'What we did not want was an enormous pedestal with something on it presuming to tell people what they ought to think' (quoted in Young, 1993, p. 28). (You can find out more about the 'Monument against Fascism' by following the link on the Study Planner of the module website.)

Another counter-monument is in Kassel, where on 9 April 1939 Nazi enthusiasts destroyed a fountain given to the city by Jewish entrepreneur Sigmund Aschrott (1826–1915) in 1908. Following a competition in 1984, the local artist Horst Hoheisel (b.1944) first created a white concrete hollow reproduction of the original fountain and then buried it upside down in the Rathausplatz, or town hall square (see Figures 5.19 and 5.20). This event took place during the Documenta 8 contemporary art festival. All that is visible now is the base of the structure, with a ring of water flowing down into the depths. The sound of the water falling and a partial glazing of the surface allow the visitor to intuit the depth of the monument. From a distance, the new fountain appears as a decorative geometric form inlaid with coloured marble. As with the Harburg monument, this ironic commentary on 'forgetting' could be understood as a fiercely challenging intellectual statement, or as an example of sealing off a disturbing memory under the cloak of artistic privilege. Hoheisel has claimed that the fountain might one day be set the 'right way up', but only when German people have changed their attitude to what happened in the Nazi period.

Figure 5.19 Horst Hoheisel, the Aschrott fountain, 1984, Kassel. Photo: Renate Lehning/Municipal Archives of Kassel, A.-c)-STR+PL Obere Königsstraße V, Aschrottbrunnen, Germany

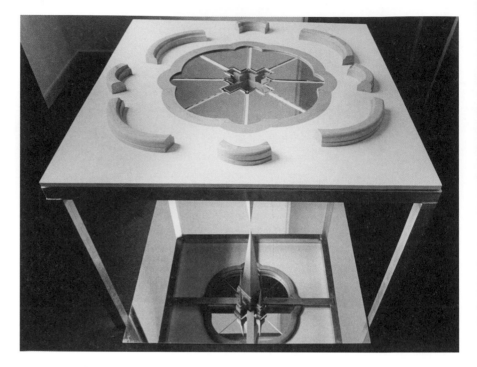

Figure 5.20 Horst Hoheisel, model of the Aschrott fountain, 1984, Kassel. Photo: Renate Lehning/Municipal Archives of Kassel, A.-c)-STR+PL Obere Königsstraße V, Aschrottbrunnen, Germany

Micha Ullman's Bibliothek memorial, Bebelplatz, Berlin

A third well-known monument, this time in Berlin, was intended to commemorate the burning of 20,000 books by fanatical National Socialist students in the Bebelplatz on 10 May 1933, an event that is often seen as a clear portent of the genocidal programme to follow. The books were selected on both ethnic and political lines – works by well-known Jews as well as by non-Jewish socialist or communist authors, who were often linked to Judaism in Nazi propaganda. The winner of the 1993 competition to design the monument was an Israeli artist, Micha Ullman (b.1939). His scheme consisted of burying a room with empty bookshelves in the Bebelplatz, with a bronze plaque embedded in the ground that includes a quote from the poet Heinrich Heine (1797–1856) dating from 1820: 'Where books are burned in the end people will burn.' Although the room is illuminated at night, little can be seen in daylight.

Figure 5.21 Micha Ullman, Bibliothek monument, Berlin, 1993. Photo: © Tim Benton

Figure 5.22 Micha Ullman, Bibliothek monument, Berlin, 1993. Photo: © Tim Benton

You should allow about
10 minutes for this
activity.

Activity

On the module website, you will find a short video clip of people looking at Ullman's Bibliothek monument. Watch this clip now and look carefully at Figures 5.21 and 5.22. How effective do you think the monument is at prompting memories of what happened in 1933?

Discussion

You will have seen from the video clip that the mysterious glass plate incites curiosity, with people trying to see what's underneath. Clearly, many tourists are brought here by guides who explain the meaning of the monument and clarify the context, located as it is in front of one of the faculty buildings of Humboldt University. But most people seem baffled by it, crouching down to peer into the gloom. With the abrasion of the glass, it is almost impossible to see the empty bookshelves except at night, when they are illuminated. Some people just walk on by; others laugh. But many pause to reflect. It seems to me that the very absence of 'content' – the books missing from the bookshelves – works rather well in causing people to pause and consider. What they make of it, of course, is difficult to assess.

The artist believes that memorials work only if they are fully autonomous works of art, unconstrained by a script or story (Ullman, 2006, p. 82). He sees his buried, empty space as something which not only comments on the burning of the books but is also a stimulus to reflection.

The act of peering down into this dimly perceptible space, while seeing oneself reflected in the glass, might prompt thoughts about whether ideas can be destroyed, but also about how one would react to an empty library. A library is where intellectuals keep the physical containers of their ideas. When a scholar dies, their library eventually becomes empty. In this sense, the monument looks forward from the burning of the books to the extermination of Jewish intellectuals in Berlin. It is like a tomb. Ullman also saw the monument as a **camera obscura**, registering those who engaged with it, just as the statues on the nearby faculty buildings had witnessed the events of the past, including the burning of the books in 1933. Ullman was later shocked by the decision of the town council to build a multi-storey car park under the square, which he considered disrespectful to his monument and the values it expressed. Despite a widespread protest, the car park was built. Ullman also hoped that the space, so close to the famous Humboldt University, would become alive with student activities, including the exchange and reading of books. At present the monument is on the tourist trail, and groups of visitors, on foot, bicycles or rickshaws, dutifully stop by and puzzle over it.

One of the reasons that memorials to Jewish memory in Germany and the former German-occupied countries have such a turbulent history is that the issues they embody are by no means resolved. The search for perpetrators of genocidal crimes continues to this day, fuelled by spectacular trials such as that in 1961–62 of Adolf Eichmann (1906–1962), one of the architects of the Holocaust, in Jerusalem. Many of those who held positions of authority in Nazi Germany and the occupied countries found a way of passing through the 'de-Nazification' processes to pick up the reins in industry, administration or government after the war. This helps to explain why the rapid growth of memorials of the Shoah came about only 20 or 30 years after the end of the war, when these men and women had retired.

The German national memorial to the murdered Jews of Europe

Designed by the American architect Peter Eisenman (b.1932), the controversial memorial to the murdered Jews of Europe situated in Berlin makes no explicit reference to the Shoah (see Figures 5.23–5.25). The 20,000-square-metre site, located not far from Hitler's former Chancellery building and bunker, houses 2711 concrete pillars, all of the same size at the base but varying in height. The visitor can enter it from any side and do whatever he or she pleases (within certain restrictions) inside the labyrinth formed by the pillars. Only on descending into the underground information centre is the story of the Shoah dramatised and explained in an extremely selective set of displays highlighting the experience of individuals and small groups in Berlin.

The history of the memorial helps to explain its form. Despite the initiative of two public figures, journalist and political activist Leah Rosh and historian Eberhard Jäckel, no agreement could be arrived at about the need for a national monument to the Shoah in Berlin until the fall of the Berlin Wall in 1989. In the part of the city controlled by communist East Germany, a memorial to victims of fascism had been created in the nineteenth-century guardhouse building, the *neue Wache*, at the east end of the main street of pre-war Berlin, Unter den Linden, with a moving statue built some years earlier by Käthe Kollwitz (1867–1945). This small but elegant building designed by the neoclassical

Figure 5.23 Peter Eisenman, German national memorial to the murdered Jews of Europe, Berlin, 2005. Photo: © Tim Benton

architect Friedrich Schinkel (1781–1841) had been adapted in the 1920s as a memorial to the fallen soldiers of the First World War. In the Nazi period, the *neue Wache* became a hall of fame for heroes, including fascist victims of street fighting during the early years of the National Socialist Party. It was thought that a new memorial focusing more specifically on the suffering caused to the Jewish people by German fascism would be appropriate.

We have already discussed the first international competition for this monument and the tensions between those on the 15-strong jury who wanted to see an intellectually and artistically ambitious project, up to date with international ideas of conceptual and minimalist art, and those who looked for instantly understandable symbols and representational associations. Among the projects submitted was a proposal to blow up the Brandenburg Gate – symbol of Prussian authority – and a project to introduce bus tours visiting all the sites of Nazi tyranny and of the persecution of Jews in Berlin. Others played on the iconography of the Star of David, standing stones and broken hearts (Young, 2002, p. 68). In March 1995 two competitors were awarded first prize, on the understanding that the project of only one of them – Christine Jacob-Marks – would be built. Her project was a 91-metre-square concrete slab, tilted to reach a height of 7.6 metres at one end, on which the

Figure 5.24 Peter Eisenman, German national memorial to the murdered Jews of Europe, Berlin, 2005. Photo: © Tim Benton

names of 4.5 million Jews would be incised. It was to incorporate 18 boulders from Masada in Israel to represent the tradition of memorial stones.

As often happens with competitions, the result was overturned by specialist and public criticism and political obstruction. A period of crisis discussions followed, including a series of widely reported international conferences in which every aspect of the project was questioned, including its very existence, in an atmosphere of increasingly bitter debate. One of the issues was whether the monument should commemorate the suffering only of Jewish people and not that of other persecuted groups – Roma and Sinti, homosexuals, political opponents and murdered civilians in the occupied countries. The explicitly Jewish iconography of many of the entries touched a nerve in this debate. Finally, a new committee of five 'experts' was given the job of selecting a design. The panel consisted of the director of the German Historical Museum in Berlin, the director of the Museum of Contemporary Art in Bonn, an art historian and a respected architectural critic, as well as the American academic James Young, as the only foreigner and Jew.

The new committee worked to define the brief, which they did in the form of probing questions which the artists interviewed had to address:

What are the national reasons for remembrance? Are they redemptory, part of a mourning process, pedagogical, self-aggrandizing, or inspiration against contemporary xenophobia? To what national and social ends will this memorial be built? Just how compensatory a gesture will it be? How anti-redemptory can it be? Will it be a place for Jews to mourn lost Jews, a place for Germans to mourn lost Jews, or a place for Jews to remember what Germans once did to them?

(Young, 2002, p. 73)

After the choice was narrowed down to two designs, the project of the American theoretician and architect Peter Eisenman and the sculptor Richard Serra (b.1939) emerged as the clear favourite. Their design took the theme of the cemetery and adapted it to incorporate 4000 concrete pillars spaced 92 centimetres apart and of varying height, ranging from a few centimetres to 5 metres, a difference accentuated by the undulating ground levels. When they were asked to adapt their design, by cutting the number of pillars to 2800 and reducing the maximum height to 3 metres, Serra refused to continue and abandoned the project. The resulting monument still covers 20,000 square metres.

Figure 5.25 Peter Eisenman, German national memorial to the murdered Jews of Europe, Berlin, 2005. Photo: © Tim Benton

A delicate issue is the status of the columns. Is the comparison with tombstones to be taken literally? If so, it would be a desecration to walk or sit on any of them. In fact they have not been consecrated, but the guardians of the site do try to stop people walking on them or jumping from stone to stone.

Mémorial des martyrs de la déportation de Paris

Another monument which takes an almost completely abstract form is the memorial to the martyrs of deportation from Paris. In 1953 Jean Cassou (1897–1986), the chief curator of the Modern Art Museum in Paris, was asked by the Association of the Deported to put together a committee and select a design to commemorate the deportation of around 160,000 people from France to Germany and the occupied territories, for forced labour or for extermination in the camps. Among these were 76,000 Jews, Roma and Sinti, some of them exiles from Germany or central Europe but most of them French, of whom only 2500 survived. Of the approximately 84,000 people deported on political or other non-racial grounds, roughly half survived. Cassou's committee began with the premise that the monument should be sculptural, and therefore looked for both an architect and a sculptor. They chose the distinguished architect Georges-Henri Pingusson (1894–1978) and the sculptor Raymond Veysset (1913–1967) (Texier, 2007, p. 99). The committee also chose the site, at the point of the Ile de la Cité, on the River Seine, just behind the cathedral of Notre Dame. Cassou had a strong idea about how the monument should fit into this highly prestigious landscape:

> It should not stand out like statues or ordinary monuments but, on the contrary, should fit into a site whose lines present a characteristic harmony. It must not break the horizontal plane formed by the terrace overlooking the river. It should therefore take the form of a slab, inviting the passer-by to reflect, as if in the presence of a tombstone. This slab should also be the roof of a crypt which could be visited and which would provide a more intimate meditation and site of a collective display [...] and I

> repeat that it is a project in which the architectural spirit of
> organisation and construction should dominate over the sculptural.
>
> (Report by Jean Cassou to a meeting of the Assemblée Générale du Réseau
> du Souvenir, 19 December 1953, quoted in Texier, 2007, p. 104)

Despite this, discussions about a possible sculpture dragged on for three years, with ideas varying from an obelisk to a representation of a crucified martyr. Pingusson's opinion was made clear in a letter he wrote on 6 December 1961 to Madame Aylé, secretary to the Réseau du Souvenir: 'The architecture must speak alone – any sculptural treatment would weaken its expressive power and constitute a chatter which would degrade the nobility of the commemoration' (quoted in Texier, 2007, p. 108).

A final attempt to incorporate sculpture involved two figures to appear in the side 'chapels' in the crypt, representing two deportees, one alive and one dead. Pingusson himself believed that these would make the message clearer. But in the end these sculptures, too, were discarded.

Pingusson's plan responded precisely to Cassou's brief. From the little grassy square a low concrete beam proclaims the title of the monument, and two narrow, steep flights of stairs lead down to a triangular courtyard, with a low window overlooking the Seine (Figure 5.26). A wrought-iron sculpture uses the iconography of the triangular badges which the victims of Nazi persecution had to wear: brown for the Roma and Sinti people, pink for homosexuals, the Star of David on a yellow background for the Jews, red for political opponents, and so forth. This triangular imagery is picked up in the crypt as well. The entrance to the crypt is framed by two massive concrete blocks which seem to crush the visitor as they enter the dark interior (Figure 5.27). Here a circular vestibule frames a long corridor lined with golden electric lights, representing the mass of people deported (Figure 5.28). Poetic statements are inscribed in the wall, quotations from well-known poets, one of whom – Robert Desnos (1900–1945) – was among the deported and died in the camps. There are no names of victims and no statistics. On either side are dark, constricted spaces which can be interpreted as chapels or prison cells (Figure 5.29). Barred doors lead to unknown destinations; heavy concrete slabs, perforated with the triangular forms, reveal the names of the main Nazi-run concentration and extermination camps. None of these named camps are in France, although, as we have seen, the Vichy regime ran many concentration camps from many of which people were sent on to Drancy, in the suburbs of Paris, for deportation to Auschwitz.

Figure 5.26 Georges-Henri Pingusson, Mémorial des martyrs de la déportation, Paris, 1962: looking down one of the flights of access stairs. Photo: © Tim Benton

Figure 5.27 Georges-Henri Pingusson, Mémorial des martyrs de la déportation, Paris, 1962: looking towards the entrance steps and showing, in the centre, the entrance to the crypt. Photo: © Tim Benton

Figure 5.28 Georges-Henri Pingusson, Mémorial des martyrs de la déportation, Paris, 1962: looking down the sanctuary of the deported. Photo: © Tim Benton

Figure 5.29 Georges-Henri Pingusson, Mémorial des martyrs de la déportation, Paris, 1962: a side 'chapel'. Photo: © Tim Benton

For many years since the end of the Second World War the French have been in partial denial about their involvement with the genocidal policies of the Nazis. For example, the widely acclaimed film by the avant-garde director Alain Resnais, *Nuit et brouillard* (*Night and Fog*, 1955), was banned from being shown at the Cannes Film Festival. One shot, showing a French soldier in a kepi (military hat) overlooking the transportation at Drancy, was censored (this scene has now been restored in a DVD version of the film). Similarly, unlike the Memorial of the Shoah Museum, no sign of Vichy participation in the genocide is referred to in Pingusson's monument. It was too early, in 1953, to acknowledge French guilt in a public memorial. Attempts at reconciliation between those who still believed that Marshal Pétain (1856–1951), the head of the Vichy regime, had been right to collaborate with the Germans and those who had actively resisted continued well into the 1950s, with amnesties granted in 1947, 1951 and 1953 for those who had been imprisoned for collaboration.

Pingusson's memorial manages to convey its message forcefully with the minimum of words and the power of suggestion. The metaphor of being forced down narrow steps and past massive concrete slabs into an underground space ending in a long corridor which can be clearly read as a funerary space works powerfully. Part of its effectiveness is the ambiguity and polyvalence of the meanings. The lateral spaces can be read as tombs, chapels or prison cells. The funerary shrine can be read as belonging to either the Roman Catholic or the Jewish tradition. Perhaps the biggest problem with the sculptural representations is the problem of identifying the subject: Jew or Christian? Resistance fighter or helpless wife and child? This memorial manages to communicate without being specific; it allows different visitors to make their own readings, based on what they know and feel about the deportations.

Conclusion

Museums and memorials to the tragedy of the Shoah exist within almost irreconcilable tensions: the wish to forget and the determination not to forget; the desire to be explicit and the need in some contexts to be ambiguous; the contradictory impulses to mourn, accuse, justify and learn. The terrible absence of Jewish people, buildings, things and cultures in the former German-occupied territories, and the continuation of anti-Semitic persecution and pogroms in many of the eastern bloc countries after the war, not to mention continuing racial prejudice in most countries, make the need for museums of this kind seem evident. But the pedagogic role usually fails to work effectively unless an emotional understanding has been built first, and it is in this role that museums and memorials face the biggest challenge. The presence of the doubters, both unreasonable fanatics and sceptical historians, provides a pressure for statistical documentation which perpetuates the maintenance of ethnic difference. Given all these pressures, and the saturation of the heritage marketplace, it seems that a mixture of the approaches available is inevitable. Explanation, emotional engagement, quiet reflection and statistical demonstration all have their place.

The importance of museums and memorials where the absence of Jewish people and culture has been represented by architectural or abstract sculptural means, testifies to the tensions involved. In Germany and eastern Europe, a straightforward pedagogic strategy, of explaining and documenting what happened, has not been readily accepted. The counter-monuments in Germany testify at once to the ambiguities of these responses and to the intellectual challenge of exhibiting absence. Hiding, instead of showing, can be a powerful form of communication. But is hiding tantamount to covering over or forgetting? The monuments we have looked at here pose these questions in a disturbing way, and it is only if the questions are debated that the strategy will prove successful in the long term.

References

Forty, A. and Kuchler, S. (1999) *The Art of Forgetting*, Oxford, Berg.

Grynberg, A. (2003) 'Du mémorial au musée, comment tenter de représenter la Shoah?', *Les Cahiers de la Shoah*, vol. 1, no, 7, pp. 111–67.

Guillemoles, A. (2010) *Sur les traces du Yiddishland: un pays sans frontières*, Paris, Les Petits matins.

Halbwachs, M. (1980) *The Collective Memory* (trans. L.A. Coser), New York/London, Harper & Row; originally published in French in 1950.

Linenthal, E.T. (1994) 'The boundaries of memory: the United States Holocaust Memorial Museum', *American Quarterly*, vol. 46, no. 3, pp. 406–33.

Nora, P. and Kritzman, L.D. (1996) *Realms of Memory: Rethinking the French Past*, New York, Columbia University Press.

Texier, S. (2007) *Les Architectes de la mémoire*, Paris, Les Editions du huitième jour.

Ullman, M. (2006) 'Bibliothek – Denkmal zur Bucherverbrennung', in Schlusche, G. (ed.) *Architektur der Erinnerung: NS-Verbrechen in der Europäischen Gedenkkultur*, Berlin, Nicolai, pp. 82–5.

Weinberg, J. and Elich, R. (1995) *The Holocaust Museum in Washington*, New York, Rizzoli.

Wieviorka, A. (2004) 'Du centre de documentation juive contemporaine de la Shoah', in Bensoussan, G. (ed.) *Génocides: lieux (et non-lieux) de mémoire*, Paris, Centre de documentation juive contemporaine, pp. 11–36.

Winter, J. (2001) 'Review of *At Memory's Edge: After-Images of the Holocaust in Contemporary Art and Architecture*', *Art Bulletin*, vol. 8, no. 2, pp. 357–8.

Winter, J.M. and Sivan, E. (1999) *War and Remembrance in the Twentieth Century*, Cambridge, Cambridge University Press.

Young, J.E. (1993) *Holocaust Memorials and Meaning: The Texture of Memory*, New Haven, CT and London, Yale University Press.

Young, J.E. (2000) *At Memory's Edge: After-Images of the Holocaust in Contemporary Art and Architecture*, New Haven, CT and London, Yale University Press.

Young, J.E. (2002) 'Germany's Holocaust memorial problem – and mine', *Public Historian*, vol. 24, no. 4, pp. 65–80.

Further reading

The following works offer an opportunity to explore issues of memory and forgetting in relation to institutions such as museums, and history from a range of perspectives including art history, anthropology and museum scholarship.

Connerton, P. (1989) *How Societies Remember*, Cambridge, Cambridge University Press.

Connerton, P. (2009) *How Modernity Forgets*, Cambridge, Cambridge University Press.

Crane, S.A. (ed.) (2000) *Museums and Memory*, Stanford, CA, Stanford University Press.

Chapter 6
Owning and displaying

Nigel Warburton

Contents

Aims

This chapter will:

- introduce ethical questions about the ownership of objects in museums

- explore the conflicting positions of cosmopolitans and those who believe in cultural patrimony in relation to cultural objects

- introduce ethical questions that arise when bodies and body parts are put on display in museums and galleries, with particular emphasis on questions of consent

- analyse some of the arguments used in debates about owning and displaying objects

- provide practice in reading critically and reasoning to a conclusion.

Materials you will need

In this chapter, you will need to listen to the following audio recordings, which can be found on the module website:

- Cosmopolitanism
- Returning remains
- Reservations about repatriation
- Ishi's brain.

You will also need the following reading, which can be found through the Open University Library website:

- Scheper-Hughes, N. (2001) 'Ishi's brain, Ishi's ashes: anthropology and genocide', *Anthropology Today*, vol. 17, no. 1, pp. 12–18.

Introduction

Most major cities of the world have museums. They typically hold a range of objects collected from around the world and in diverse circumstances. London's British Museum, for example, is a treasure trove of archaeological finds from Egyptian, Roman, Greek, Assyrian, Mexican and many other sites, as well as a hoard of gifts and acquisitions with varying provenance. Some of these are ancient, others more recent; some are valued because of the insights they give into another culture, others primarily for their beauty (though, obviously, these aren't mutually exclusive qualities). Oxford's Pitt Rivers Museum, discussed in Book 1, houses a wide range of artefacts – in this case, mostly acquired by a single collector and displayed in keeping with his particular typological system of classification.

Many objects in museums, though, are hotly contested. In recent years their ownership, location and display have become sources of contention. This may be because they were acquired either through looting, or through dubious 'deals' with people who had little choice but to sell, deals that were tantamount to (or actually) extortion, made by owners whose descendants now want the objects returned; or because other nation-states or peoples believe they have a prior right to objects that are part of their heritage, regardless of whether or not the objects were acquired legally and in freely chosen transactions. These are not merely intellectual debates about rights and responsibilities: for some people their notion of cultural identity is centred on the symbolic importance of the artefacts or human remains of their ancestors being treated with appropriate respect and being displayed in a context that is controlled by those who they see as the rightful owners of such things. Such objects can exert power long after they have been removed from the historical, social and geographical contexts in which they were created – or, in the case of human remains, lived.

The debates around such objects are focused on moral questions about who should own what and why. Even where there is a straightforward answer to the legal question of ownership, though, the moral issues may remain. Just because a museum is the legal owner of a particular piece, it doesn't follow that all issues have been settled. There can still be the important matter of whether the law in question is fair and just.

The second part of this chapter looks at a related and more specific question about the ethics of the display of human bodies and parts of bodies. The BODY WORLDS exhibitions of the German anatomist Gunther von Hagens (b.1945) display 'plastinated' dissected corpses (see Figure 6.1). (**Plastination** is a process, developed by von Hagens, of preserving human bodies, muscles and organs by saturating them with polymer resin.) By 2010 more than 33 million visitors had been drawn to these travelling exhibitions of human remains. They exert a fascination that goes far beyond interest in the anatomical details they reveal. Yet there are questions about the degree to which some of the earlier body 'donors' were genuinely donors: that is, whether they consented to this post-mortem use of their flesh and bones. As of 2010, however, as many as 12,000 people had signed consent forms for their bodies to be plastinated after their deaths. The fact of informed consent removes many moral obstacles to this use of bodies.

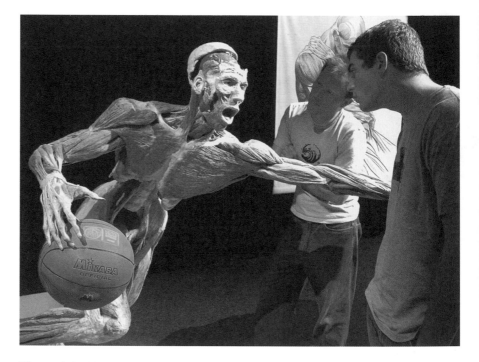

Figure 6.1 'The Basketball Player', and visitors, BODY WORLDS, Los Angeles, 2004–05. Photo: © Gunther von Hagens' BODY WORLDS, Institute for Plastination, Heidelberg, Germany; www.bodyworlds.com

The question of respecting the intentions of those whose bodies are on display in museums is an interesting one. The philosopher Jeremy Bentham (1748–1832) had a strong desire to display his body after death as what he called an **auto-icon** (see Figure 6.2).

Figure 6.2 Jeremy Bentham's 'auto-icon'. University College London. Photo: © 2010, UCL Learning & Media Services, All Rights Reserved. Image cannot be copied or used in any other form without express permission of the copyright holder

But many of those whose bodies and body parts are now exhibited in glass cases had known intentions that their corpses not be disturbed. No buried pharaoh would have wanted to end up partly unwrapped in a department of Egyptology thousands of miles from his kingdom, with his mummified toe protruding from the wrapping. In more recent cases some groups argue for the repatriation and reburial of the body parts of their ancestors. Using audio and textual sources, including searching the OU Library, we shall be considering two such cases: that of the Torres Straits Islanders and their attempts to repatriate their ancestors' remains, and that of Ishi, an indigenous Yahi Native American man whose brain was, until recently, kept in an American museum. Such questions about ownership, implied consent and the ethics of display are surfacing with increasing frequency in the twenty-first century.

In this chapter you will explore what Philosophy, as a discipline, can contribute to such debates. Philosophers are interested in analysing the underlying assumptions and arguments of a question, and in contextualising this within broader philosophical discussions. Above all, the study of Philosophy emphasises thinking for yourself – although this is not to suggest that philosophers have a god-like ability to see through the complexities to the 'correct' answer that they can then present to you on a plate. The point of this chapter is not to tell you what you ought to think about the issues it raises; but rather to provide you with an overview of what some of the key questions are and to encourage you to think through the arguments, drawing your own conclusions. Although this chapter, and the audio recordings that accompany it, ranges far wider than just Philosophy, the emphasis throughout will be on the sorts of critical skills of argument and analysis that philosophers characteristically employ, or at least aim at.

6.1 Cosmopolitanism and cultural patrimony

You may already be aware of some of the issues surrounding the ownership of objects such as the Benin bronzes (Figure 6.3) and the Parthenon marble sculptures (Figure 6.4). The Benin bronzes are striking plaques and heads that were made around the sixteenth century and looted by a British expeditionary force in the nineteenth century. They have subsequently found their way into a number of museums around the world, including the British Museum. There is a polarised debate about whether they should remain there, or should be returned to their geographical site of origin in Nigeria. (If you have studied AA100, you will be familiar with the terms of this debate.) The contemporary Nigerian playwright Wole Soyinka (b.1934) has given a clear statement on why these particular objects have been considered so important and why, for some people, their current location is so controversial:

> When I see a Benin Bronze, I immediately think of the mastery of technology and art – the welding of the two. I think immediately of a cohesive ancient civilisation. It increases a sense of self-esteem, because it makes you understand that African society actually produced some great civilisations, established some great cultures. And today it contributes to one's sense of the degradation that has overtaken many African societies, to the extent that we forget that we were once a functioning people before the negative incursion of foreign powers. The looted objects are still today politically loaded. The Benin Bronze, like other artefacts, is still very much a part of the politics of contemporary Africa and, of course, Nigeria in particular.
>
> (Quoted in *A History of the World in 100 Objects*, 2010)

Perhaps more famous than this is the ongoing dispute about whether the ancient frieze sculptures that were part of the Parthenon in Athens, but are now housed in the British Museum, should be shipped back to Greece to be installed in a specially created museum next to their original location.

Figure 6.3 Relief plaque, bronze. From Benin City, Nigeria. British Museum, London, Af1913,1211.1. Photo: © The Trustees of the British Museum

These debates are particular and much-discussed examples of a more general philosophical question about whether such highly significant objects should be thought of as belonging to humanity as a whole rather than to particular nations or peoples. Cosmopolitans believe that as well as our individual identities stemming from where we were born and live, our cultural, religious or non-religious background, and numerous other facets of each person's being, we should recognise that from a moral point of view we are all members of one global community.

Figure 6.4 Parthenon frieze from the Parthenon Gallery, Acropolis Museum, Athens. Photographed by Nikos Daniilidis. Photo: © Acropolis Museum

'I am a citizen of the world'

We are all human beings with a shared humanity. When asked where he was from, the ancient Greek philosopher Diogenes (*c.* 412 BCE–323 BCE) famously declared, 'I am a citizen of the world.' That is the spirit of cosmopolitanism: a philosophical position that both recognises and celebrates individual differences, and yet emphasises our shared humanity.

For cosmopolitans, such as the philosopher and writer Kwame Anthony Appiah (see Section 6.2), the consequence of recognising that significant archaeological finds are part of the common culture of humanity, as well as belonging to particular cultural contexts, is key. They draw the conclusion that it is better for humanity if such objects are widely available for viewing by being on public display in museums around the world, rather than simply being returned to their sites of origin. Others, who argue for the importance of what they call **cultural patrimony**, disagree, and for many reasons.

Cosmopolitanism

Cosmopolitanism is a philosophical position that emphasises our common humanity despite cultural differences, that sees each of us as primarily citizens of the world, and that regards the common good in terms of the global as well as the local. For Appiah, a prominent cosmopolitan thinker, this means allowing people to live according to the customs of their community, while recognising their equality and shared interests as human beings.

Cultural patrimony

Patrimony is property that is legally passed on from generation to generation. Those who defend an idea of *cultural* patrimony argue that particular cultures, or in some cases nations, have a right of ownership of objects that originated from that culture or nation. They often believe that this right overrides any other considerations about who owns objects and where they might be displayed.

In the first part of this chapter we will be analysing some of the cosmopolitan arguments for world museums containing and displaying works from many cultures alongside each other, together with the sorts of counter-argument raised by those who see cosmopolitanism as a thinly veiled reassertion of the cultural imperialism which first led to works of national importance being removed from the sites where they feel they belong. Cosmopolitans see their position as both rational and practical; those who disagree see them as the new imperialists who, by arguing for the retention of objects of profound symbolic and aesthetic significance, are continuing a tradition of systematically harming less powerful cultures. This makes it sound as if there is a simple polarised debate, but in fact the arguments on both sides of this issue are more subtle than this. What is at stake here, though, is nothing less than the moral foundations of museums. There is no assumption of a 'right' answer in what follows: the aim is to introduce competing viewpoints and relevant case studies in order to provide you with materials from which you can draw your own conclusions.

6.2 Appiah on cultural patrimony

In this section, we'll be looking closely at Appiah's arguments about cultural patrimony. In order to understand them we need to appreciate both his angle and the angle of those he is arguing against.

Activity

To begin with, listen to the audio recording 'Cosmopolitanism', which you can find on the module website. This is an interview with Appiah, exploring his idea that important archaeological finds belong to humanity, and not necessarily to the countries that happen to exist in the geographical locations in which these objects were found.

You should allow about 30 minutes for this activity.

Do you agree with Appiah's approach as it comes across from the audio? Even if you do, can you think of some counter-arguments to it? Write down a few notes before reading the discussion section below.

Discussion

Here are some possible responses to Appiah. You may have come up with variations on these, or additional points:

1 Perhaps nations or ethnic identity *are* more fundamental than any notion that we are all part of humanity. In other words, Appiah's whole argument rests on his belief that cosmopolitanism is the correct ethical stance to take on a wide range of questions, including the question of cultural patrimony, and that general assumption can be challenged. If you don't accept his cosmopolitan stance about the importance of making cultural objects available to all humanity, then you won't necessarily agree that some objects would be better located away from their places of origin rather than in them.

2 Most of the objects in question were acquired in dubious circumstances, often as a result of imperial colonisation, and many were looted. The museums' right of ownership should be challenged in such situations. Even if the objects in question were acquired legally, the power relations between buyer and seller may have been so unequal as for this to have been a kind of extortion. Furthermore, given the harm done by empire, successor states have a duty to make amends for the crimes of their forebears. One symbolic way of doing this would be to return important objects to their original locations.

3 The meaning of such objects is tied to their context. African sculpture needs to be seen in Africa, where there is likely to be a greater

continuity and understanding of local religion and society than, for example, in the United Kingdom, where such objects are more likely to be aestheticised and their original meanings obscured.

4   Another point, related to the previous one, is that the question of which artefacts should be considered works of art is a more contentious one than, perhaps, Appiah believes. Some of the objects that he describes, such as the Benin bronzes and Nok sculptures, may have had ritual significance beyond the sort of aesthetic contemplation that he describes in the audio. If that is so, it is not obvious to regard as watertight his arguments that as works of *art* they should, if possible, be distributed across the globe for wider appreciation. If they're not works of art in any straightforward sense, then arguments for universal access that depend on the belief that works of art are made to be viewed are weakened.

Reading Appiah

Listening to the audio recording should have given you a good overview of Appiah's approach to the issue. We are now going to look closely at his written defence of his stance on the ownership and display of such objects.

I shall now take you stage by stage through Reading 6.1, 'Whose Culture Is It, Anyway?'. Don't simply skim ahead to the discussion sections. Try to answer the questions I ask in the activities before doing that. The questions below are the sorts of question you should be asking yourself when reading *any* piece of argumentative prose. Most of them are intended to help you clarify precisely what Appiah's arguments are, to understand the position of those he opposes, and to become aware of how he uses particular examples to build his case. There are also questions that encourage you to reflect critically on his arguments and to think through the best arguments that can be made against his case. It is only by exploring the arguments and evidence on both sides of such a question that we can hope to arrive at anything other than dogmatic conclusions.

Who is Kwame Anthony Appiah?

Kwame Anthony Appiah (Figure 6.5), born in 1954, is Professor of Philosophy and Law at New York University in the USA. He has written on a wide range of subjects, including race and identity. Raised in Kumasi in Ghana, he is related to Asante kings on his father's side. His mother's family is of English origin. He attended university in England and now lives in the USA. If you want to read more about Appiah, follow the link on the Study Planner of the module website.

Figure 6.5 Kwame Anthony Appiah, former Laurance S. Rockefeller University Professor of Philosophy and the University Center for Human Values, Princeton University, New Jersey, USA. Photo: © Princeton University, Office of Communications/Denise Applewhite (2005)

You should allow about
15 minutes for this
activity.

Activity

Turn to Reading 6.1, 'Whose Culture Is It, Anyway?', by Appiah. This is an extract from his book *Cosmopolitanism: Ethics in a World of Strangers* (first published in 2006).

Read through the extract now. Don't worry if you can't follow all Appiah's arguments on this first reading. We shall be analysing several of his arguments closely. The point of the first reading is to get an overview of Appiah's position. Make sure you read through to the end of the piece before going back and attempting the questions below. As a general study skill, reading swiftly through an article or chapter before looking closely at its detail is a good way of getting your bearings. Here you should be trying to appreciate what the author's main conclusion is, and some of the arguments, evidence and even rhetoric that he uses to nudge you towards accepting his conclusion.

Don't continue until you have read the extract through. Then move on to the activities below, referring back to Reading 6.1 as directed. The point of these questions is not just to help you find your way through the reading, but also to suggest the kinds of question you should be asking yourself when reading other prose. Passive reading – letting the ideas wash over you – isn't enough. In the humanities it is extremely important to develop the skill of *active* reading – critical engagement with the text – both to understand as much as possible about an author's intentions and to engage with the arguments and assumptions that the author is making, thinking of counter-arguments and possible criticisms and, at times, identifying flaws in the author's reasoning along the way.

Activity

Now re-read the first part of Reading 6.1, entitled 'The spoils of war'. Answer the following questions:

1   Why do you think Appiah begins with the example of objects taken from Kumasi?

2   Why does he describe Baden-Powell's boast as 'almost comical'?

3   What is the main point Appiah is making with his discussion of archaeological finds in Mali?

Discussion

1   As we have seen, Appiah was born in Kumasi and is related to
    Asante kings. By beginning with an example that you would expect
    him to feel very strongly about, the looting of objects that belonged to
    his own forebears, his own 'cultural patrimony' as it were, he makes a
    strong rhetorical point. If he is prepared to see even the looted
    property of his own ancestors as part of a common heritage of
    humanity, rather than something that should necessarily be returned
    to its original location, it is difficult to accuse Appiah of simply siding
    with the imperialists. This isn't overtly stated, but it is my
    interpretation of how this first example functions.

2   Appiah is drawing our attention to the irony of Baden-Powell saying
    there was no 'attempt at looting' when, from our perspective today,
    the whole activity was nothing else but looting. If we are charitable to
    Baden-Powell, we might point out that what he meant by 'looting' in
    this context was stealing for personal gain, rather than following
    orders and collecting the 'indemnities' for the British government –
    something that many today would see as officially sanctioned looting.

3   Appiah points out that Mali is not in a position to enforce laws that are
    designed to prevent archaeological finds being exported. But nor can
    it finance archaeological digs. He also acknowledges that the illegal
    export of such finds is a kind of theft that parallels imperialist looting
    in the past.

Activity

Re-read the second section of Reading 6.1, entitled 'The patrimony
perplex'. Write down short notes answering the following questions:

*You should allow about
30 minutes for this
activity.*

1   What does 'patrimony' usually mean?

2   What are the two senses of 'cultural patrimony' that Appiah identifies?

3   Why does he point out that Nigeria is less than a century old? What
    difference does he believe that makes to the debates about cultural
    patrimony?

4   Whether or not you agree with Appiah, can you think of any
    arguments that could be made against his claim that it is better to
    think of the possessors of Nok sculptures as 'trustees for humanity'?

Discussion

1   Patrimony is property that is passed down from generation to
    generation. It legally belongs to those who inherit it. If you are not

clear about what 'patrimony' usually means, then it will be very difficult to follow Appiah's thread.

2   Appiah identifies two senses of this term that are, he says, conflated. Getting clear about what Appiah means in this passage requires a bit of effort. If you skim over this passage too quickly you might miss the distinction he is making.

His first sense of 'cultural patrimony' is the more general sense. It derives from the fact that human beings make objects that are invested with significance. Human culture is a manifestation of human creativity. In order for objects to be interpreted, knowledge of social and historical conventions is required. But 'culture' in this sense, at least as I interpret this passage, is what humanity inherits from the particular contributions made in specific places.

The second sense that Appiah identifies here is the sense of 'culture' that refers to a specific group as 'a culture'. This is the particular group which created the objects in question. But, more important for Appiah's argument, this sense of 'cultural patrimony' assumes that the culture in question has a trans-historical identity; that is, it exists across time, not just at the moment at which the objects were created.

So Norway's cultural patrimony in the second sense is the set of cultural objects (and practices, perhaps) that rightly belong to Norway, whereas the cultural patrimony of Norway in the first sense would be the contribution that Norway has made to human culture.

3   Here Appiah is questioning the assumption built into the second of his two senses of 'cultural patrimony', namely that cultures have a trans-historical existence that gives them rights of ownership of objects. Modern Nigeria is very unlike the culture that produced the Nok sculptures (and the creators of the Nok sculptures definitely did not make them for Nigeria, as Nigeria didn't then exist). In other words, Appiah is questioning the assumption that geographical locations guarantee any cultural continuity or similarity and is thereby undermining at least some claims for cultural ownership of objects produced there in earlier times.

4   The point of this activity is to think of possible responses, not necessarily responses with which you agree. A variety of responses are possible, some of which can easily be countered. Here are two ways in which Appiah's assumptions might be questioned (but you might have come up with better ones).

First, if a people own something, they don't have to see themselves as 'trustees for humanity'. Ownership rights override other considerations. They should be free to do whatever they like with their own possessions, including destroying them. In other words, it is possible to question Appiah's assumption that humanity has some kind of claim on objects that belong to particular groups.

Second, nations and groups are more fundamental units for humanity than the totality of human beings. Nations are and should be self-determining, and there is no legitimate position from outside nations that imposes responsibilities on how these nations treat their legitimate property.

Activity

Re-read the third section of Reading 6.1, entitled 'Precious bane'. Jot down some thoughts in response to the following questions before reading the discussion:

You should allow about 30 minutes for this activity.

1 What does 'bane' mean?

2 What does Appiah's choice of the word 'crowd' in the phrase 'the cultural-patrimony crowd' reveal about his attitude to those who argue for cultural patrimony?

3 Why does Appiah believe that it is not obvious that all significant archaeological finds should remain exactly where they are found?

Discussion

1 'Bane' is an archaic word that means poison or something that destroys.

2 The word 'crowd' is pejorative here and suggests that Appiah does not hold these people's views in high esteem. In writing an academic essay about cosmopolitanism, for example, it wouldn't be appropriate to refer to cosmopolitans as 'the cosmopolitan crowd'. This is a question of tone. Appiah's tone in this chapter is polemical: he is making a strong and (he hopes) persuasive case for his conclusions in a book written for general readers. In a more academic context he would have been much less likely to have used the word 'crowd' to refer to those with whom he disagreed.

3 We've already seen that Appiah believes that sometimes the interests of humanity are best served by making significant objects available to a wide range of people by placing them in museums around the world. Here he presents an argument that a controlled form of legal export of archaeological finds from Mali would have produced better consequences than insisting that all objects stay in the country in which they were found. This approach would also have allowed

Malians to import works of art that would have enriched their aesthetic experience.

There is no space to reproduce all of Appiah's article here. In the remaining pages, which we have omitted, he touches on further themes. For example, one important section is where he explores three circumstances in which he believes the repatriation of objects does make sense. These are (1) when there is an aesthetic argument for repatriation (as when the work is site-specific); (2) when the object is of particular contemporary cultural or religious ritual significance; and (3) when the object in question was stolen. Appiah also suggests that a good way for European museums to make restitution to societies that Europeans plundered in earlier times would be not simply to return objects that originated in those places and were stolen from there, but to help stock the museums of those societies with examples of good art from around the world.

Whether or not you agree with Appiah's cosmopolitan approach to questions of cultural heritage, these activities should have helped you to achieve a clear idea of what he believes and why. They should also have helped you to understand the sorts of criticism that might be made of some of his arguments.

6.3 A different sort of afterlife: owning and displaying human remains

At the end of the audio recording 'Cosmopolitanism', Appiah explains that he thinks questions about the ownership and display of human remains should be treated differently from questions about works of art removed from their original cultural and geographic contexts. The rest of this chapter focuses on questions about the ownership of parts of the body and how they are treated.

Activity

Listen again to the last few minutes of the audio recording 'Cosmopolitanism'. Write a brief summary in note form of Appiah's position on the return of human remains and how he defends it. Do you agree with him?

You should allow about 30 minutes for this activity.

Discussion

Here is my summary:

Appiah points out that different societies have different attitudes to the remains of their dead. Those who are descended from the dead are more concerned with the remains of their ancestors than with others. The interests of those who think of themselves as descendants of these people should have a major influence on what happens to these remains. These interests – which take many forms, including symbolic or religious – need to be weighed against scientific interests in the remains. The weight of descendants' interests is stronger when only a short time has elapsed since their ancestors' deaths and when a people believe a certain sort of reverence towards remains to be central to their culture.

If you disagree with Appiah's position, be sure to state your reasons clearly.

Bentham's auto-icon

As was mentioned in the introduction, the philosopher and legal reformer Jeremy Bentham, who is famous for his utilitarian philosophy (you will recall from Chapter 1 that this is the idea that the right course of action is the one that maximises happiness for the greatest number of people), notoriously made arrangements for his body to be displayed as what he called an auto-icon after his death. You can still see it in University College London today, though Bentham's mummified head, originally on display (see Figure 6.2), has had to be removed due to decay.

Bentham was explicit in his instructions about what should happen to his body after his death, as can be seen from this extract from his final will (dated 1832, the year of his death):

> My body I give to my dear friend Doctor Southwood Smith to be disposed of in [the] manner hereinafter mentioned[.] And I direct that as soon as it appears to any one that my life is at an end my executor or any other person by whom on the opening of this paper the contents thereof shall have been observed shall send an express [message] with information of my decease to Doctor Southwood Smith requesting him to repair to the place where my body is lying and after ascertaining by appropriate experiment that no life remains it is my request that he will take my body under his charge and take the requisite and appropriate measures for the disposal and preservation of the several parts of my bodily frame in the manner expressed in the paper annexed to this my will and at the top of which I have written 'Auto-Icon'[.] The skeleton he will cause to be put together in such manner as that the whole figure may be seated in a Chair usually occupied by me when living in the attitude in which I am sitting when engaged in thought in the course of the time employed in writing[.] I direct that the body thus prepared shall be transferred to my executor[.] He will cause the skeleton to be clad in one of the suits of black occasionally worn by me[.] The Body so clothed together with the chair and the staff in my later years borne by me he will take charge of[.] And for containing the whole apparatus he will cause to be prepared an appropriate box or case and will cause to be engraved in conspicuous characters on a plate to be affixed thereon and also on the labels on the glass case in which the preparations of the soft parts of my body shall be contained as for example as in the manner used in the case of wine decanters my name at length with the letters ob. followed by the day of my decease[.] If it should so happen that my personal friends and other Disciples should be disposed to meet together on some day or days of the year for the purpose of commemorating the Founder of the greatest happiness system of morals and legislation

my executor will from time to time cause to be conveyed to the room in which they meet the said Box or case with the contents there to be stationed in such part of the room as to the assembled company shall seem meet.

(Quoted in Marmoy, 1958, p. 80)

Bentham's last wishes have been realised and respected. His friend Dr Thomas Southwood Smith (1788–1861) publicly dissected Bentham's body and gave a lecture over the open corpse. The flesh was removed from the bones and the head mummified. The glass eyes that Bentham had bought for the purpose were inserted, and the skeleton dressed in Bentham's clothes and posed in a seated position. The head had not kept its shape well during the mummification process, so a wax version was made to sit on top of the skeleton. The mummified one was placed at Bentham's feet. The whole was placed in a glass case to produce a distinctive kind of statue – one made out of the remains of a human being.

This object eventually ended up in the possession of University College London, where it is still on display. Many myths have grown up about it, including that Bentham is given a vote at important university meetings, and that students once kidnapped Bentham's mummified head and played football with it. Neither of these stories is true, though the head was once kidnapped but soon returned.

Activity

Write down a few notes in response to these questions:

Is Bentham's explicit consent to the subsequent use of his body important in deciding questions about the rightness or wrongness of putting it on display? If so, why?

Discussion

In many areas of life, explicit consent prevents a harm or even a crime being committed. So, for example, someone may consent to have sex with another person of legal age; but if someone has sex with another person against their will, that is rape. There is widespread agreement, too, that, other things being equal, we should try to respect the clearly expressed wishes of the dead about what should happen to their possessions after death. There is an interesting question about whether someone's body is really their possession in the way that their money and house are. But if it is their possession, then surely we should try to respect their desires for what should happen to their body, unless, of course, that would result in danger or harm to other people, or would involve a crime being committed.

In Bentham's case, his explicit instructions rightly carried weight with his friends, who took care that they were acted on. Contrast this with the treatment of the bodies of various pharaohs and other significant ancient Egyptians. The body of King Tutankhamun (reigned *c.*1361 BCE–*c.*1352 BCE) (see Figure 6.6), for instance, has been unwrapped and extensively investigated, his probable cause of death ascertained (a combination of a failing immune system, a leg fracture and malaria), and his genetic relationship to other bodies preserved in museums deciphered from his DNA. Like Bentham, these ancient Egyptians, too, made elaborate plans for what should happen after their deaths. But unlike Bentham, who was an atheist, they believed in an afterlife and in the importance of the preservation of their bodies and grave contents as an important prerequisite for their entering it. Many museums around the world now house mummified bodies of people who certainly did not consent to their last remains being put on display.

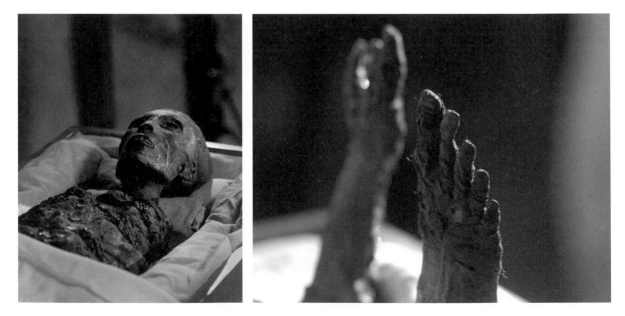

Figure 6.6 The mummy of King Tutankhamun in his tomb, photographed in 2008. Photos: © Barry Iverson/Alamy

Activity

On what grounds do you believe museum curators feel justified in overriding the wishes of ancient Egyptians who clearly did not consent, and would not have consented, to having their bodies put on display? You might want to have a look around at some museum websites, such as that of the British Museum in London, to see how such exhibits are presented.

Discussion

The usual justifications given for displaying and investigating Egyptian mummies are archaeological and scientific. From an archaeological point of view, detailed investigation of burials reveals a great deal about past cultures; and this is particularly so when, like Tutankhamun's, graves contain large numbers of well-preserved objects. The display of mummified bodies serves an educational role. From a scientific perspective, understanding more about diet, health, genetic relationships, and so on, both informs archaeology and helps us understand the past of humanity.

Two case studies

Torres Straits Islanders' remains

In March 2011 London's Natural History Museum agreed to return the bones of 138 indigenous people that had been removed from the Torres Strait Islands (Figure 6.7) in the nineteenth century and had been held in the museum collection. This followed 18 months of negotiations, as part of a campaign by the descendants of these people for the bones to be returned. The bones have particular significance because the islanders believe that the souls of the dead cannot rest while parts of their body are far from home. Richard Lane, the then director of science at London's Natural History Museum, explained the competing views which needed to be taken into account:

> Considering the return of ancestral remains is a complex and sensitive issue that seeks to balance the Museum's commitment to the scientific study of human diversity and origins with different cultural perspectives on meaning, value and duties with respect to remains. In their deliberations, Trustees acknowledged the strong feelings of connection of the community to the remains and noted the continuing responsibility by the community for the care of the remains.

> (Quoted in Natural History Museum, 2011)

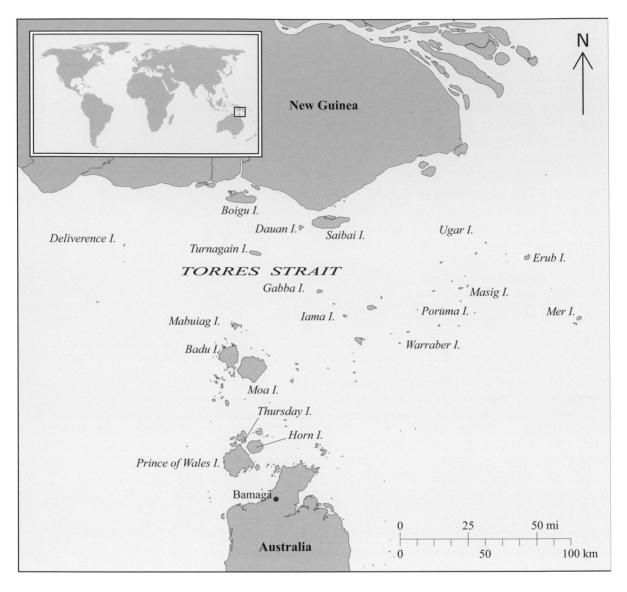

Figure 6.7 Map showing the Torres Straits Islands

Activity

Now listen to the audio recording 'Returning remains', which you can find on the module website. In this recording, Torres Straits Islanders Ned David and Seriako Stephen discuss the agreement to repatriate the remains of their ancestors from the Natural History Museum.

As you listen, make notes on why these Torres Straits Islanders were so keen to have these body parts returned.

You should allow about 30 minutes for this activity.

Discussion

The key reasons for wanting these body parts returned include the following:

- It was important to the Torres Straits Islanders that their ancestors' remains should be laid to rest in an appropriate way and in an appropriate place. They believed that until the remains were returned, their ancestors' spirits would not fully be at rest.

- These remains reflected a spiritual and cultural connection between present-day Torres Straits Islanders and their ancestors.

- The symbolic value of the return of the remains as an act of restitution and reparation was extremely important to the Torres Straits Islanders. The act of returning the remains was seen as an attempt to make amends for past European wrongs.

Activity

Now listen to the audio recording 'Reservations about repatriation', which you can find on the module website. In this recording, the sociologist Tiffany Jenkins (author of *Contesting Human Remains in Museum Collections*, 2011) discusses the return of body parts from museums. According to her, too much weight has been given to the Torres Straits Islanders' claims.

As you listen to the recording, make notes on whether you agree with Jenkins. If you don't, say why not.

You should allow about 30 minutes for this activity.

Discussion

The key questions in this area concern how to balance the competing claims of scientific researchers and those who want to return bones and skulls to their place of origin. Jenkins suggests that those who want such parts returned may be over-optimistic about the consequences of success. But what is her evidence? Is that a convincing argument? Who should have the power to decide what happens in these cases: those who have historically held power, or those whose ancestors' remains are under discussion? If you found yourself disagreeing with Jenkins, make sure that you are clear about why you disagree, and think about how she might respond and how you could respond to her.

Ishi's brain

Ishi was an indigenous American of the Yahi tribe who was captured and displayed as a living exhibit in a San Francisco museum in the early twentieth century. After his death, and against his wishes, his body was preserved for research purposes. The distinguished anthropologist Nancy Scheper-Hughes discusses what happened to his brain in the audio recording 'Ishi's brain' and in an article which you can access from the OU Library website (see Figures 6.8 and 6.9). The point of including this second case study is to provide you with a rich example to focus your thoughts about the issues we have discussed throughout this chapter. I have deliberately refrained from unpacking what is at stake here.

Figure 6.8   Nancy Scheper-Hughes, Berkeley, California 2010

Figure 6.9 Photograph of Ishi. Courtesy of the Phoebe A. Hearst Museum of Anthropology and the Regents of the University of California, 15-5910

Activity

You should allow about an hour for this activity.

First of all, listen to the audio recording 'Ishi's brain', which you can find on the module website. In this recording, Scheper-Hughes talks about Ishi and the fate of his body. Then, when you have listened to the recording, you should find and read an article by Scheper-Hughes published in the journal *Anthropology Today*.

To find the article, go to the journals search page of the OU Library website (a direct link to this page has been provided on the Study Planner of the module website). Enter the title of the journal: 'Anthropology Today'. You can then follow the link to the journal on JSTOR. Browse down to the issues published in 2001 and select 'no. 1', which contains the article. The full bibliographical details are:

- Scheper-Hughes, N. (2001) 'Ishi's brain, Ishi's ashes: anthropology and genocide', *Anthropology Today*, vol. 17, no. 1, pp. 12–18.

You should read from the paragraph beginning 'This much is certain ...' (at the bottom of p. 14) to the end of the article.

You can use this case study to practise applying the sort of critical reading that we used for Appiah's writing in the first part of this chapter. Try to read and listen actively rather than passively, making sure that you follow the point of what is being written or said. As you do so, ask yourself clarificatory questions, try to think of counter-arguments and counter-examples, and imagine how Scheper-Hughes might reply to them. You should also think about how this case relates to themes such as consent, ownership, reparation and the nature of museum displays: the themes that have recurred throughout this chapter.

Discussion

The point of this activity is to put into practice some of the skills of reading and critical engagement that have been foregrounded in earlier parts of this chapter. There are many different questions you could ask yourself here. Cultivating a style of active reading where you seek not only to understand, but also to engage with, the author's position is central to studying Philosophy in particular and the Humanities in general.

Conclusion

There are few simple answers in most of these cases. Yet, through careful examination of arguments and assumptions, it is possible to clarify the reasoning behind competing claims, and to excavate the theoretical underpinnings of what might seem like simple assertions of different viewpoints. The aim here is not to prove that one side or the other is right; nor is it to tell you how to weight the different arguments. The point of this chapter is to equip you with some examples and ideas that might help you clarify what you believe about these issues concerning the afterlife of objects, and to provide the material for you to make a case for your own conclusions.

References

A History of the World in 100 Objects (2010) BBC radio series, episode 77, 'Benin plaque: the oba with Europeans' [Online]. Available at http://www.bbc.co.uk/ahistoryoftheworld/about/transcripts/episode77/ (Accessed 17 September 2014).

Appiah, K.A. (2007) *Cosmopolitanism: Ethics in a World of Strangers*, Harmondsworth, Penguin.

Jenkins, T. (2011) *Contesting Human Remains in Museum Collections: The Crisis of Cultural Authority*, London, Routledge.

Marmoy, C.F.A. (1958) 'The "auto-icon" of Jeremy Bentham at University College London', *Medical History*, vol. 2, no. 2, pp. 77–86.

Natural History Museum (2011) 'TSI joint announcement', press release, 10 March.

Scheper-Hughes, N. (2001) 'Ishi's brain, Ishi's ashes: anthropology and genocide', *Anthropology Today*, vol. 17, no. 1, pp. 12–18.

Further reading

These works provide an opportunity to explore issues of heritage, display and ownership in more detail. Through them you will be able to develop your skills of critical reading and cultivate a sensitivity to the ethical and philosophical dimensions of the study of Material Culture.

Appiah, K.A. (2010) 'Cosmopolitanism' [an interview], in Edmonds, D. and Warburton, N. (eds) *Philosophy Bites*, Oxford, Oxford University Press, pp. 47–57; based on a podcast audio interview available at http://www.philosophybites.com/2008/03/anthony-appiah.html (Accessed 17 September 2014).

The British Museum Trustees (n.d.) 'The Parthenon sculptures: the position of the Trustees of the British Museum' [Online]. Available at http://www.britishmuseum.org/the_museum/news_and_press/statements/parthenon_sculptures/trustees_statement.aspx (Accessed 17 September 2014).

Cuno, J.B. (2008) *Who Owns Antiquity? Museums and the Battle over Our Ancient Heritage*, Princeton, NJ, Princeton University Press.

Eakin, H. (2009) 'Who should own the world's antiquities?', *New York Review of Books*, vol. 56, no. 8, 14 May [Online]. Available at http://www.nybooks.com/articles/archives/2009/may/14/who-should-own-the-worlds-antiquities/ (Accessed 17 September 2014).

Von Hagens, G. (2008) *BODY WORLDS: The Original Exhibition of Human Bodies*, 13th edn, Heidelberg, Arts & Sciences Verlagsgesellschaft mbH.

Reading 6.1 'Whose Culture Is It, Anyway?'

Source: Appiah, K.A. (2007) *Cosmopolitanism: Ethics in a World of Strangers*, **Harmondsworth, Penguin, pp. 115–36; footnotes omitted.**

The Spoils of War

In the nineteenth century, the kings of Asante – like kings everywhere – enhanced their glory by gathering objects from all around their kingdom and around the world. When the British general Sir Garnet Wolseley destroyed Kumasi in a 'punitive expedition' in 1874, he authorized the looting of the palace of the Asante king Kofi Karikari. At the treaty of Fomena, a few months later, Asante was required to pay an 'indemnity' of 50,000 ounces (nearly one and a half tons) of gold, much of which was delivered in the form of jewelry and other regalia. A couple of decades later, a Major Robert Stephenson Smyth Baden-Powell (yes, you know him as the founder of the Boy Scouts) was dispatched once more to Kumasi, this time to demand that the new king, Prempeh, submit to British rule. Baden-Powell described this mission in his book *The Downfall of Prempeh: A Diary of Life with the Native Levy in Ashanti, 1895–96.*

Once the king and his Queen Mother had made their submission, the British troops entered the palace, and, as Baden-Powell put it, 'the work of collecting valuables and property was proceeded with.' He continued,

> There could be no more interesting, no more tempting work than this. To poke about in a barbarian king's palace, whose wealth has been reported very great, was enough to make it so. Perhaps one of the most striking features about it was that the work of collecting the treasures was entrusted to a company of British soldiers, and that it was done most honestly and well, without a single case of looting. Here was a man with an armful of gold-hilted swords, there one with a box full of gold trinkets and rings, another with a spirit-case full of bottles of brandy, yet in no instance was there any attempt at looting.

This boast will strike us as almost comical, but Baden-Powell clearly believed that the inventorying and removal of these treasures under the orders of a British officer was a legitimate transfer of property. It wasn't looting; it was *collecting*. In short order, Nana Prempeh was arrested and taken into exile at Cape Coast. More indemnities were paid.

There are similar stories to be told around the world. The Belgian *Musée Royal de l'Afrique Centrale*, at Tervuren, explored the dark side of the origins of its own collections in the brutal history of the Belgian Congo, in a 2001 show called 'ExItCongoMuseum.' The Berlin Museum of Ethnology bought most of its extraordinary Yoruba art from Leo Frobenius, whose methods of 'collection' were not exactly limited to free-market exchange.

The modern market in African art, indeed in art from much of the global south, is often a dispiriting sequel to these earlier imperial expropriations. Many of the poorest countries in the world simply do not have the resources to enforce the regulations they make. Mali can declare it illegal to dig up and export the wonderful sculpture of Djenné-Jeno. But it can't enforce the law. And it certainly can't afford to fund thousands of archaeological digs. The result is that many fine Djenné-Jeno terra-cottas were dug up anyway in the 1980s, after the publication of the discoveries of the archaeologists Roderick and Susan McIntosh and their team. They were sold to collectors in Europe and North America who rightly admired them. Because they were removed from archaeological sites illegally, much of what we would most like to know about this culture – much that we could have found out by careful archaeology – may now never be known.

Once the governments of the United States and Mali, guided by archaeologists, created laws specifically aimed at stopping the smuggling of the stolen art, the open market for Djenné-Jeno sculpture largely ceased. But people have estimated that, in the meantime, perhaps a thousand pieces – some of them now valued at hundreds of thousands of dollars – left Mali illegally. Given these enormous prices, you can see why so many Malians were willing to help export their 'national heritage.'

Modern thefts have not, of course, been limited to the pillaging of archaeological sites. Hundreds of millions of dollars worth of art has been stolen from the museums of Nigeria alone, almost always with the complicity of insiders. And Ekpo Eyo, who once headed the National Museum of Nigeria, has rightly pointed out that dealers in New York and London – dealers including Sotheby's – have been less than eager to assist in their retrieval. Since many of these collections were well known to experts on Nigerian art, it shouldn't have taken the dealers long to recognize what was going on. Nor is such art theft limited to the Third World. Ask the government of Italy.

Given these circumstances – and this history – it has been natural to protest against the pillaging of 'cultural patrimony.' Through a number of declarations from UNESCO and other international bodies, a doctrine has evolved concerning the ownership of many forms of cultural property. It is that, in simplest terms, cultural property be regarded as the property of its culture. If you belong to that culture, such work is, in the suggestive shorthand, your cultural patrimony. If not, not.

The Patrimony Perplex

Part of what makes this grand phrase so powerful, I suspect, is that it conflates, in confusing ways, the two primary uses of that confusing word 'culture.' On the one hand, cultural patrimony refers to cultural artifacts: works of art, religious relics, manuscripts, crafts, musical instruments, and the like. Here 'culture' is whatever people make and invest with significance through the exercise of their human creativity. Since significance is something produced through conventions, which are never individual and rarely universal, interpreting culture in this sense requires some knowledge of its social and historical context. On the other hand, 'cultural patrimony' refers to the products of *a* culture: the group from whose conventions the object derives its significance. Here the objects are understood to belong to a particular group, heirs to a trans-historical identity, whose patrimony they are. The cultural patrimony of Norway, then, is not just Norway's contribution to human culture – its voices in our noisy human chorus, its contribution, as the French might say, to the civilization of the universal. Rather, it is all the artifacts produced by Norwegians, conceived of as a historically persisting people: and while the rest of us may admire Norway's patrimony, it belongs, in the end, to them.

But what does it mean, exactly, for something to belong to a people? Much of Norway's cultural patrimony was produced before the modern Norwegian state existed. (Norway achieved its modern independent existence in 1905, having been conjoined with either Denmark or Sweden – with the exception of a few chaotic months in 1814 – since the early fourteenth century.) The Vikings who made the wonderful gold and iron work in the National Museum Building in Oslo didn't think of themselves as the inhabitants of a single country that ran a thousand miles north from the Oslo fjord to the lands of the Sámi reindeer herders. Their identities were tied up, as we learn from the sagas, with lineage and locality. And they would certainly have been astonished to be told that Olaf's gold cup or Thorfinn's sword belonged not to Olaf and Thorfinn and their descendants but to a nation. The Greeks claim the Elgin marbles, which were made not by Greece – it wasn't a state when they were made – but by Athens, when it was a city-state of a few thousand people. When Nigerians claim a Nok sculpture as part of their patrimony, they are claiming for a nation whose boundaries are less than a century old, the works of a civilization more than two millennia ago, created by a people that no longer exists, and whose descendants we know nothing about. We don't know whether Nok sculptures were commissioned by kings or commoners; we don't know whether the people who made them and the people who paid for them thought of them as belonging to the kingdom, to a man, to a lineage, to the gods. One thing we know for sure, however, is that they didn't make them for Nigeria.

Indeed, a great deal of what people wish to protect as 'cultural patrimony' was made before the modern system of nations came into being, by members of societies that no longer exist. People die when their bodies die. Cultures, by contrast, can die without physical extinction. So there's no reason to think that the Nok have no descendants. But if Nok civilization came to an end and its people became something else, why should those descendants have a special claim on those objects, buried in the forest and forgotten for so long? And, even if they do have a special claim, what has that got to do with Nigeria, where, let us suppose, a majority of those descendants now live?

Perhaps the matter of biological descent is a distraction: proponents of the patrimony argument would surely be undeterred if it turned out that the Nok sculptures were made by eunuchs. They could reply that the Nok sculptures were found on the territory of Nigeria. And it is, indeed, a perfectly reasonable property rule that where something of value is dug up and nobody can establish an existing claim on it, the government gets to decide what to do with it. It's an equally sensible idea that the object's being of cultural value places on the government a special obligation to preserve it. Given that it is the Nigerian government, it will naturally focus on preserving it for Nigerians (most of whom, not thinking of themselves as heirs to Nok civilization, will probably think it about as interesting as art from anywhere else). But if it is of cultural value – as the Nok sculptures undoubtedly are – it strikes me that it would be better for them to think of themselves as trustees for humanity. While the government of Nigeria reasonably exercises trusteeship, the Nok sculptures belong in the deepest sense to all of us. 'Belong' here is a metaphor, of course: I just mean that the Nok sculptures are of potential value to all human beings.

That idea is expressed in the preamble of the Convention for the Protection of Cultural Property in the Event of Armed Conflict of May 14, 1954, which came out of a conference called by UNESCO.

> Being convinced that damage to cultural property belonging to any people whatsoever means damage to the cultural heritage of all mankind, since each people makes its contribution to the culture of the world. …

Framing the problem that way – as an issue for *all* mankind – should make it plain that it is the value of the cultural property to people and not to peoples that matters. It isn't peoples who experience and value art; it's men and women. Once you see that, then there's no reason why a Spanish museum couldn't or shouldn't preserve a Norse goblet, legally acquired, let us suppose at a Dublin auction, after the salvage of a Viking shipwreck off Ireland. It's a contribution to the cultural heritage of the world. But at any particular time it has to be in one place. Don't Spaniards have a case for being able to experience Viking craftsmanship? After all, there's already an awful lot of Viking stuff in Norway. The logic of 'cultural patrimony' would call for it to be shipped back to Norway (or, at any rate, to Scandinavia): that's whose cultural patrimony it is.

And, in various ways, we've inched closer to that position in the years since the Hague convention. The Convention on the Means of Prohibiting and Preventing the Illicit Import, Export and Transfer of Ownership of Cultural Property, adopted by the UNESCO General Conference in Paris in 1970, stipulated that 'cultural property constitutes one of the basic elements of civilization and national culture, and that its true value can be appreciated only in relation to the fullest possible information regarding its origin, history and traditional setting'; that 'it is essential for every State to become increasingly alive to the moral obligations to respect its own cultural heritage.' And a state's cultural heritage, it further decreed, included both work 'created by the individual or collective genius of nationals of the State' and 'cultural property found within the national territory.' The convention emphasized, accordingly, the importance of 'prohibiting and preventing the illicit import, export and transfer of ownership of cultural property.' A number of countries now declare all antiquities that originate within their borders to be state property, which cannot be freely exported. In Italy, private citizens are free to own 'cultural property,' but not to send it abroad.

Precious Bane

Plainly, special problems are posed by objects, like Viking treasure and Nok art, where there is, as the lawyers might say, no continuity of title. If we don't know who last owned a thing, we need a rule as to what should happen to it now. Where objects have this special status as a valuable 'contribution to the culture of the world,' the rule should be one that protects that object and makes it available to people who will benefit from experiencing it. So the rule of 'finders, keepers,' which may make sense for objects of less significance, will not do. Still, a sensible regime will reward those who find such objects, and give them an incentive to report not only what they have found but where and how they found it.

For an object from an archaeological site, after all, value comes often as much from the knowledge to be gleaned by knowing where it came out of the ground, what else was around it, how it lay in the earth. Since these articles usually don't have current owners, someone needs to regulate the process of removing them from the ground and decide where they should go. As I have said, it seems to me reasonable that the decision should be made by the government in whose soil they are found. But the right conclusion for them is not obviously that they should always stay exactly where they lay. Many Egyptians – overwhelmingly Muslims who regard the religion of the pharaohs as idolatrous – nevertheless insist that all the antiquities ever exported from its borders are really theirs. You do not need to endorse Napoleon's depredations of North Africa to think that there is something to be said for allowing people in other countries the chance to see close up the arts of one of the world's great civilizations. And it's a painful irony that one reason we've lost information about cultural antiquities is the very regulation intended to preserve it. If, for example, I sell you a figure from Djenné-Jeno with evidence that it came out of the ground in a certain place after the regulations came into force, then I am giving the authorities in the United States, who are committed to the restitution of objects taken illegally out of Mali, the very evidence they need.

Suppose that, from the beginning, Mali had been encouraged and helped by UNESCO to exercise its trusteeship of these Djenné-Jeno terra-cottas by licensing digs and training people to recognize that objects removed carefully from the earth with accurate records of location are worth more, even to collectors, than objects without this essential element of provenance. Suppose they had required that objects be recorded and registered before leaving, and stipulated that if the national museum wished to keep an object, it would have to pay a market price for it; the acquisition fund being supported by a tax on the price of the exported objects. The digs encouraged by this regime would have been worse than proper, professionally conducted digs by accredited archaeologists. Some people would still have avoided the rules. But mightn't all this have been better than what actually happened? Suppose, further, that the Malians had decided that, in order to maintain and build their collections, they should auction off some works they own. The cultural-patrimony crowd, instead of praising them for committing needed resources to protecting the national collection, would have excoriated them for betraying their heritage.

The problem for Mali is not that it doesn't have enough Malian art. The problem is that it doesn't have enough money. In the short run, allowing Mali to stop the export of a good deal of the art in its territory does have the positive effect of making sure that there is some world-class art in Mali for Malians to experience. (This doesn't work well everywhere, since another feature of poor countries is that it's hard to stop valuable materials from disappearing from national collections and reappearing in international auction houses. That's especially true if the objects are poorly cataloged and worth many times the total annual salaries of the museum staff; which explains what has happened in Nigeria.) But an experience limited to Malian art – or, anyway, art made on territory that's now part of Mali – makes no sense for a Malian than for anyone else. New technologies mean that Malians can now see, in however imperfectly reproduced a form, great art from around the planet. If UNESCO had spent as much effort to make it possible for great art to get into Mali as it has done to stop great art from getting out, it would have been serving better the interests that Malians, like all people, have in a cosmopolitan aesthetic experience.

Living with Art

[…]

In the spirit of cosmopolitanism, you might wonder whether all the greatest art should be held in trusteeship by nations, made widely available, shared across borders through traveling exhibitions, and in books and Web sites. Well, there's something to be said for the exhibitions and the books and the Web sites. There is no good reason, however, to think that public ownership is the ideal fate of every important art object. Much contemporary art – not just paintings, but conceptual artworks, sound sculptures, and a great deal more – was made for museums, designed for public display. But paintings, photographs, and sculptures, wherever they were created and whoever imagined them into being, have become one of the fundamental presences in the lives of millions of people. Is it really a sensible definition of great art that it is art that is too important to allow anybody to live with?

Afterword

Across Book 4 we have invited you, through the careful study of a series of case studies, to think critically about context. In the first three chapters you encountered a range of voices and texts – a novel, pamphlets, reports and various newspaper articles – which all referred to the anxieties and discontents of the new industrialised and highly urbanised society of the nineteenth century that was emerging at that time in the north of England. The task there was to develop your imaginative and interpretive skills in dealing with different kinds of textual evidence and to deploy those skills in such a way as to reconstruct how that past was understood by those who lived and participated in it, as well as to recognise some of the different interpretive strategies employed by historians and literary specialists to understand it.

In the first three chapters of Book 4 you learned that through collating and combining overlapping historical sources such as newspaper articles and political reports and pamphlets, you could develop an understanding of a particular moment in time. In other words, through textual forms of evidence the past was made available to the present. However, you also learned the importance of situating textual forms of evidence in their time such that they performed a dual function: first, they opened up the past to interpretation, and, second, they formed the context for interpreting other textual forms of evidence from the same historical moment. You also saw how, in this process of interpretation, the past and present interact: current debates about the nature of the economy and society inform the kinds of questions historians ask about the past.

You learned, too, that the meaning and significance of a novel lies not only in the novel itself but also outside it, in its reception by historically constituted publics. Moreover, the novel itself – in this case, *Hard Times* by Charles Dickens – became a further piece of textual evidence that enriched your understanding of the issues and debates of the nineteenth century. Across all these chapters you developed not just disciplinary-specific skills of interpretation, but also your ability to think interdisciplinarily, through reflection on the importance of history to the understanding of a nineteenth-century novel and on the relevance of a literary source to the interpretation of a historical period.

In the final three chapters of Book 4 you were invited to think about context through a collection of rather more explicitly interdisciplinary case studies in which context was much less clearly defined. In these three chapters you encountered a range of visual, anthropological and architectural sources which led you to consider the sometimes violent disruptions to context that can dramatically change the meaning or significance of an object, voice or text and how that object, voice or text is interpreted. The task here was to develop the skill of critical reflection. In these chapters you learned the importance of reflecting on your own experiences in your studies. As you worked through chapters on the tourist gaze, the role of museums and monuments in the transmission of social memory and the ethics of display, you reflected on processes and events in which you yourself are implicated – as a tourist, as an inheritor of a common European past and as a moral agent. In these chapters your implication in the issues they covered suggests that the definition of context as a relationship between words, images and objects includes you (and indeed us) – or, rather, includes the questions you ask and the interpretations you make in the course of your studies. In other words, whether you are studying a historical novel, a newspaper article, a museum collection or a procession or a ritual, context includes not only relevant historical and cultural facts but also you as the interpreter. Context, then, turns out to be an essential tool for analysis in the Arts and Humanities, yet it is unstable and uncertain, fluid and fractured, and subject to the critical decisions of the interpreter who must decide which contextual elements to privilege.

Glossary

American civil war

A conflict between southern and northern states in America, 1861–65.
A confederacy of southern states wanted to separate from the north in
protest at President Lincoln's plans to limit slavery. This secession was
considered to be a rebellion by the north, and war ensued. In Britain
many liberals supported Lincoln's wish to end slavery, though some
aristocrats sympathised with the slave-owners' objection to government
interference.

Anti-Corn Law League

A movement campaigning against the Corn Laws. The movement was
dominated by manufacturing interests and was largely led from
Manchester. It achieved success in 1846 when the Corn Laws were
repealed.

authenticity

The term may imply the provenance or genuineness of an object. It
may also imply that a range of cultural and/or religious values allegedly
invested in an object may be destroyed through its commodification.

auto-icon

The term used by the philosopher Jeremy Bentham (1748–1832) to
describe turning his dead body into a self-memorial by having it
preserved and put on public display.

bourgeoisie

Originally a French word meaning the middle strata or group in society,
this word was later used by Karl Marx (1818–1883) and Friedrich
Engels (1820–1895) to refer to the owners of the means of production,
businesspeople, bankers and employers. The term is used more
generally in contemporary and historical writing to refer to a broader
section of the middle class, including lawyers, doctors, civil servants and
other members of the professions. In Marxism, this social group is seen
as sustaining and supporting businesspeople and employers through a
shared commitment to capitalism. (See **capitalist**.)

camera obscura

A dark space in which an image is projected from outside via a pinhole in one of the walls.

capitalist

Someone who believes in the superiority of capitalism, a political and economic system where the means of production are privately owned and where prices and costs are determined by competition rather than by regulation.

Chartists

Members of the Chartism movement, active in the 1830s and 1840s, which was a movement for the reform of Parliament. Its goal was the implementation of the six points of the People's Charter: universal male suffrage; equal electoral districts; a secret ballot; annual elections; no property qualification for Members of Parliament; and payment of Members of Parliament. Chartism attracted mass support, chiefly among the working class(es). A number of huge petitions were presented to Parliament.

commodification

The process through which a place, object or culture is transformed into a commodity.

commodities

Objects, items or services that are produced for general sale.

Corn Laws

A series of laws which kept grain prices high by imposing a duty on imports whenever the domestic price of grain fell below a fixed level. The Corn Laws were designed to protect landowners and farmers against cheap foreign grain. They therefore benefited rural areas and landowners, as opposed to cities and grain consumers. The Corn Laws were repealed in 1846 following the successful campaign of the Anti-Corn Law League.

cosmopolitanism

A philosophical position that emphasises our common humanity despite cultural differences, that sees each of us as primarily citizens of the world, and that regards the common good in terms of the global as well as the local. For Kwame Anthony Appiah (b. 1954), a prominent cosmopolitan thinker, this means allowing people to live according to the customs of their community, while recognising their equality and shared interests as human beings.

counter-monument

The term used to describe a number of monuments and memorials in the postwar period commemorating the Shoah, or Holocaust.

cultural patrimony

Patrimony is property that is legally passed on from generation to generation. Those who defend an idea of *cultural* patrimony argue that particular cultures, or in some cases nations, have a right of ownership of objects that originated from that culture or nation. They often believe that this right overrides any other considerations about who owns objects and where they might be displayed.

culture

The values and practices of social groups.

diaspora

The dispersion of the Jews from the land of Israel over the centuries. The term can also refer to the spread of any people from their original homeland.

didactic

Intended to instruct or teach.

electoral reform

In the early nineteenth century only a small minority of men could vote for Members of Parliament. During the nineteenth and early twentieth centuries a series of Electoral Reform Acts gradually extended the franchise. The most important were those of 1832, 1867 and 1918. Under the 1832 Act, most middle-class men were given the vote and some of the most blatant anomalies were removed. In 1867 many urban working-class men were admitted to the franchise. However, it was not until the 1918 Act that all men and most women won the vote (the age qualification for women was higher until 1928).

Factory Acts

Legislation that limited the hours that women and children could work in factories. Acts also attempted to regulate conditions in factories by subjecting them to inspection.

Holocaust

The term used in some countries to describe the mass murder of Jews, Sinti and Roma people (see Shoah).

identity

This term is used to signify what makes individuals the same as, or different from, other people. Identifying markers include characteristics such as gender, class and race. Historians look at language to see how people in the past define themselves in relation to other people. As such, identity is used to look at the relationship between individuals and social groups.

Liberal

A person who adheres to Liberalism, a political philosophy whose supporters believe in the rights and freedom of the individual. Nineteenth-century Liberalism was closely associated with the values of the industrial middle class. It promoted free trade, political economy and freedom from government interference. The Liberal Party developed from the Whigs, in a bid to balance the aristocratic and industrial interests of the party after the Reform Act of 1832.

Marxism

A political and economic theory based on the ideas of Karl Marx (1818–1883) and Friedrich Engels (1820–1895), and developed by their followers. Marxism provides the intellectual foundation for communism.

mechanics' institutes

Adult education establishments, originally focusing on scientific and technical subjects. However, their scope was broad and they often housed important libraries, hosted lecture courses on a range of subjects, and catered for the needs of mainly working-class people studying in their spare time.

nationalism

A collection of discourses and practices through which histories are written, displayed, taught and learned; associated with the rise of nation-states in the nineteenth century. It is also closely associated with the creation of mass education, museums, monuments and heritage sites.

omniscient

The term 'omniscient' when applied to a narrator literally means that the narrator is 'all-knowing'. Fictional works written in the third person often employ an omniscient narrator, who is capable of telling the reader the unspoken thoughts and feelings of characters in the narrative, and is able to anticipate events.

pauper

Someone with no means of livelihood who is dependent on others. The term was much used in the nineteenth century to describe people who came into contact with the Poor Law.

pilgrimage

Among Christians, a pilgrimage is a journey undertaken in fulfilment of a vow for devotional or penitential reasons. The journey is typically to a place where relics or sacred objects are kept, or which are associated with miracles or specific holy persons.

plastination

A process used by the German anatomist Gunther von Hagens (b.1945) to preserve human bodies, muscles and organs by saturating them with polymer resin.

political economy

The study of the production of wealth and economics in relation to political, social and moral systems. Political economy can be liberal, believing in the principle of *laissez-faire* (leaving the market to regulate itself through 'natural law' and competition), or it can be socialist, believing that the state should regulate the market in order to distribute wealth equally. In the nineteenth century the term is associated with *laissez-faire* political economists who were the most predominant in debate.

Poor Law

The system to provide relief to the poor. The costs of the system rose dramatically in the early nineteenth century as poor harvests, wars and an increasingly commercial agriculture pushed more rural workers into poverty. In 1834 a new Poor Law was introduced to try to limit demand. Under the new system, a distinction was made between those unable to work and the 'able-bodied', who were to be provided with relief only in workhouses. These were designed to be so unattractive that independent work was always preferred.

profane

The term implies a realm of everyday human interactions with objects which are not subject to any special rules or prohibitions. (See **sacred**.)

proletariat

Wage earners, those without property who have to sell their labour to survive. The term is from ancient Rome, but was used by Friedrich Engels (1820–1895) and Karl Marx (1818–1883) to mean the working class(es).

realism

A mode of writing that appears to render actual life as authentically as possible. It depends on literary conventions such as close, accurate description and largely unobtrusive methods of narration. A secondary meaning of realism relates to subject matter that is everyday and unheroic. As a critical term, realism is particularly associated with nineteenth-century fiction, but it is a wide-ranging and complex concept, used in discussion of other literary genres (especially drama) and in other periods.

rhetoric

The use of artfully constructed language, designed to persuade an audience.

Roma

Another term for Romani, used specifically to refer to those living in central and eastern Europe.

romance

A term that refers to a long literary tradition reaching back to medieval tales (such as stories of Arthurian knights), through to fantasy genres of various kinds. The fictional characters who populate romances are usually idealised, settings are often remote, and events are often subject to supernatural interventions.

Romani

A mainly European socio-cultural group associated with a non-settled way of life whose members have long been subject to persecution by settled populations. The Romani trace their origins to south Asia.

sacred

The term implies a distinct realm of human interactions with objects heavily regulated by special rules and prohibitions. (See profane.)

satire

The use of exaggeration to expose faults and failings (either individual or social). Satire is often humorous, but its main purpose is to ridicule or deride.

Shoah

The preferred term in many European countries to describe the Holocaust: the mass extermination of Jews, Sinti and Roma people during the period of Nazi rule in Germany, particularly between 1941 and 1944.

shtetl

A village or small town with a predominantly Jewish population. The term is often used of a settlement (especially in central or eastern Europe) in a surrounding area whose population is largely non-Jewish.

Sinti

Romani people, living in central and eastern Europe.

slavery

A state of servitude in which a person is defined as the property of an owner and bound to serve them. Slavery was the antithesis of free labour (on which capitalist economies were supposed to be based). Slavery was outlawed in the British empire in 1834 after active campaigning by reformers such as William Wilberforce (1759–1833). Radical political movements of the early nineteenth century used the language of slavery to denounce the factory system. Referring to factory workers as 'white slaves' also exposed the hypocrisy of the middle classes, who campaigned against slavery in the Caribbean but said little about the exploitation of the British poor in factories. This was a particularly controversial point in Lancashire, where industry was highly dependent on cotton from the southern states of America, which were known for their use of slave labour.

socialist

A person who adheres to socialism, a political philosophy whose supporters believe that freedom and equality are best ensured through the collective responsibility for work and welfare.

source

A word used by historians to describe where information is taken from. This might be written texts, but might also include spoken ones ('oral sources') or artefacts. A distinction is often made between primary sources, which were created in the period studied, and secondary sources, which are later comments or interpretations, including those of other historians.

stamp duty

A tax on documents and publications.

tourist gaze

A distinct way of looking at places, objects and culture associated with tourism. (See **touristification**.)

touristification

The transformation of a place, object or culture in order to make it attractive to tourists. (See **tourist gaze**.)

utilitarian economists

Economists who applied the ethical philosophy of utilitarianism, based on the idea that our human instincts cause us to seek pleasure and avoid pain, to economics. Utilitarians thought that self-interest is what determines our actions and choices. In the early nineteenth century, the philosopher and reformer Jeremy Bentham (1748–1832) applied utilitarian ideas to a range of economic and social issues, with the aim of promoting 'the greatest good of the greatest number'. John Stuart Mill (1806–1873) offered modified versions of Bentham's views.

Vichy regime

The French government of 1940–44 which collaborated with the German occupying army during the Second World War. Headed by

Marshal Philippe Pétain (1856–1951), it was based in the town of Vichy in southern France.

working class(es)

People in the lower ranks of society who exchange labour for income, such as artisans, labourers and factory workers. The plural is used by some historians to reflect the diversity of the labouring classes, their work, politics and culture. Some historians, such as E.P. Thompson (1924–1993), use the singular 'working class'. This assumes that a collective identity was formed out of the diverse experience of work.

Acknowledgements

Chapter 6

Scheper-Hughes, N., 'Ishi's Brain, Ishi's Ashes: anthropology and genocide', *Anthropology Today* Vol. 17, Issue 1, pages 12–18, February 2001. Royal Anthropological Institute of Great Britain and Ireland, John Wiley and Sons, UK. Reproduced with permission of Nancy Scheper-Hughes.

Reading 6.1

Appiah, K.A. (2007) 'Whose culture is it, anyway?', *Cosmopolitanism: Ethics in a World of Strangers*, Published by Penguin, UK, and W.W. Norton & Company, USA.

Index

political economy 27–8, 31, 32–3, 34, 36, 129, 151, 307
  Anti-Corn Law League 22, 31, 133, 303
  see also capitalism; Chartism; communism; economic liberalism; economic systems; Factory Acts; Marxism; socialism; strikes; wage reductions
politics *see* electoral reform; political economy
polyphony 96–7
Poor Law 25, 307–8
Poovey, Mary 24
population growth 17–18, 27
Prempeh I (King) 292
Preston Lockout 68, 71–4, 101–4, 131
print culture *see* Book History; broadside ballads; libraries; literacy; newspapers
profane, the 168–70, 190, 308
proletariat 13, 41, 42–43, 308
  see also working class
public culture *see* civic culture
publishing industry *see* Book History; broadside ballads; libraries; literacy; newspapers

Quarry Bank Mill 15, 16, 28

Rachael (Dickens character) 93
reading, active and passive 274, 288
realism (in literature) 81, 82, 85, 308
  non-realism 86, 88, 89, 97
Reform Acts 141, 142, 143, 146, 305
  see also electoral reform
relic, Warsaw milk churn as 212, **213**, 214, **214**
  see also memory; museums
religion vi-vii, 167, 168–70
  didactic novels 75
  objects and tourism 167, 168–70, 195, 198
    commodification and authenticity 192–4, 195
    megaliths of Flores 186–91, **187**, 192, 193, 194, 195
    shrine of St Sara vi, 180, 181–6, 187, 191, 192, 193, 195
  religious tourism 173, 179–80
  in strike committee's rhetoric 72–3, 102
  see also Christianity; Hinduism; pilgrimage
Rendall, Jane 150
Resnais, Alain 251
revolution 9, 12, 43, 115, 130
  in Europe 118, 127, 128–9, 151

  see also class; economic systems; electoral reform; riots
Reynolds's Weekly Newspaper 142, 143, 155
rhetoric 66, 308
Ringelbaum, Emanuel 212, **213**, **214**
riots 138–40, **139**, 141, 142, 143, 155
  see also class; revolution
rituals 116
  see also anthropology; pilgrimage; shrine of St Sara
Roma (Romani), 308, 309
  Holocaust and 206, 230, 232, 245, 247, 248, 306
  shrine of St Sara and 180–3, 184, 185, 186, 191
romance (genre) 82, 84, 308
Romani *see* Roma
Rose, Mary B. 28
Rose, Sonya 134
Rosh, Leah 243
Ross, David 33–5, 36, 51–2, 142
Rummel, Rudolph Joseph 231
Russia 72

sacred, the 167, 168–70, 176, 185, 190, 195, 309
Safdie, Moshe 220
Sara, St *see* shrine of St Sara
satire 86, 309
savings banks 128, 141, 151
Scheper-Hughes, Nancy 286, **286**, 288
Schinkel, Friedrich 244
Schneersohn, Isaac 223
Schopenhauer, Johanna 15
Second World War 233
  see also Holocaust; Vichy regime
secularisation 172
'self-help' 130, 131, 141, 152
serfdom 72, 101
Serra, Richard 246
Shakespeare 65–6
Shalev-Gerz, Esther 238
Shoah 205–6, 309
  see also Holocaust
shrine of St Sara vi, 180–4, 195
  as cultural spectacle 183–6, 187, 191, 192
shtetls 221, 309
Simmons, James Richard 75
Sinti 206, 230, 232, 245, 247, 248, 306, 309
Sivan, Emmanuel 216
Slackbridge (Dickens character) 71, 90, 91, 92
slavery 72, 138, 139, 142, 154, 303, 309–10